THE DEMOCRATIC CITIZEN

*Social Science and
Democratic Theory in the
Twentieth Century*

THE DEMOCRATIC CITIZEN

CITIZEN

*Social Science and
Democratic Theory in the
Twentieth Century*

DENNIS F. THOMPSON

Princeton University

CAMBRIDGE
AT THE UNIVERSITY PRESS
1970

Published by the Syndics of the Cambridge University Press
Bentley House, 200 Euston Road, London N.W.1
American Branch: 32 East 57th Street, New York, N.Y.10022

© Cambridge University Press 1970

Library of Congress Catalogue Card Number: 76–128633

Standard Book Number: 521 07963 2

Composed in Great Britain by
Alden & Mowbray Ltd at the Alden Press, Oxford

Printed in the United States of America

FOR CAROL

Contents

Contents

Conclusion   181

Preface

This book brings together some aspects of social science and democratic theory as practised in twentieth-century Britain and the United States. I approach this enterprise as a political theorist, but I expect that some political theorists will feel that I have shown excessive respect toward social science. At the same time, some social scientists may complain that I have overly simplified their findings and that I have presented too little data analysis in these pages. The risk of studies such as this is that critics on both sides may be right. If this book provokes others to forge links more firmly anchored to both sides, I shall be sufficiently gratified.

I wrote a preliminary statement of some of the arguments in this book at Balliol College, Oxford, in 1964 and presented them in a paper at the annual meeting of the American Political Science Association in New York in 1966. The book itself is a revision of my doctoral dissertation completed at Harvard in 1967. Chapter 2 of this book appeared in a somewhat different form in *Frontiers of Democratic Theory*, edited by Henry Kariel and published by Random House in 1970. A small part of Chapter 4 appeared in *Public Policy*, vol. xv, edited by John Montgomery and Arthur Smithies and published by the Harvard University Press and the Kennedy School of Government in 1966.

I have benefited greatly from comments and criticisms on various versions of this study, most especially from Carl J. Friedrich, Sanford V. Levinson, Walter F. Murphy, Thomas N. Scanlon, Judith N. Shklar, Patricia Skinner, Edward R. Tufte, W. L. Weinstein and Pennie Woodbury. They deserve no blame for any of the errors I may have made here. I am grateful to Donald Stokes for letting me see his and David Butler's *Political Change in Britain* before it was published; and similarly to Edward Tufte for giving me an early draft of his and Robert Dahl's *Size and Democracy*. Financial support at various stages of this project came from Harvard University, Princeton University and the National Endowment for the Humanities.   D.F.T.

Introduction

Twentieth-century students of politics are divided into two camps. The first camp, the more fashionable, is inhabited by those who pursue political research largely with the tools of contemporary social science, especially quantitative methods. The second camp is inhabited by those who mostly use traditional methods of political inquiry, both normative and empirical. There have been occasional skirmishes between the two camps, usually fomented by people in one camp who feel threatened by the other. And there have been pleas for peace missions to bring the camps together, by those who feel at home in both. Yet, even though large numbers of students of politics do not swear unqualified allegiance to either camp, very few have tried to work out the details of a rapprochement between them.[1]

This book suggests how such a rapprochement can be achieved in one part of an important area of political studies—liberal democratic theory and practice. The part is the present status and future of citizenship as expressed in democratic theory in the twentieth century and as revealed by the findings of social science in recent years.

The book has two aims: to show how evidence from social science may or may not be useful in developing a theory of democracy that is oriented toward citizenship; and to suggest how this theory can be reconciled with such evidence. These aims will be carried out by constructing and applying a schema which combines the evidence and the theory concerning democratic citizenship.

The nature and scope of this study thus depend on how democratic citizenship, democratic theory and social science are construed. All three therefore need to be explained at the outset.

DEMOCRATIC CITIZENSHIP

The book is about only those portions of democratic theory and social science which deal with the democratic citizen. It is this

I

portion of the theory that is regarded as most fundamental by the theorists who are oriented toward citizenship, and also this portion of social science which is most fully covered by empirical studies.

'Citizenship' is not meant to suggest merely those rights possessed by a passive subject by virtue of residing under a particular territorial jurisdiction. Nor is it meant mainly to connote patriotism or loyalty to a nation-state. 'Citizenship' as used here refers to the present and future capacity for influencing politics. It implies active involvement in political life. This idea of citizenship naturally evokes the ideas of citizenship in the traditions of thought extending back through Rousseau and Machiavelli to the ideals of Athenian democracy.[2] However, citizenship in twentieth-century democratic theory in two respects suggests more than the Greek idea of citizenship. First, according to the modern idea, *all* individuals are to engage in the activities of citizenship; there are no exceptions, such as slaves. Second, modern citizenship suggests that citizens are in their political activities to express not only public but also the personal interests of individuals and groups. In another respect, the twentieth-century idea of citizenship suggests less than the Greek idea. The modern conception allows for less active involvement since in a large, industrialized state it is impossible for all citizens to be consulted on most of the decisions which have to be made. Nevertheless, some forms of twentieth-century democratic theory more closely reflect the ancient ideals of citizenship than other forms do. Theorists who in this study are called citizenship theorists remain dissatisfied with the low levels of citizen involvement in modern democracies and emphasize the importance and the possibility of expanding citizenship. Those theorists who here are called elitist democratic theorists do not stress the need for greater citizenship.

The standards of citizenship will be expressed here as forms of participation, discussion and voting; and as forms of equality which refer to the distribution of these activities. The kinds and degrees of citizenship which are necessary for a political system to attain various kinds and degrees of democracy is a central question in this essay. 'Democratic' is added to 'citizenship' to indicate that citizenship is a feature of the democratic system. To say that a system is democratic is to imply not only that the system is responsive to the interests of most of the citizens but also that the citizens share in governing (if only by selecting in a competitive system who shall govern between elections). To what extent and for what purposes citizens should share in governing depends on how citizenship is interpreted in light of empirical evidence. Thus, the meaning of 'democratic' as applied to citizenship should become clear in the course of this study.[3]

But plainly the democratic citizenship discussed here is not a sufficient condition for a system to be called democratic. Citizenship alone does not guarantee that governments are and can be responsive to citizens' desires and needs. To determine the degree of responsiveness, we should have to examine much more closely the historical record and the present state of processes and institutions such as legislatures and parties, as well as the links between such institutions and citizens. We should also need to look at the results of particular policies and decisions generated by political systems. However, the problem of citizenship as defined here should take precedence over these other problems. Citizenship is a precondition of influencing these processes and institutions. If citizens participate, we cannot say for certain without further information about institutions that citizens effectively influence government. But if citizens do not or cannot participate, we can say with more assurance that they are not likely to influence politics.

Although 'democratic' is an abbreviation of 'liberal democratic', the idea of liberty is not of central concern here. The distinctive problems of liberty arise where liberties conflict. In an inquiry which deals with characteristics of citizenship which all citizens do or should possess, the question of the nature and resolution of conflicts among citizens or between citizens and authorities is not salient. Citizenship, though it contributes to liberty, is logically prior to it: people must participate before conflicts arise. It may be said, of course, that citizens without citizenship are not really free; but in this case the problem of liberty coincides with the problem of democratic citizenship.

SOCIAL SCIENCE

The findings of social science which this essay uses are mostly drawn from studies conducted by those social scientists often called, rather inelegantly, behavioralists.[4] Behavioralism in this context is not a philosophical doctrine which holds that all statements about human activity, including mental activity, can be reduced without loss of meaning to statements about physical behavior. It is rather a methodological orientation which assumes that a fruitful (perhaps the most fruitful) way to explain and predict human activity is systematic study of behavior using techniques and procedures which follow, as far as possible, the methodological canons of the natural sciences. Plainly such an orientation embraces quite a bit of variety. Not only do the natural sciences themselves vary in their methodology, but so do the ways in which their canons can be applied to social phenomena. Behavioral social science, then, does not refer to a unified school of social scientists who agree on methods. Indeed behavioralism is, as Robert Dahl observes, more a mood than an approach. Nevertheless, the studies from social science which figure in this essay do share one salient feature—the use of quantitative methods. Since many social phenomena cannot be manipulated like phenomena in a laboratory, social scientists wishing to emulate the natural sciences apply controls to their data, rather than to the phenomena. Hence, statistical techniques become essential. A second common (but less essential) feature of these behavioral studies is that they concentrate more on individuals and social groups than on institutions, ideologies, or events. Consequently, such studies of politics make more use of sociology, social psychology and psychology than other forms of political inquiry normally do. 'Social science' in this book usually refers to studies which have these two features.

The basis for many of the studies cited here is the panel survey, in which the same carefully selected sample of persons is interviewed at different times. Studying the same subjects under different conditions is assumed to be a way of approximating one aspect of the controlled experimentation of some of the natural sciences. This essay focuses on the major panel studies of voting conducted in Britain and the United States, beginning with the study of Erie County, Ohio, in 1940 by Paul Lazarsfeld and his associates and continuing through the leading recent studies such as those by the Survey Research Center at the University of Michigan. These studies constitute the most sustained investigation of problems which are most relevant to a theory which is oriented toward citizenship. However, the voting studies are not the only part of social science employed in this book. Where problems arise which require evidence that cannot be extracted from voting studies, other studies are enlisted, though nearly all fall within the category of behavioral social science.

In the chapters that follow, it will become clear that a number of limitations of behavioral social science arise when it is applied to democratic theory. However, a few limitations are inherent in the behavioral studies themselves. Although many of the social scientists considered here have come to realize that more traditional methods of political science, particularly historical analysis, are not outmoded by the newer methods, the findings of social science generally do not reveal much historical perspective. Most of the studies have been conducted under fairly stable social and political conditions rather than under what have been called 'heated conditions'.[5] There is, furthermoer, not very much reliable data on citizens' attitudes and formation of opinions over long periods of time. Thus, the available findings by no means exhaust the range of political experience even in developed democracies. These present inadequacies of social science mean that the effort in these pages to bring together democratic theory and social science must be tentative.

DEMOCRATIC THEORY

The democratic theory with which the findings of social science are confronted here is drawn from the writings of thirteen twentieth-century theorists who, from various perspectives, orient their theories toward democratic citizenship. These theorists will be called citizenship theorists. Citizenship theory is characterized by certain presuppositions and standards of citizenship to be developed and examined in detail throughout this study.

5

Another kind of democratic theory—elitist theory—will occasionally be mentioned to illustrate the absence of the presuppositions of citizenship. But elitist democratic theory will not be confronted with social science. The disagreement between elitist and citizenship theorists, as we shall see, does not turn on whether one theory can accommodate empirical evidence better than the other.

However, if citizenship theory could not be reconciled at all with the findings of social science, we should hardly find it acceptable, whatever our attitude toward elitist theory. Perhaps the most potent criticism of citizenship-oriented theory, including traditional democratic theory of earlier centuries, is that it cannot cope with the seemingly pessimistic picture of democratic citizens evoked by contemporary social science. To show, as this study seeks to do, that citizenship theory can accommodate the findings of social science is to strengthen that theory considerably. However, this study is not a complete defense of the theory. The presuppositions on which the theory rests are not fully justified, and not all the objections against this form of democracy are considered. Nor is this study completely a defense. Citizenship theory is criticized and amended in a number of important respects.

Citizenship theorists, like many political theorists of the past, are not hostile to empirical evidence. They not only could approve the rise of social science but some of them actually encouraged it. Indeed, some—most notably Charles Merriam and Graham Wallas—were pioneering spirits (if not exactly faithful practitioners) of behavioral social science. The currently fashionable division of political studies into normative and empirical branches distorts the nature of citizenship theory, just as it obscures the nature of traditional political theory. Citizenship theorists, along with theorists of the past who contributed to democratic thought, are as much concerned with describing and explaining as with prescribing and evaluating. Nevertheless, the fact remains that for various reasons (to be discussed in Chapter 2) citizenship theorists do not incorporate social science into their theories, and social scientists shun many of the concerns of citizenship theory.

In many discussions of the normative implications of empirical studies, actual theorists are seldom cited. A classical theory of democracy, constructed from fragments of the most optimistic eighteenth- and nineteenth-century democratic ideology, becomes the target for attack. Such a straw-man theory is easily demolished.[6] If theories actually held by serious writers are considered, as is done here, a theory of democratic citizenship looks much more respectable. However, the reason that twentieth-century theorists rather than earlier writers appear in this study is not that the earlier theorists are less realistic or less respectable. A study of some earlier theorists would probably yield the same results as this analysis.[7] The reason for choosing twentieth-century theorists is that since they write in a context which more nearly coincides with the context of the empirical studies, they respond more directly to the problems raised by those studies. With twentieth-century theory, it is not necessary, as it would be with earlier theory, to speculate on what a particular theorist *might have* said when faced, for example, with the consequences of universal suffrage.

All the citizenship theorists considered here wrote in a British or an American setting, with the exceptions of Hans Kelsen and Alf Ross. These two writers are included because their work is so often mentioned in Anglo-American discussions, though it is shaped by their Austrian and Danish experiences respectively. American theorists are chosen mainly because the largest number of extensive empirical studies have been conducted in the United States. British theorists and studies are also included because British and American democratic thought in this century have so interpenetrated one another that discussion of one without reference to the other is difficult. Not only a common language but also similar outlooks and practices, as many observers have pointed out, have encouraged this.[8]

The treatment of citizenship theory here is not a historical or sociological study of the development of ideas. The similarities and the continuities, rather than the differences and changes, are the chief concern. The common recurrent themes in the writings of all these theorists are used throughout this book to create a portrait of citizenship theory in the twentieth-century.

Since this book treats citizenship theory largely as a single body of thought, we should first notice some important differences among the theorists. Citizenship theorists view democracy from three different perspectives—scientific, religious and humanist.

In the work of theorists who view democracy from a scientific perspective, two conceptions of science have been prominent: science as a method or attitude; and science as a body of knowledge. It is the first conception which dominates the thought of John Dewey, Hans Kelsen, Alf Ross and Thomas Vernor Smith. These theorists see democracy as the application of the scientific method to social problems or at least as the expression of scientific tolerance and tentativeness in political life.[9] Science as a body of knowledge, especially as applied in technology, is for Charles Merriam as important to democracy as the scientific method.[10] From Graham Wallas, a British sociologist who early recognized the significance of his discipline for political theory, comes a warning that laboratory science often ignores the valuable emotional aspects of life in a democracy. He believes, however, that a properly conceived *social* science can serve as a firm basis for democracy.[11]

From a religious perspective, democracy is seen both to originate historically in religious ideas and practices; to be modeled on a religious congregation; or to be based on divinely grounded natural law. A. D. Lindsay, who stresses the Puritan foundations of democracy, argues for the first two of these views, while Yves Simon, who emphasizes the Thomist basis, supports the third view.[12]

The humanist perspective on democracy is characterized by a concern with human values derived from secular not supernatural or transcendental sources; and the belief that the features of social life in primary groups—such as the family and small associations—also ought to be fostered in more inclusive groups. This perspective is represented by Carl Friedrich, Robert MacIver, Leonard Hobhouse, and the British socialists G. D. H. Cole and Harold Laski.[13] To be sure, Laski's political thought ranges, in various periods, from pluralist to anarchist and Marxist. But throughout his writings, as Michel Fourest argues, humanism persists. Even in his Marxist period, Laski made it clear that his opposition to Western democracy was to its institutions, not its humanist values.[14]

8

No argument in this study depends on which, if any, of these perspectives ought to support the theorists' views of citizenship. The study focuses on what all these theorists have in common— their shared commitment to the presuppositions and standards of citizenship. Nevertheless, noticing the different perspectives of the theorists not only underscores the variety concealed under the label 'citizenship theory'.[15] It also suggests that the theorists' agreement on the presuppositions and standards of citizenship is all the more remarkable. In the first chapter, I shall explore this agreement on the presuppositions; and in later chapters, the standards that they support.

I Presuppositions

Theories of democracy qualify as forms of citizenship theory insofar as they presuppose the autonomy and the improvability of citizens; and posit the standards of citizenship which follow from these two presuppositions. The presupposition of autonomy entails that citizens be treated as the best judges of their own interests. The presupposition of improvability holds that citizens be treated as capable of showing better political and social judgment than they do at any present time.

This chapter explores the general nature and the content of these presuppositions and shows how they are reflected in the writings of the citizenship theorists presented in the Introduction. It also demonstrates the significance of the absence of the presuppositions by briefly discussing elitist democratic theory. And finally, it indicates how the presuppositions support the standards of citizenship.

THE NATURE OF PRESUPPOSITIONS

Almost any statement we make, question we ask or theory we hold presupposes something, takes something for granted.[1] For example, the question 'Is citizens' apathy caused by lack of education?' presupposes that there are apathetic citizens. But such a presupposition is subject to further empirical inquiry; it is a relative presupposition. Some of our presuppositions, however, are absolute; they are not subject to further empirical inquiry which could affect whether or not we accept them. The principle 'everything that happens has a cause' is an example. If we discovered an event that appeared not to have a cause, we would not give up this principle but rather we would conclude that our search for a cause had not been sufficiently thorough. Such a presupposition is not simply an empirical generalization since it determines how we proceed in verifying generalizations. It is not a logical tautology since its contradictory is not self-contradictory. Nor is the presupposition an evaluative statement in any straightforward way since it shapes how we see the world as it *is*.

In these respects, the presuppositions of autonomy and improvability are very much like absolute presuppositions. These presuppositions of citizenship serve, usually implicitly, as regulative principles in the theory, enjoining theorists to seek evidence to show that citizens recognize their own interests and are capable of improving their political abilities. For example, if theorists find a citizen who apparently errs in his judgment of his own interest, they do not reject the presupposition of autonomy but instead search for further reasons why the judgment may be in his interest.

Our acceptance of the presuppositions of a theory of democracy, then, does not depend mainly on evidence from social science. The presuppositions at root represent fundamental attitudes toward politics and social life generally. A complete defense of the presuppositions of citizenship would require a portrayal, in literary and philosophical terms, of a vision of a society of autonomous and improvable men. Thus, the terms of discourse in which much political theory has been traditionally presented are not obviated by the use of modern social science in democratic theory. But even if the presuppositions themselves can normally claim empirical immunity, many of the conditions and ideals of citizenship, which are partly based on them, cannot. The particular content of these conditions and ideals is very much affected by the findings of social science, as we shall see in later chapters. Moreover, even the presuppositions, though themselves never empirically testable, might be eventually abandoned as irrelevant, should the conditions and ideals which follow from them persistently clash with social science.

The presuppositions of democratic theory are less comprehensive and universal than absolute presuppositions, such as the presupposition of causality, in metaphysical theories. The presuppositions of democratic theory would not be offered as valid for all historical periods or cultures, as metaphysical systems usually are. Nor would democratic theorists claim, as metaphysicians often do, that only by accepting their presuppositions can the world, or human action, be fully intelligible. Democratic theorists need claim only that with a theory reflecting their presuppositions one is more inclined to notice certain features of social and political life which it is desirable to see—not that one inevitably or necessarily overlooks those features if one adopts a theory with different presuppositions. The connection in democratic theory between presuppositions and the theory or its implications is therefore best understood in linguistic and psychological terms. Although presuppositions arise out of certain facts and values, once accepted the presuppositions shape the language and conceptual categories of a theory so that certain kinds of facts and values are more accessible in thinking about politics. Because of their presuppositions, what citizenship theorists stress differs from what other theorists stress.

The linguist Edward Sapir's remarks on the general impact of language on thought serve as a good description of how pre-suppositions, embodied in a language of democratic theory, can affect the way we see and evaluate the world:

> language ... can discover meanings for its speakers which are not simply traceable to the given quality of the experience itself but must be explained to a large extent as the projection of potential meanings into the raw material of experience ... forms [of language] predetermine for us certain modes of observation and interpretation.[2]

Little solid evidence, admittedly, can be found to show that linguistic differences sustain fundamentally different world-views, as Benjamin Whorf argued. What we do find is that some differences between languages and within one language require speakers to pay more attention to different categories. The 'cognitive availability' of certain categories and distinctions probably affect people's recall ability, ease of communication and generally their dispositions to think in certain patterns; such effects may impinge upon problem-solving and creative thought.[3] As linguistic differences affect one's way of looking at the physical world, so the differences between political theories which share the presuppositions of citizenship and those which do not probably shape one's way of viewing the political world. However, the content of the presuppositions of citizenship must be explored before their impact on views of democratic politics can be illustrated.

PRESUPPOSITIONS OF CITIZENSHIP

Despite the divergent perspectives from which citizenship theorists approach democracy, they all share a commitment to the presuppositions of autonomy and improvability. To be sure, the theorists may find different origins and foundations for these presuppositions. Scientific democrats would, for example, ground the presupposition of autonomy on scepticism toward any claim to permanently superior competence on matters about which some-one else has more immediate experience. Religious democrats would found autonomy on a belief in the inviolability of the individual soul or the sanctity of the inner light of conscience. Humanist democrats would see autonomy as the recognition of the moral worth of secular man. But as far as citizenship theory is concerned, these differences are not so important as the similarities among the theorists.

The presupposition of autonomy, treating each citizen as the best judge of his own interest, places few restrictions on what counts as being in a citizen's interest. Interests should be under-stood as whatever wants or desires a citizen expresses in the political process in which claims are made; or if he is not engaged in such processes, whatever wants or desires he would be likely to express were he so engaged.[4] Thus, some unexpressed desires count as interests. As we shall see in Chapter 3, this allows us to challenge the argument that persons who do not participate know their own interest best and therefore need not be encouraged to participate. What is in a citizen's interest is not limited to satisfaction of material desires. Psychic satisfactions—such as those a member of an ethnic group may derive from voting for one of his own kind— must surely count, at least if basic needs are satisfied. Moreover, we do not require that a citizen in making judgments about his interest should also impartially take into account other people's interests. This further moral element has traditionally been included in the idea of autonomy by some philosophers. It is retained in the idea of autonomy as used here, but mainly as an ideal. The primary meaning of the presupposition is the minimal content of autonomy understood in terms of self-interest (which of course *may* include satisfaction from seeing others' interests satisfied). Finally, yet another meaning which is sometimes associated with 'autonomy'—complete independence from other persons—is not intended here at all. Autonomy in most democratic theory is now assumed to arise only in a social context. An individual's view of his interests is shaped and influenced by others, especially groups to which he belongs or with which he identifies, though he must not be coerced or manipulated.

If a citizen is to be treated as the best judge of his own interest, how can we say, as we sometimes wish to, that citizens are mistaken about what is in their interest? To say that a person is the best judge of his own interest does not necessarily imply that he is always correct in his judgment. He may be the best judge but turn out to be wrong. We may say that we know better than a citizen what is in his interest in some particular instance. However, to be consistent with the presupposition, we must interpret this to mean that we believe that he will in the future agree that we knew better. Until he does agree, we must treat his view of his interest as better than ours at least on decisions about who shall govern and for what broad purposes. There is no doubt some flexibility here. Citizenship theorists reject what Simon calls the 'coach-driver' theory, which asserts that political leaders must slavishly follow the wishes of citizens all the time. There is room for leadership, though it must be tested in a reasonable period of time against the verdict of citizens.[5]

A belief in the capacity of citizens in general to improve their judgment about what is in their interest is the basis of the presupposition of improvability. This presupposition, an attenuated version of older democratic doctrines of progress, encourages us to attribute deficiencies that citizens may have to social and political conditions, which can be improved. This presupposition thus provides important backing for the ideals of citizenship.

These two presuppositions together dispose citizenship theorists to treat citizens' political choices at any time as being in their interest, and also to seek changes which would enable citizens to judge better in the future what is in their interest. The presuppositions infuse all the standards of citizenship, as we shall see in the last section of this chapter. However, in the writings of citizenship theorists, the presuppositions and standards are not laid out systematically and often are not even explicitly stated. The presuppositions are reflected most clearly in the general demand for greater political involvement of ordinary citizens. This can be shown first for the presupposition of autonomy and then more briefly for improvability.

AUTONOMY

Among scientific democrats, Dewey is the only one who presents an epistemology that can be construed as supporting the autonomy of the ordinary citizen. For the presupposition is reflected not only in Dewey's political theory, but in an indirect way in his whole philosophical system. 'The philosopher of the plain man', he has been called. It has been said, for example, that Dewey's attacks on dualism, such as the distinctions between theory and practice, knowledge and opinion and ends and means, are 'attacks upon an aristocratic leisure-class condescension toward the world of the masses of men'.[6] While this is not the primary purpose of his attack on dualisms, clearly if such dualisms cannot be maintained, no class can easily find philosophical backing for claiming superior competence. Dewey is suspicious of writers like Walter Lippmann who dislike what the public chooses as much as the uninformed way in which they choose it. Dewey believes that asking people what they want, not telling them what they need or what is good for them, is 'an essential part of the democratic idea'. More inclined to criticize than assimilate earlier democratic theory, Dewey nonetheless insists that traditional theory was correct in demanding that all citizens take part in democratic processes. It is not sufficient that government should result in the highest social good—unless all citizens share 'in selecting governors *and* determining their policies'.[7]

In the theories of Kelsen and Ross, the presupposition of autonomy is revealed most clearly in an inclination to favor the greatest possible involvement of all citizens in the political life which affects them. Indeed, for Kelsen direct democracy is the ideal form of democracy, and representative democracy is 'a considerable weakening' of the demand that all citizens should actively help determine policies. Furthermore, Kelsen distrusts those who say that the problem of democracy is the problem of effective leadership because he thinks they neglect the much more important problem of activating citizens.[8] Ross too gives the latter problem priority, but he recognizes a need for leadership and prefers representative democracy.[9]

The whole orientation of Merriam's democratic theory, focused primarily on the ordinary citizen, indicates his commitment to autonomy. His concept of democracy, summed up in his often repeated 'five assumptions of democracy', largely concerns the consent, equality and perfectibility of citizens. Much of one of his major works, *Political Power*, views power 'from the point of view of those upon whom power is exercised rather than from that of the authoritarians themselves, from below rather than from above'. The same theme also underlies his discussions of planning. One might expect that a theorist so enamored of the uses of technology as Merriam is would be content if democratic leaders effectively applied it for the benefit of all. But Merriam, like Ross, insists that 'popular participation' by the 'bulk of the community' is the essential part of the idea of democracy. Although 'leadership is one of the basic factors in the organization of life', Merriam thinks that one of the prime aptitudes of a leader is the ability to sense what the public want. Political leaders are 'in large measure followers and interpreters' rather than the 'inventors'.[10] In a similar way, Merriam's colleague, Thomas Vernor Smith, holds that 'each man is the best judge of what he desires'. This is true even though only a very few people are very good at making such judgments.[11]

More than most other citizenship theorists, Wallas faces up to the difficulties that the findings of social science create for a belief in the autonomy of citizens. But he does so explicitly as a democrat, and his orientation is favorable toward the idea of citizenship. A chief goal of politics in his view is to increase the 'political strength of the individual citizen', even though he stresses that there are limits to the demands that should be made upon the citizen. The fact that his most important book is addressed to politicians does not detract from his concern for the ordinary citizen. For the essence of his message is that if politicians would treat citizens as intelligent human beings with a capacity for reason and a need for some emotion, then citizens would tend to act that way.[12]

Among religious democrats, the commitment to the presupposition of autonomy is strongest in Lindsay's theory. The opinions of the 'plain man', according to Lindsay, must be treated with the utmost respect. Lindsay argues that 'the claims of the ordinary plain man to have some share in the government of his country can be justified' partly because he knows 'where the shoe pinches'—he knows his own interest best. Democracy needs skill and leadership, Lindsay realizes, but appreciation of these qualities must be combined with a 'reverence for the common humanity of everyday people'. If the voice of the people is not quite the voice of God, no one else has a better claim to speak for Him.[13]

Similarly, Simon trusts the voice of 'the people', in terms of whom he defines democracy. A somewhat romantic affection for ordinary men marks much of his writing. Ordinary men, though not uncorrupted, are more realistic; they 'hold in check' the 'sort of destructiveness proper to the intelligentsia'. If the authority of leadership is necessary in modern democracies, leaders must be 'in communion' with the common man, be able 'to feel the rags on his back' and the pinch of his 'worn-out shoes'. Direct democracy, the 'archetype of all democratic organizations', requires, Simon admits, 'special historical conditions' that no longer exist, but it should be approximated in our time by establishing strong local government in a federal structure.[14]

In humanist democracy, the presupposition of autonomy again shows itself in the overriding importance assigned to the ordinary citizen. In Friedrich's theory, the common man, viewed primarily as 'a man of character rather than of intellect', is the protagonist. Since character means 'consistent loyalty to believed standards', what counts in a democracy is what the common man aspires to, not what a rationalist set of standards might dictate he should want. Not only should the ordinary citizen control his governors but he should participate in governing as well. Since there are more opportunities for such participation in the 'communal life' of 'small towns', Friedrich favors strong local government in a federal political structure.[15]

Although MacIver says that the people are prejudiced and often deceived, he goes so far as to find reason for praise in the fact that they do not deceive anyone else, as corrupt rulers do. It is not only a presupposition of autonomy, but also more specifically a fear of 'irresponsible power' that makes MacIver recommend that we should take the risk of trying to educate the ordinary citizen. But this education is to enable him to get what he wants, not to train him to seek what the 'enlightened' think he should want. Furthermore, a government must have more than the consent or the popular support of ordinary citizens; it must enlist their active participation, though to decide the 'broad march of politics', not specific issues of day-to-day policy.[16]

Hobhouse was strongly influenced by the metaphysical theory of the state, but he insists, against it, that 'the individual citizen be the paramount value in democratic theory'. This insistence, as he develops it, indicates that he presupposes autonomy. Hobhouse recognizes that most ordinary citizens, who are not very interested in politics, must at times be led. But leaders and activists should occupy themselves 'in convincing the people and carrying their minds . . . [rather] than imposing on them laws they are concerned only to obey and enjoy'—and presumably this can be done only insofar as citizens are persuaded to participate in politics.[17]

In none of his writings does Laski give up the presupposition of autonomy. When he condemns traditional democratic institutions, it is in the name of the traditional democratic values of citizenship. Even when he is profoundly despondent about the 'rows on rows of tired faces' in the London tube, this merely makes him 'more urgently democratic'. A chief object of his pluralism is to enlist the active involvement of all citizens in political processes; this is why he praises private associations, urges devolution and decentralization.[18] In his quasi-anarchist writings, Laski asserts that the ordinary citizen is 'ultimately the supreme arbiter of his behavior'. Consequently, Laski urges an increase in 'civic interest and knowledge', and a restoration to the citizen of 'his personal initiative and responsibility'. All citizens have an obligation to participate in politics, especially to protest wrongful actions. Even in his 'revolutionary' writings, Laski's concern for the autonomy of the ordinary citizen keeps him in the ranks of citizenship theorists. One of the main reasons he urges socialist reforms and occasionally proposes revolution to overthrow capitalism is to make 'the participation of the common man in the operation of his government . . . wider and more profound'.[19]

The dispersal of power recommended by Cole is meant, as in Laski's pluralism, to give citizens more of a chance to express their political interests. Cole's abiding concern for the ordinary citizen, a reflection of the presupposition of autonomy, is revealed in other ways, for example in his lengthy history of *The Common People*, and in his *Guide to Modern Politics* addressed to the common man. The trouble with present democracy and democratic theory is that they assign 'to the ordinary citizen little more than a privilege . . . of choosing his rulers, and [do] not call upon him, or assign to him the opportunity, himself to rule'.[20] Both Cole and Laski, more explicitly and more strongly than other citizenship theorists, wish to see a radical extension of the present political role of citizens in a democracy.

IMPROVABILITY

Citizenship theorists do not always clearly distinguish their confidence in the present abilities of citizens from confidence in potential abilities. This is because the theorists believe that treating citizens now as if they are the best judges of their own interests is the best way to improve their competence in the future. The presupposition of improvability, therefore, is an essential companion of the presupposition of autonomy. Unless citizens' competence can be assumed to be improvable, citizenship theorists would be less likely to look favorably on the political behavior which citizens exhibit at present. Because the two presuppositions are so intimately connected, much of what was cited in the previous section as a reflection of the commitment to autonomy is also a sign of a belief in improvability. However, the presupposition of improvability as a form of the idea of progress does need some further discussion.

Citizenship theorists presuppose that both the democratic citizen and the democratic community are, if not perfectible, then improvable through human effort. Although these theorists almost never suggest that this improvement is inevitable, some think that progression toward democratic ideals is more likely than retrogression. The very difficulty of attaining democratic ideals constitutes a challenge to pursue these ideals more actively. In the twentieth century when pessimism marks most political theory, this attenuated belief in progress must be regarded as optimistic.

Citizenship theorists who discuss progress vary in the degree of optimism which they express, and in what they are optimistic about. Few are so hopeful as Merriam: not only will science and social arrangements eradicate disease and poverty; they will also 'conquer the jungles' of the 'inner life of the personality, so long filled with vile broods of haunting fears and doubts of dreads' and release the 'sunlight of happiness'. At times Merriam even sees an 'inexorable and inevitable' progress with intelligence triumphing over 'ignorance and error'.[21] Simon, in contrast, argues that the 'moral progress' of the common man is not automatically ensured by scientific progress, which engenders 'greater evil' as well as 'greater good'. Still, he is hopeful that men will be able to restrain the evil forces and release the good ones.[22] Wallas believes that our democratic social heritage—accumulated ideas, habits and institutions—is 'constantly expanding'. If the expansion is not inevitable at every stage, it is bound to be upward in the long run because each generation hand on to their children more than they received from their parents.[23] Both he and Hobhouse locate the source of progress in the development of the capacity of men to adjust to their environments and to get along with one another— what Hobhouse calls the 'growth of the humanitarian spirit' and the 'harmonious development of human life'.[24] MacIver does not think that the 'growth of the democratic spirit' will be ineluctably aided by the trends of history such as social mechanization, but he does believe that 'whatever dangers [such trends] threaten can be controlled by the same unresting intelligence that created it'.[25]

The commitment to improvability as applied specifically to the political competence of the citizen is best illustrated by Dewey's writings. 'We have every reason to think', Dewey writes, 'that whatever changes may take place in existing democratic machinery, they will be of the sort to make the interest of the public a more supreme guide and criterion on governmental activity. . . In this sense, the cure for the ailments of democracy is more democracy'. Dewey is not blind to the faults of the public opinions of ordinary men. He praises Lippmann's indictment of the public, but he refuses to accept Lippmann's constructive proposals which imply that nothing much can be done to enlighten ordinary citizens. Dewey's commitment is also reflected in his espousal of socialist reform. Although he does not completely embrace democratic socialism, his tendencies in this direction are motivated largely by his belief that socialist measures are best calculated to remove the barriers to the development of the ordinary citizen's intelligence.[26]

The belief in the improvability of the democratic citizen accounts for the extreme importance nearly all citizenship theorists attach to education. It is education in various forms which is the chief instrument of this progress. The kinds of education that are thought appropriate range from Merriam's 'civic education', which includes instruction in the techniques of political organization as well as enlightenment about social trends, to Wallas' 'cultural transmission' of 'proper moral and intellectual ideals necessary for democracy'. Each theorist has his recommendations for educational reform—for example, Dewey pleads for the teaching of the social content and unity of everyday experiences and the cultivation of a critical and inquiring habit of mind.[27] A principal purpose of all these reforms is to make ordinary citizens more competent in political affairs, and most theorists are confident that citizens will respond successfully to proper education, though some like Laski insist that social and economic reform is a prerequisite. For many theorists the best form of democratic education is more democracy—giving citizens more political responsibilities.[28]

To call for more and better education has always been one of the favorite defenses of believers in progress, especially advocates of democracy. In the eighteenth and nineteenth centuries when educational opportunities were limited, it was plausible enough to expect that educational expansion would alleviate some of the defects of popular government. But how long can one use this defense? How long can one plead for more time to allow democratic education to yield returns? Probably the answer is—indefinitely. There will always be some social deficiency that a theorist will cite as an impediment to the enlightenment of citizens. As long as such impediments exist, no factual evidence about the ignorance and foolishness of citizens is likely to shake the belief that citizenship theorists have in this attenuated notion of progress. The belief is sustained by a presupposition which cannot normally be undermined by empirical evidence because it influences what evidence is considered significant.

ELITIST DEMOCRATIC THEORY

The significance of the commitment to the presuppositions of citizenship can be underscored by looking at theories of democracy which do not share that commitment to the same extent. In the twentieth century many democratic theorists, impressed by the need for leadership and disillusioned by the failure of many citizens to engage actively and responsibly in politics, shift the focus of their theories from the ordinary citizen to elites or leaders. Since these theorists usually stipulate that the political elite be not entirely closed or unified and that it be subject to some control by means of free elections, these theorists remain in this sense democrats. But since they do not hold the presuppositions of citizenship, they must be considered elitist democratic theorists. The political thought of Walter Lippmann and Joseph Schumpeter serve as examples of this elitist orientation to democracy, which pervades much of contemporary political science.[29]

A deep distrust of citizens' political desires and judgment signals the virtual absence of the presupposition of autonomy in elitist democratic theory. For Lippmann, this distrust stems from two weaknesses of citizens. First, since 'the pictures inside people's heads do not automatically correspond with the world outside', citizens' judgment is distorted; people tend to think, for example, in stereotypes. This defect by itself would not place the citizen in a worse position than his leaders, for Lippmann believes that every representation of the world suffers from this weakness (even scientific models). However, a second weakness turns the first into a disability which specially affects ordinary citizens. Because the 'self-contained community' where political matters were familiar to everyone has vanished, only a few people have the time and ability to adjust their mental pictures to a remote and complex reality. From this descriptive account, Lippmann is led to prescribe that those few people with well-adjusted mental pictures constitute, or decisively influence, the political elite. The elite should not be very sensitive to popular demands. Citizens should intervene 'only when there is a crisis of maladjustment, and then not to deal with substance of the problem but to neutralize the arbitrary force which prevents adjustment'. When Lippmann writes that 'statesmanship' is 'giving the people not what they want but what they will learn to want', he does not mean simply that the rulers should look beyond the next election. He means that they should penetrate to citizens' 'real and permanent interest'. 'The People', in whose name an elite rules, are not today's voters but a Burkeian 'community of the entire living population, with their predecessors and successors'.[30]

For most of the same reasons as Lippmann, Schumpeter distrusts citizens' judgment about their own interests. His celebrated definition of the democratic method as a 'competitive struggle' among elites for 'the people's vote' is not only a description of how democracies work, but also evidently a prescription about how they ought to work. 'Democracy *means only* that the people have the opportunity of accepting or refusing the men who are ruling them'. Schumpeter maintains that once voters elect a government, they must not exert pressure (even in the form of letters and telegrams) until the next election. No 'political back-seat driving' is allowed. Also, Schumpeter would 'reduce the pressure on the leading men [in politics] by appropriate institutional devices'. Opportunities for participation beyond voting are apparently limited to seeking positions in the elite. But Schumpeter believes that accessibility to elites must not be too easy, for he wishes elites to maintain semi-aristocratic values and beliefs. British society between the Wars represents Schumpeter's notion of a proper degree of accessibility.[31]

That elitist democratic theorists are not committed to the presuppositions of improvability shows up both in a general doubt about the political potential of citizens and in the nature of the specific reforms these theorists propose. Even while concentrating on description and explanation, elitist democratic theorists strongly imply that the weaknesses of citizens which they describe are permanent and that therefore injunctions to alter these characteristics are futile. Schumpeter's theory is almost wholly intended to show how *in spite of* the weaknesses of citizens democracies manage to operate tolerably well; hence, his theory is not suited for the discovery of facts which could assist movement toward greater citizenship. Schumpeter criticizes Graham Wallas, whose descriptive theory he admires, for insisting on seeing 'some blue sky in the midst of clouds of disillusioning facts'. Lippmann is even more explicit: 'No progress can be made toward [the] unattainable ideal' of educating 'a people for self-government'. His view is that a democratic theory, if it is to be realistic, must by-pass not treat the ills of citizens he describes.[32]

Without the presupposition of improvability, elitist democratic theory makes some areas for reform and research seem more urgent than areas which citizenship theory stresses. Citizenship theory leads naturally to concern for improving conditions under which citizens can more actively govern themselves. Elitist theory leads in contrast to efforts toward improving the quality of leaders and the conditions under which they operate. The weaknesses of citizens are skirted, not ameliorated. Lippmann's main reforms, for example, would be the development of a 'public philosophy' among members of the elite, and the institution of 'intelligence bureaus', whose members with life tenure would oversee bureaucracies so as 'not to burden every citizen with expert opinions on all questions'. Schumpeter also wishes to make politics more professional; he would encourage only those persons who would make politics a full-time career to assume responsible positions in democratic government. As for citizens, they need only exercise 'democratic self-control' by not getting very involved in politics.[33]

Since excellence and expertise in political leadership is important, why criticize a theory which mainly focuses on leadership? One reason is that the presuppositions of a democratic theory should draw attention to those important changes which are most in danger of neglect. Elitist democratic theory reinforces the potent historical pressures toward centralized, bureaucratic power that make citizens feel remote from politics and that discourage citizenship. Citizenship theory resists these pressures, and yet does not and cannot ignore the importance of leadership. These same pressures which tend to emasculate citizens raise elites to such prominence that any democratic theorist, whatever his presuppositions, is forced to recognize the need for competent leadership.

Another general reason for eschewing elitist democratic theory is the severe tension that arises in the theory between the democratic element, which preserves elections, and the elitist element which justifies sharp limits on electoral and other forms of participation. The elitist element is so strong that it calls into question the *raison d'être* of permitting popular participation at all. If citizens are so incorrigibly incompetent that their role must be limited, what *reason* (as distinct from cause) can be given for members of an elite to pay any attention at all to the results of elections? If the electoral verdict and other expressions of citizens' desires are not rational, a system which forces elites to heed such expressions is profoundly irrational. To justify injecting a dose of elitism into their democratic theory, these theorists paint such a pessimistic picture of citizens that any reason for retaining a strain of democracy disappears. When autonomy is not to some extent presupposed, participation seems pointless.

A number of other more specific complaints can be made against elitist democratic theory.[34] In the course of this book, many of these will be incidentally raised—for example, the elitists' misunderstanding of the nature of ideals, their exaggerated fear of media manipulation, their inordinate faith in elite consensus and expertise. But it is not possible in this study to provide a complete rebuttal of elitist democratic theory. Nor would it be worthwhile to compare the respective capacities of elitist and citizenship theory to deal with the findings of social science. For the dispute between the two theories ultimately turns on what presuppositions should characterize democratic theory, and that dispute, as we have noticed, cannot be finally settled by the empirical studies on which this book concentrates.

The contrast between elitist and citizenship theory is sometimes exaggerated. Citizenship theorists could and do accept some of the account of the weaknesses of citizens which elitist theorists present. Moreover, much of the elitist attack on traditional democratic theories simply does not apply to citizenship theorists. Indeed, no serious democratic theorist ever demanded, for example, 'omni-competent citizens', an ideal so grandly described by Lippmann that he admits that he himself could never attain it.[35] Nevertheless, this brief look at elitist democratic theory should indicate that the presuppositions of citizenship do make a difference. Citizenship theory with its presuppositions of autonomy and improvability does draw our attention to the capacities of citizens for greater political involvement. Elitist democratic theory, resisting those presuppositions and the standards of citizenship that accompany them, does not.

REVIEW AND PREVIEW OF CITIZENSHIP

The presupposition of autonomy, enjoining us to treat citizens as the best judges of their interests, is revealed by the distrust of theories which would remake the citizen according to some rationalist ideal of what is in his interest. Most citizenship theorists prefer to say that democracy should give a citizen what he wants, not what others think he should have. Self-realization and development of individuals are not to be directed toward some preconceived end set by the theorists but to ends largely shaped by the aspirations of citizens. Although citizenship theorists substantially qualify the portrait of the common man as a rational, self-sufficient individual, their commitment to the modified view of him is not qualified very much at all. The presupposition is also reflected in the belief that substitutes for citizens in political activity are to be avoided as far as possible. For most theorists, the demand that citizens take a large part in political processes does not entail a particular set of institutions, such as government by referenda or public opinion polls. Certainly not all the theorists agree that the demand for participation implies unqualified majority rule or direct democracy even in principle.[36] Nor does citizenship theory deny that leadership is essential in a democracy. But it does insist not only that leaders share the values and beliefs of the ordinary citizen, not only that they remain sensitive to his needs, but also that leaders strive to activate the inactive citizen.

The presupposition of improvability can be seen in the theorists' commitment to progress, attenuated though the idea of progress is. Less concerned with explaining or defending than with transforming democracy, citizenship theory does not treat present defects as inevitable but seeks to correct them by educating the citizen and by encouraging him to become more competent in political affairs. The defects are not to be circumvented by lessening his political responsibility or the need for his involvement in politics. The presupposition of improvability sustains the expectations that change can be favorable to democratic ideals and that efforts toward achieving the ideals, though difficult, will not be futile.

Whether or not a theory is based on the presuppositions of citizenship does make a difference. The impact of their absence in elitist democratic theory should suggest the impact of their presence in citizenship theory. Furthermore, these presuppositions protect citizenship theorists from prematurely rejecting their view of citizenship in face of the findings of social science. They escape what in the next chapter will be identified as descriptivism. The standards of citizenship which the presuppositions partly support are thus more secure. However, these standards are significantly affected by empirical evidence in ways that will be the principal focus of the rest of this essay.

The standards of citizenship can be presented as sets of conditions and ideals for four aspects of citizenship—participation, discussion, rational voting and equality. Citizenship theorists do not set out their view of citizenship in this way; nor do they explicitly distinguish four standards. But this is an appropriate way in which to bring together the content of citizenship theory and social science.

One way the standards of citizenship are related to the presuppositions is through what may be called the democratic objective. All the standards in some form aim at this objective among others. Since the democratic objective refers to an aggregation of what everyone, or as many people as possible, will consider to be in their own interest, the objective plainly is supported by the presupposition of autonomy. The presupposition of improvability, however, reminds us that any present expression of interests may not be the most satisfactory, and that greater involvement in politics should allow citizens to recognize their interests more clearly. Here some of the ideals of citizenship promote such improvement.

The standards are related to the presuppositions not only through the democratic objective, but also more directly. The demand for *participation*, it should already be clear from the discussion in this chapter, itself expresses a belief in autonomy and improvability. Presupposing autonomy, theorists urge that as far as possible a citizen should articulate his own interests in the political processes which shape the fundamental choices in a system. If each citizen is to be treated as the best judge of his own interest, it follows that no one is a completely adequate substitute for him, assuming that his view of his interest sometimes differs from those held by others. Presupposing improvability, theorists see greater participation as a means to greater political competence.

Since political *discussion* is a form of participation, the standards of discussion are also partly founded on the two presuppositions in the same way that the demand for participation is. There is a further connection between the presuppositions and discussion, however. The commitment to discussion as a method of resolving differences and modifying interests reflects the belief that a citizen's interests and desires ultimately must be changed only by him, not manipulated or coerced by an external agent. Furthermore, the process of discussion is believed to encourage a citizen, on his own or looking to his reference groups, to modify his views about his interests where his views are faulty. Both these beliefs about the nature of the changes which properly conducted discussion engenders are thus partly sustained by the presuppositions of autonomy and improvability.

Rational voting can be assumed to take place if citizens are presupposed to be the best judges of their own interests. And if citizens' competence is improvable, efforts to modify the conditions under which voting decisions are formed will make voting more rational. Voting is crucial in citizenship theory since it is the one political act which all citizens can be expected to perform. For this reason, it can give a sense of purpose and direction to other political activities, and can serve as an avenue to more active expression of political interests. However, it is not only as an expression of choices or interests that voting is important. The act of voting allows citizens to feel that they have played a part in the process which produces the electoral result. The result can thus be certified in their minds as legitimate. The more the whole process leading up to the electoral results fulfills all the other standards of citizenship, the more legitimate citizens will feel it to be and the more legitimate it will be.

Finally, the standards of *equality* are based partly on a commitment to autonomy. Presupposing autonomy, citizenship theorists tend to think that all citizens are equally entitled to decide matters of fundamental political and social choice, and therefore that all the activities of citizenship should be equally distributed. Furthermore, the presupposition inclines some citizenship theorists, notably Laski and Cole, to urge radical alterations in the political and social structure so as to provide more nearly equal exercise of power by all citizens. All efforts to realize equality of citizenship are further supported by the presupposition that citizens' competence is improvable.

Each of the four aspects of citizenship can be expressed in three modes which indicate the various ways in which citizenship is manifested in a democracy; the ways it could be manifested; and the ways it might be. A schema for these modes of citizenship will be developed in the next chapter, and applied using empirical studies in the subsequent four chapters.

2 *Schema*

If the standards in citizenship theory are to be confronted with some findings of social science, citizenship theory should be presented within a schema which distinguishes various kinds of standards according to the degree to which such evidence affects them. The chief aim of this chapter is to develop such a schema by defining and elaborating three kinds of standards of citizenship.

The schema is not founded on approaches adopted by citizenship theorists. These theorists, as well as many others, tend toward one of two extreme approaches to relating evidence and value standards —prescriptivism or descriptivism. The first task in this chapter is to argue against these approaches. The next is to describe a more balanced approach which should underlie the schema that brings the findings of social science to bear on the standards of citizenship.

PRESCRIPTIVISM AND DESCRIPTIVISM

Faced with a conflict between democratic theory and evidence from social science, many writers tend either to discount the evidence or to give up the theory. Prescriptivism represents the first tendency; descriptivism, the second. Neither constitutes a satisfactory approach.

Prescriptivism in its extreme form maintains that all value standards of citizenship theory should be treated as prescriptions that are immune to challenge by evidence from social science. The standards in citizenship theory, it would be said, are 'prescription[s] for a worthwhile polity which should be sought after'. No evidence about what men do or can do in present polities could ordinarily undermine such prescriptions.[1]

The trouble with prescriptivism is that it overlooks the fact that most democratic theorists insist that some of their value standards are closely related to present political reality. Only a few standards in citizenship theory are as insulated from the findings of social science as prescriptivism suggests. In the case of many other standards, citizenship theorists would agree with Dewey's view that in seeking 'a measure for the worth of any given mode of social life', we should not

> set up, out of our heads, something we regard as an ideal society. We must base our conception upon societies which actually exist, in order to have any assurance that our ideal is a practicable one. . . . The problem is to extract the desirable traits or forms of community life which actually exist, and employ them to criticize undesirable features and suggest improvement.[2]

Neither do religious theorists let their interest in perfection blind them to modifying standards in face of what Simon calls 'factual necessities'.[3] Even Laski, who because of his antipathy toward existing institutions and conditions might be expected always to object to relating standards to present reality, does not entirely give up hope of reform within the existing social and political framework.[4]

Descriptivism in its pure form asserts that the findings of social science refute or support the standards of citizenship in just the way such evidence would refute or support a descriptive or explanatory proposition. For instance, some writers argue that since electoral studies show that voters do not consider the public good, the proposition that they should do so is somehow falsified.[5] The trouble with descriptivism is that it ignores the fact that citizenship theorists do not offer this proposition, or any other value standard, as a description or explanation of anything. The standards of citizenship, though affected by evidence, express evaluations and prescriptions which cannot be treated simply as empirical generalizations.

Neither citizenship theorists nor elitist democratic theorists actually adopt either prescriptivism or descriptivism in their pure forms. However, elitist theorists, as we have seen, generally place too much weight on behavioral findings in assessing most value standards, and hence tend toward descriptivism. Had citizenship theorists integrated evidence from social science into their theories, their general approaches would most likely have led them toward either descriptivism or prescriptivism.

Theorists such as Lindsay, Dewey, Friedrich and MacIver who emphasize shared values or operative ideals tend toward descriptivism.[6] For the question of what ideals are held by members of a community, though different from empirical questions about what the members of a community do, can be answered solely by analysis of empirical evidence. These theorists do not, like some descriptivists, make the simple mistake of supposing that empirical evidence about what men do falsifies value standards, but they tend to assume that (properly analyzed) evidence about what men value fully determines and justifies value standards.

Other citizenship theorists tend toward prescriptivism because their general approaches do not reveal the importance of evidence from social science. Some Thomist natural law theorists, for example, consider the question of how far democratic ideals are actually realized to be casuistry, not genuine political philosophy.[7] Socialist humanism deals in broad historical generalizations susceptible to some kinds of significant empirical study but not to the findings of less sweeping inquiries conducted by most social scientists. Scientific theorists might be expected to have a better record on this score, but they do not. Kelsen is so intent on keeping his theory 'pure' (i.e. non-ideological and non-factual) that his treatment of democracy almost never mentions any empirical objections to democratic ideas.[8] Similarly, Merriam is, as one commentator notes, 'far more interested in using "science" as a concept of a general political theory than in being scientific himself'.[9]

Even though the standards of citizenship partly rest, as we have seen, upon presuppositions that ultimately cannot be refuted by social science, we can reasonably expect some detailed evidence to be given in support of the specific forms which the standards take. Since the presuppositions are compatible with a wide range of possible forms and degrees of citizenship, evidence from social science is needed to formulate and adequately defend the specific standards of citizenship. If we recognize the relevance of social science and at the same time maintain some independence of value standards from the evidence, we can avoid the exaggerations of prescriptivism and descriptivism to which many democratic theorists are prone. We must stress, as descriptivism does too little and prescriptivism too much, a *disparity* between evidence from social science and value standards in citizenship theory. At the same time, we must emphasize, as prescriptivism does too little and descriptivism too one-sidedly, an *interplay* between the evidence and the standards. The schema to be proposed here assumes both the disparity and the interplay between evidence and value standards. The next two sections explain and defend these two assumptions.

THE DISPARITY BETWEEN EVIDENCE AND STANDARDS

The presuppositions of citizenship, as we have seen, are normally unaffected by empirical evidence from social science. Since the value standards in citizenship theory are partly based on the presuppositions, they are partly protected from refutation by social science. The value standards in citizenship theory are conditions and ideals which are used to prescribe and evaluate. Evidence from social science is expressed by propositions which describe or explain. It is clear, at least *prima facie*, that evaluating and prescribing are different kinds of linguistic activities from describing and explaining, however mingled these activities may be in actual discourse. It is not so clear, however, exactly how the differences between these activities should be characterized, how important they are or what implications follow from them. This set of problems is enormously complex and has occupied English-speaking moral philosophers more than any other single problem in this century.[10] Without pretending to settle these problems here, we need to establish a disparity between value standards and evidence in citizenship theory. We must maintain that standards cannot be completely justified by reference to any set of findings from social science. The methods for justifying the standards and the findings that constitute the evidence, despite some overlap, do not entirely coincide.[11]

The justification of a finding in social science always depends on an observational test or on other propositions which are subject to such tests. The justification of a value standard in citizenship theory depends not only on observational tests but also on a human decision to accept some higher-order principle, such as a presupposition, from which the standard follows. Admittedly, findings in social science also presuppose the acceptance of certain higher-order principles, such as the principle of induction or the laws of logic, which cannot be established by observational tests. But the same principles must be taken for granted in the justification of value standards, since empirical evidence is almost always an ingredient in this process too. In justifying value standards there are *additional* principles which require a decision not based on observation—most obviously the presuppositions of citizenship.

The general philosophical perspectives of citizenship theorists indicate that they do not share a common view of the relation between value standards and evidence, even though very few of them explicitly discuss it. The views range from those of natural law theorists such as Simon, who rejects any fundamental division between empirical evidence and value standards, to those of the positivists such as Ross and Kelsen, who rigidly maintain such a division.

Dewey, who is one of the few citizenship theorists to give this question any serious attention, would probably object to the disparity between standards and evidence as presented here.[12] For Dewey, justifications of evidence and value standards both terminate in observations or predictions of consequences. Dewey is correct in asserting that the consequences of acting upon any value standard must be considered carefully. But ultimately a value standard rests upon a human choice that no amount of evidence about consequences can finally determine. Even if we know all the consequences of acting on a certain value standard and what consequences we desire, we still must decide between competing standards. If, for example, we wish to hold a standard which prescribes equal political participation by all citizens, and (let us assume) we discover that this will impede the adoption of certain liberal programs which we also desire, we must decide whether or to what extent this value of equality surpasses the values which the liberal programs would further. Complete empirical knowledge about consequences, though necessary for a reasoned decision, does not dictate the final decision. In citizenship theory, we must consider other value standards and the presuppositions.

Thus because of the necessity of making decisions that are never fully justified on the basis of observations alone, the methods for justifying value standards in citizenship theory cannot be identified with the methods for justifying evidence from social science. A disparity exists between the standards and evidence in the sense that the standards cannot be justified solely by reference to the findings of social science.

Some writers object that most of the propositions in social and political inquiry fuse empirical and valuational elements in such a way that they can be separated, if at all, only at the cost of serious distortion.[13] This objection cannot be answered convincingly in *general* terms. However, it can be undermined, if we can show, as I intend to do in this study, that in assessing a *particular* theory the two elements can be meaningfully distinguished.

Even though we must reject the view that empirical and valuational elements are inseparably fused in political inquiry, we need not reject the argument which the view is sometimes used to support. This argument is that social science cannot be 'value-free' because values affect the selection of problems and the interpretation of data in social science.[14] Even though this argument is sound, we may still recognize the disparity between value standards and evidence from social science. One social scientist may hold values which, for example, incline him toward elitist democratic theory, while another holds values which support citizenship theory. Each emphasizes different problems in his research and finds different implications in it, but both can agree on what the data describe. Indeed, these hypothetical social scientists correspond fairly well to Walter Lippmann and Graham Wallas.

THE INTERPLAY BETWEEN EVIDENCE AND STANDARDS

Although values no doubt influence empirical inquiries, the important interplay between value standards and evidence in citizenship theory should occur in assessing value standards. The standards, as well as the presuppositions, affect what evidence we consider and how we interpret it, and the evidence affects the way we formulate and appraise the standards (though normally not the presuppositions).

This interplay cannot be recognized if evidence is not brought to bear on the value standards of democratic theory in the first place, and citizenship theorists who are prone to prescriptivism therefore have inhibited a proper understanding of this interplay. But many social scientists also share the blame. In contemporary social science, the disparity between evidence and value standards is blown up into a rigid dichotomy. Many social scientists have taken only too seriously Max Weber's strictures against confusing empirical and valuational inquiry. They have shunned systematic evaluation and prescription and have refused to integrate their findings with valuational theory.[15] It is sometimes forgotten that Weber himself rejected the view that social scientists must eschew evaluation and prescription.[16] Nothing in the disparity between standards and evidence, as presented here, precludes applying the conclusions of social science to a systematic democratic theory which is primarily evaluative and prescriptive.

While the value standards in such a theory must ultimately rest upon human decisions which are not based on evidence alone, an intelligent decision results only from a complex process of reasoning which can hardly be said to yield arbitrary or irrational conclusions.[17] A value standard must be justified by reasons, in accordance with some systematic procedure, which should show whether the standard is consistent with other standards and with the basic presuppositions, and whether it is supported by empirical evidence. The last four chapters of this study illustrate some forms which this reasoning about value standards may take. In this process, an interplay between evidence and standards is essential.

In general, evidence from social science can support or weaken value standards of citizenship in two ways. First, evidence can show whether a standard is realized, or is likely to be realized. If, for example, evidence suggests that all the changes designed to realize a prescription for greater citizen participation in present social conditions are not likely to do so, the prescription, though not refuted, becomes less tenable. Exactly why the prescription should be thus weakened is not easy to explain, but it no doubt arises from the assumption, built into at least some uses of our concept of choice, that we cannot sensibly be asked to choose to do something that is very likely to be impossible. Admittedly, not all moral or political prescriptions are confined to the realm of what is possible or likely. The saints and heroes of moral life have their counterparts in the revolutionary radicals of political life. But a large number of prescriptions of democratic theory are intended to be realized. For these, evidence which indicates that they are probably unrealizable, though not necessarily decisive, is damaging.

We cannot specify in any precise way the degree to which a prescription is supported or weakened by a piece of evidence showing that it is unlikely to be realized, even if the evidence is reliable and quantitatively expressed. For it is not merely a matter of judging the probability of whether the means will realize the end posited by the prescription; the means themselves have to be judged by value standards. Moreover, the role of the standard in the whole theory must be taken into account. Although we can never say exactly how much a standard is weakened by being shown to be unlikely to be realized, we can certainly say that such a standard is less acceptable than if it were shown to be likely to be realized.

The second general way in which evidence can be used to support or weaken standards of citizenship is by showing what consequences would follow from realizing (or from not realizing) the standard. The consequences may follow either from the practice specified in the standard itself (for example, greater participation) or from the means thought to be necessary to realize the standard (for example, greater social equality to increase participation). In either case, if the consequences which follow from realizing the standard are less desirable than not realizing the standard, then normally the standard is not acceptable, or is at least weakened. Here again, there is room for imprecision, not only in weighing the likelihood of certain consequences but also in weighing the consequences themselves.

This account of the general ways in which evidence affects value standards does not fully represent the interplay that should occur in justifying a value standard. It is not simply a matter of clarifying a *particular* value standard and deciding, after using evidence in the two ways, whether the standard is acceptable. Consideration of evidence, as well as conceptual analysis of the standard, often opens up new possibilities or difficulties that may not have been apparent when a standard is considered by itself. These new possibilities or difficulties may force a revision of the standard, either because a revised standard seems more feasible, has more desirable consequences or is more compatible with other standards and with the presuppositions in the theory. The revised standard may then require analysis and may call for further empirical investigation. At the same time, investigating unforeseen possibilities may turn up implications for *other* standards in the theory. These implications will have to be explored before we can be satisfied that the standard with which we began, even if it is revised, is justified. The procedure may often not be complete for one standard until all the standards in the theory are similarly examined.

Only by actually demonstrating how standards are revised and assessed in the whole theory of citizenship can the procedure for justifying standards be adequately explained. However, we are not therefore forced to abandon completely the hope for some general outline of a procedure. By specifying the major types of standards in citizenship theory, and the ways in which evidence can affect each type, we can develop a schema in which a procedure for justifying the standards can be systematically presented.

THE SCHEMA

In the schema, three modes of citizenship are represented by three kinds of standards of citizenship—conditions, constructive ideals and reconstructive ideals. Each of the four aspects of citizenship yields standards, partly based on the presuppositions discussed in Chapter 1, in each of the three modes.

Aspects of citizenship yielding standards	Modes of citizenship		
	1	2	3
Participation	Conditions	Constructive ideals	Reconstructive ideals
Discussion	Conditions	Constructive ideals	Reconstructive ideals
Voting	Conditions	Constructive ideals	Reconstructive ideals
Equality	Conditions	Constructive ideals	Reconstructive ideals

Conditions

Conditions concern citizenship as it exists, constructive ideals concern citizenship as it could be in present social and political structures, and reconstructive ideals concern citizenship as it might be in a new structure. Evidence from social science (in its present state of development) is most relevant for justifying a condition, less relevant for a constructive ideal and least relevant for a reconstructive ideal.

CONDITIONS

A condition stipulates that in particular democratic systems a certain aspect of citizenship must fulfill specified functions according to weak or minimal criteria. To decide whether the functions are fulfilled, we judge whether evidence from social science indicates that the functions are performed in the manner that citizenship theory implies; and approximately to the extent that the theory implies.

In formulating a condition, we deliberately try to find criteria which preserve at least a minimum of the valuational content of citizenship theory and which at the same time can be met at present in Britain and the United States. (These particular democratic systems appear here not for any reasons inherent in the schema but for the reasons of intellectual convenience given in the Introduction). Thus, formulating a condition is neither a purely empirical nor a purely evaluative operation, but requires an interplay, described in the previous section, between evidence and value standards. The condition is brought into conformity with the evidence, but in a way and within the limits set by the standards and presuppositions of citizenship theory. In treating conditions in this way, we avoid both prescriptivism and descriptivism.

The purpose of postulating conditions that can be satisfied is to escape the distortion that would result from denying that systems commonly regarded as democratic by political scientists and others exhibit any democratic citizenship at all. There is little to be gained from the semantic imperialism that would appropriate the term 'democratic' for only those activities of which one *fully* approves. Moreover, the presupposition of autonomy instructs us to respect whatever citizenship is manifest now. But equally we must stress that the conditions are based on weak or minimal criteria so as to avoid the implication that the kind and extent of citizenship that has been achieved is completely satisfactory. For this implication would violate both presuppositions of citizenship. The need for further improvement thus implied by the conditions is made explicit by the ideals of citizenship.

Political systems are sometimes evaluated according to how well they satisfy conditions that are supposed to be empirically necessary for the persistence of democratic systems.[18] These prerequisites, such as the proper distribution of income or cultural and psychological traits, should not be the primary interest in a theory which is meant to evaluate citizenship. The stability for which such empirical conditions are necessary is better treated in citizenship theory as only one objective or function of the conditions for citizenship. It is a subsidiary objective because most citizenship theorists have properly been more concerned about the quality of citizenship and how it can be improved in a democratic system than about how the system manages to persist at all.

Some political scientists employ empirical conditions to evaluate the quality of processes in developed democracies in a way that, for a different reason, is inadequate for a theory of citizenship. The trouble is that these political scientists would transform the evaluation of citizenship into a purely empirical enterprise. Robert Dahl's eight minimal conditions for a polyarchy, for example, are arbitrary points on continua that could quantitatively express, for instance, the extent of voting or the extent to which citizens possess equal information. Dahl concedes that to use his criteria or conditions to evaluate political systems, we may have to make judgments that at least at present cannot be expressed meaningfully in purely quantitative or even empirical terms. However, he apparently does not think that this difficulty represents an insurmountable obstacle to formulating in purely empirical terms a democratic theory which can be used to evaluate political systems.[19] Certainly we should encourage efforts to develop quantitative indices and weighting procedures for the purposes of evaluation. But if my earlier account of the disparity and the interplay between evidence and standards is correct, then the difficulties in operationalizing evaluative criteria cannot be avoided by greater scientific sophistication. They are inherent in any democratic theory which recognizes that evaluation cannot be based on empirical findings alone.

THE DEMOCRATIC OBJECTIVE

Of the objectives or functions toward which the conditions are directed, one which appears in some form in all democratic theory is the democratic objective. The democratic objective stipulates that a political system produce rules and decisions which, of all practical alternatives, are those which will satisfy the interests of the greatest possible number of citizens. This objective is implicit in the standards and presuppositions of citizenship theory.[20] The full meaning of the objective will become clear when the conditions of citizenship are analyzed in the following chapters. However, four possible misunderstandings can be forestalled.

In the first place, the democratic objective is not the only important objective with which citizenship theory deals. It has pre-eminence in the first mode in the schema only because it happens to be the one which almost all democratic theorists agree is a significant part of the purpose of democracy. Other objectives toward which conditions are directed, such as individual self-realization, may be equally important.

In the second place, the democratic objective is not a static concept—a simple aggregation of preferences that are expressed at a particular time. The future tense of the term 'will satisfy' in the definition of the objective suggests that citizens can alter their views of what their interests are. Also, because of the way the concept is embedded in the theory of citizenship, it takes into account the circumstances in which interests are formed and changed. As we shall see, even the failure of some citizens to express interests does not prove that these citizens would not express interests if they were to participate in politics.

In the third place, the principle of relative majority rule, which stipulates that the alternative preferred by the greatest number of voters be selected, cannot be considered either a sufficient or always a necessary criterion for the democratic objective. The principle is not a sufficient criterion because other standards of citizenship must also be met before the democratic objective is satisfied. The principle is not always a necessary criterion because it may be qualified or suspended if it conflicts with the standards, especially the standard of equality. Since the equality standard requires that all citizens be treated equally not merely in the counting of votes but in all aspects of citizenship, it implies that minorities must be protected even though they lose elections. The majority principle must not prevent present minorities from becoming future majorities, must not violate the basic rights of permanent minorities and (perhaps) should not prevent intense minorities from overruling indifferent majorities on particular issues.[21] Although the many social and institutional mechanisms which would qualify or suspend the principle of majority rule cannot be examined here, plainly the majority principle in citizenship theory is subordinate to the equality standard and other standards.[22]

In the fourth place, it is not easy to evade the logical paradoxes which mathematical theorists have found in deriving a collective choice from a set of individual preferences (as the democratic objective in principle would require). Given certain seemingly reasonable conditions, not only the majority principle but all methods for deriving a collective choice from a set of individual preferences will, for some set of preference orderings, always produce paradoxical results (for example, a collective ordering of *A* to *B*, *B* to *C*, and *C* to *A*). Kenneth Arrow, the most prominent expositor of these paradoxes, thinks that the 'Anglo-American two-party system' escapes the paradoxes since they do not arise when voters are limited to only two choices.[23] But even if we agree that the British and American systems are two-party systems, the problem comes up again when we ask if the party systems offer voters genuine choices. In principle, an adequate answer to this question would require a derivation of a collective choice from sets of individual preferences among a range of alternatives greater than two. If we suppress the problem at the electoral stage of the political process, it intrudes again at the nomination stage.

The paradoxes can be avoided if we apply the majority principle only where individual preference orderings are not very dissimilar (in a way that can be mathematically defined). However, there is not sufficient empirical evidence to indicate how common this unacceptable dissimilarity is in preference orderings in actual democracies. It is not yet possible, therefore, to regard these paradoxes as insignificant. However, since citizenship theory focuses on electoral processes where those logical problems are not so acute, we need not pursue them in the form raised by Arrow. This should not obscure the fact that they remain a serious difficulty for any democratic theory.[24]

THE CONCEPT OF AN IDEAL

An ideal in citizenship theory pictures a desirable state of affairs which is not yet realized. It may also explicitly or implicitly prescribe that we strive to realize that state of affairs, and it may evaluate the present state of affairs in which the ideal is not realized.

Ideals thus differ from conditions in that ideals need not be realized to be justified. Once an ideal in citizenship theory is realized, it is properly speaking no longer an ideal from the perspective of any current version of the theory. While in ordinary discourse we sometimes speak of an ideal which is realized now (e.g. 'This is the ideal time for the election'), we do not do so if, as in citizenship theory, we can specify a state of affairs which is superior to the realized state of affairs in the same or similar respects.

The prescriptions expressed or implied by an ideal refer to striving to realize an ideal, not necessarily realizing it. Even for those ideals that are intended to be realizable, we must focus on whether citizenship is moving toward an ideal rather than how far citizenship presently falls short of an ideal. Usually an ideal in citizenship theory is too vague to serve as a standard against which to measure the precise amount of change, though the ideal is definite enough to indicate the kind and direction of change that is desired. If we were to restrict citizenship theory to ideals which are capable of precise formulation, we would tie the theory too closely to present political knowledge. If a satisfactorily large gap is to exist between ideals and present political life, we must be able to prescribe, for example, greater participation, without having to specify exactly how much more.

The concept of an ideal proposed here is broader than the common notion of an ideal as the 'best attainable'. For any desirable state of affairs, even less than the best, may be the subject of an ideal so long as it is not realized. Nor does the concept exclude, as some philosophers' concept of an ideal would, claims based merely on interests or wants.[25] The concept also extends beyond two other concepts of an ideal—operative ideals and myths—which some citizenship theorists adopt. Arguing that political theory should be conceived as ideals that are 'operative in men's minds', A. D. Lindsay writes:

> The thing that matters to the state or any association is not what political theorists think about it but what its own members suppose it to be: their beliefs about it and their loyalties to the purposes it is supposed to support, in virtue of which they go on paying their taxes or subscriptions and act as loyal members of it.[26]

Similarly, MacIver defines 'myths' as 'value-impregnated beliefs and notions that men hold, that they live by or live for'.[27]

One reason citizenship theory should not be limited to these ideals is that they would reduce valuational inquiry to an almost purely empirical operation of analyzing what people believe and what functions their beliefs perform. To concentrate on operative ideals and myths would be to evade inquiring whether the beliefs people hold can be justified as democratic theory. A second objection to confining democratic theory to operative ideals and myths is that the beliefs people express are not sufficiently analytical or unprosaic to form the basis for a democratic theory that would satisfy academic theorists. The operative ideals of most men are indistinct clichés. The political theorist may conceive of his task as making such ideals explicit, but he is more often actually propounding ideas of his own or other political theorists—ideas which bear only a vague resemblance to the 'ideals that are operative in men's minds'. And that is as it should be. The ideals of democratic theory, even of a theory which exalts the ordinary citizen, need not be limited to what the ordinary citizen espouses.

The general concept of an ideal takes two forms in citizenship theory. The first will be called a constructive ideal because the non-radical changes to which it refers can be built upon present social and political structures. The second form will be called a reconstructive ideal because the radical changes to which it refers challenge rather than build upon present structures.

CONSTRUCTIVE IDEALS

In the second mode in the schema, a constructive ideal pictures a state of affairs that is intended to be realizable by trends and non-radical reforms. Such an ideal requires either a greater degree of whatever the corresponding condition stipulates—for example, more participation by more citizens; or a stronger form or kind of whatever the condition stipulates—for example, more debate where the condition requires only non-manipulated discussion.

At least by implication, a constructive ideal also prescribes these changes required by the state of affairs it pictures. The range of the prescribed changes extends from a point just beyond the status quo to a point just before radical reform would be necessary to promote the ideal further. Although a constructive ideal is thus restricted to changes which can be effected by non-radical reforms or by trends, it does not exclude non-radical reforms that might cause other subsequent changes which *are* radical. For example, an increase in voting turnout which could be accomplished without radical reform might create a new bloc of voters which would subsequently use its power to bring about radical social and political changes.

We should not expect to discover objective criteria which would empirically distinguish radical and non-radical change in all or most possible instances. For what counts as radical change naturally depends upon the perspective from which one views a change and on what stakes one has in the change. But the absence of criteria is not a serious difficulty in citizenship theory where substantial agreement exists on what changes are to count as radical. Let us settle for a formal definition: A reform is radical if it requires a qualitative change in an existing economic, social, or political structure of a nation-state. This definition, though obviously incomplete, at least directs our attention to the structure in which a reform takes place, and this is not an unimportant consequence. For the question of whether or not a reform is radical is often confused with whether the rate of a change is gradual or sudden, or whether the way in which a change is implemented is peaceful or violent.[28] It cannot be argued *a priori* that non-radical reform is always peaceful and gradual, and radical reform always violent and sudden. These are largely empirical issues (though evidence from social science may not resolve them, as we shall see below).

Why should the idea of non-radical or moderate change as expressed in constructive ideals be given a prominent place in citizenship theory? First, the relative stability that is preserved by moderate change is an important value not only in most developed democracies but also in most citizenship democratic theories. Although stability is not sacrosanct, it must not be discounted. Second, evidence from social science would be much less relevant to assessing the ideals of citizenship if we allowed only radical ideals because, as we shall see, the link between any such evidence and the ideal is tenuous. Third, disillusionment with democracy and democratic theory, as several citizenship theorists observe, may result from expecting too much. Thomas Vernor Smith writes: 'If one cannot gain heaven, it is foolish to despair if there still remain in one's hands the means of avoiding hell.'[29] This limbo conception of democratic ideals may not adequately represent the noble aspirations of all citizenship theory, but it should not be charged with fostering complacency. On the contrary, such a conception has motivated constructive proposals for reform (such as MacIver's 'program for the control of inter-group discrimination in the United States') which though not radical are far from contented defenses of the status quo.[30] Furthermore, moderate reform need not lull citizens into complacency and stifle radical reform. In fact, some moderate reform raises expectations and generates demands for radical reforms, as I shall argue in Chapter 6.

To justify a claim that a constructive ideal is realizable, we need evidence to reveal *trends* which, if continuing, tend to realize the ideal; and to suggest that certain non-radical *reforms*, if effected, tend to realize the ideal. In addition to evidence about reforms and trends, evidence sometimes has to be used to show that promotion or realization of a particular constructive ideal would not be undesirable, or would not conflict with presuppositions and with other ideals. Notice that evidence about the reforms does not, strictly speaking, include evidence which would show whether and exactly how the reforms could be implemented. This study is not a handbook for reform. Only a few of the many possible changes in democratic life are used to illustrate their general role in citizenship theory.

Constructive ideals, as defined here, thus escape the defects of both prescriptivism and descriptivism. Since a constructive ideal must be supported by findings showing that it is realizable or that its realization is desirable, it is not immune to evidence from social science, as prescriptivism implies all ideals are. But neither is a constructive ideal fully determined or justified by such evidence, as descriptivism implies. For the ideal is partly supported by presuppositions which affect what findings are considered significant and how they are interpreted. In assessing a constructive ideal, then, we must allow for both a disparity and an interplay between the ideal and evidence.

RECONSTRUCTIVE IDEALS

Conditions remind us how far the standards of citizenship theory have been realized, and constructive ideals suggest what more could be done within an existing structure. Reconstructive ideals, the third mode in the schema, point out how much more remains to be done. Even if a democracy satisfied all the conditions and realized all the current ideals of citizenship, the presuppositions of citizenship would still direct further efforts toward autonomy and improvability. The reconstructive ideals at any particular time embody this ceaseless discontent.

Unlike a constructive ideal, a reconstructive ideal pictures a state of affairs that cannot be realizable without radical reform; or may not be realizable with any reform. In either case, the ideal is justifiable with little or no reference to evidence from behavioral social science as it now exists. Hence, prescriptivism seems to be nearly true of reconstructive ideals, though it is mistaken if applied to other standards in citizenship theory. Descriptivism is most obviously misleading in the case of reconstructive ideals.

Advocates of reconstructive ideals sometimes insist, as G. D. H. Cole does about Guild Socialist ideals, that they are 'eminently practical'. But also like Cole, most advocates recognize that the social structure will have to be transformed to effect such ideals.[31] This is why reconstructive ideals that are meant to be realizable receive little support from evidence drawn from social science. Since such evidence is based on studies conducted within the present structure, it would be unduly risky to extrapolate from this evidence to conclusions about citizenship in some future re-constructed society. Many of the factors that are assumed to be constant in these studies would have to be treated as variables if we were to take account of the possibility of radical reform. The voting studies, for example, assume as constant certain features of the context in which voting decisions are made; for example, findings about voter behavior in national elections assume a relative salience of national parties and candidates, which is largely a result of a centralized political structure. Were we to try to transform such constants into variables so that the findings would be applicable to all structures, the findings would be much less reliable and conclusive than they are now.

From evidence about radical reforms in sub-structures of society (for example, decentralization in a particular factory), we might be able to gain some hint of what effects analogous reforms in the whole structure would have. But even here, transferring findings in a sub-unit to a whole society may not be warranted. Evidence might show, for example, that citizens have a greater 'sense of efficacy' in a factory where decision-making is decentralized. But even if the whole society were decentralized so that there were no dominant points of power to which citizens could refer, citizens might feel less effective with respect to politics. A reconstructive ideal characteristically is so forward-looking that there is no exact instance or adequate analogy of its realization. Lacking such instances and analogies, advocates of reconstructive ideals turn not to social science but to historical, philosophical and even literary inquiry. The justification of such ideals requires an exercise of imagination that goes beyond what social science can warrant; it depends on a vision of historical forces and reconstructed societies that cannot be fully captured in any quantified general-ization.

Similarly, evidence from social science is misapplied if directed against two beliefs about the way in which radical reform must be implemented. Laski and others sometimes assert that radical reform must overturn the economic structure since economic factors are the most fundamental determinants of social and political life.[32] Even if we could unambiguously distinguish economic from other factors conceptually, the statistical problem of 'multicollinearity' would stifle any efforts to show comprehensively that economic factors are or are not more significant determinants or causes of particular phenomena than are other factors. When a number of economic variables are highly correlated with non-economic variables, it is often impossible to make reliable inferences about the relative contributions of these two sets of independent variables to the determination of any dependent variables.[33]

A second belief—that violence is necessary for radical change— usually stems either from a reaction to repeated failure in trying to reform a system peacefully; or from an interpretation of history which alleges that all significant radical change in the past has come by violent means.[34] Social science cannot destroy even the historical grounds for this belief because its proponents can always deny, usually with good reason, that any findings of social science are seriously incomplete and frequently misleading when applied to broad historical generalizations.[35]

If evidence from social science is of little help when reconstructive ideals are proposed as realizable programs for radical reform, it is of even less use when the ideals are presented as critical challenges which are not meant to be realizable by means of any reform. An ideal of complete decentralization of governmental decision-making may be practically unrealizable in any social and political structure. The ideal nonetheless serves as a reminder that citizenship in present structures falls far short of what would be desirable; it gives impetus to efforts to reconstruct society for the radical expansion of citizenship. A dialectic is thus generated between the ideal and the existing political life. In such a dialectic, it is desirable to have an ideal which pictures a state of affairs as far removed as is coherently possible from existing political reality. The more remote the ideal, the more ideological pressure it brings against the status quo, and if ideals have effects on men's minds, the more likely it is that some kind of reform will take place. Moreover, the further the ideal from the status quo, the further will be the resolution of the dialectic from the status quo. It follows, then, not only that a justifiable reconstructive ideal may be unrealizable but also that it may be more justifiable to the extent that it is more difficult to realize. If, for example, the pressures for coordination and planning in the present structure of industrialized society make decentralized organization more difficult, this is all the more reason for urging a reconstructive ideal of decentralization. Insofar as more practicable ideologies are needed to move men to action, we can always turn to constructive ideals and the less extreme reconstructive ideals. And these may be even more acceptable and attainable when the more extreme reconstructive ideals are seriously proposed.

That reconstructive ideals can receive less support from social science than conditions and constructive ideals does not make reconstructive ideals any less valid. They are sustained by the presuppositions of citizenship, and in some respects are, as we have noticed, more faithful to these presuppositions than are the conditions and constructive ideals. That reconstructive ideals are somewhat remote from the existing state of citizenship is no cause for criticizing these ideals, though it is cause for criticizing the present state of citizenship.

Although reconstructive ideals are relatively unaffected by evidence from social science, they may be weakly challenged or supported by such evidence in three ways. First, it may be alleged that even a partial increase in an activity urged by a reconstructive ideal would be undesirable. In such cases, the evidence cited to support the desirability of a reconstructive ideal will often be the same as the evidence cited to support the desirability of a corresponding constructive ideal. Second, some very limited support for a reconstructive ideal may come, as I suggested above, from evidence showing favorable effects of a reform analogous to, but on a smaller scale than, or in a different context from, the reform implied by the ideal. Finally, evidence may play a minor role in conceptual analysis which shows whether the ideal is internally coherent, or whether it conflicts with other ideals deemed equally or more desirable.

Without reconstructive ideals, a democratic theory is devoid of vision. It fails to serve as a guide for the radical changes which full realization of democratic ideals requires. A theory of citizenship bereft of these ideals fails to express the full import of the pre-suppositions of autonomy and improvability. By concentrating on constructive ideals, a democratic theory becomes too cautious and may miss opportunities for demanding desirable change.[36]

With *only* reconstructive ideals, a democratic theory spells disillusionment.[37] That is for instance the result of the shift in emphasis from constructive to reconstructive ideals at one point in Laski's thought. Similarly, treating all democratic ideals as reconstructive ideals is the fault of Sartori's analysis of the logical relations of ideals and reality. To say that all ideals are 'predestined not to succeed' and they are 'not . . . designed to be converted into reality' is to ignore the role of constructive ideals.[38] Without the backing of the less visionary but more widely acceptable constructive ideals, a democratic theory might be more readily dismissed and less widely acted upon. Reconstructive ideals unsupported by constructive ideals are as inimical to a satisfactory citizenship theory as are constructive ideals unsupported by reconstructive ideals. A balanced democratic theory should include both kinds.

CONCLUSION

The schema proposed here defines the standards of citizenship in terms of three modes, according to the degree to which evidence from behavioral social science is relevant to them. Conditions which stipulate functions or objectives in citizenship theory are the most affected by such evidence. The evidence significantly shapes how the conditions must be formulated if they are to be satisfied. The most common (but not the only) objective to which the conditions refer is the democratic objective, requiring that rules and decisions satisfy the interests of the greatest possible number of citizens. Constructive ideals, which prescribe a greater degree or a stronger form of what the conditions demand, partly depend on evidence which indicates whether they are realizable by certain non-radical changes. Reconstructive ideals picture a state of affairs which is not realizable within present social and political structures. These ideals are, therefore, less affected by evidence from social science than are the conditions or the constructive ideals but are not therefore any less acceptable.

The schema seeks to avoid both the prescriptivist approach, which treats all ideals as immune to evidence from social science, and the descriptivist approach, which treats ideals as falsifiable in the same way as generalizations in social science. Most democratic theorists including citizenship theorists are prone to one of these two approaches. In appraising the value standards of citizenship, these theorists consequently attach either too little or too much significance to the findings of social science. A more balanced approach, which underlies the schema presented here, recognizes both the disparity and the interplay between evidence and value standards. Value standards cannot be justified solely by evidence, but evidence does play an important role in justifying standards. Such evidence helps to formulate and assess conditions and constructive ideals, though these conditions and ideals (as well as the presuppositions) also influence the selection and interpretation of the evidence.

In the next four chapters, standards for the four aspects of citizenship—participation, discussion, rational voting, and equality —will be presented in each of the three modes in the schema and will be confronted with some findings of social science.

3 Participation

The demand for a high level of participation by citizens, as Chapter 1 revealed, is a prominent theme in citizenship democratic theory. The forms of participation which are most common in modern democracies are activities, such as voting and discussion, which are connected with the electoral processes. This chapter, and the next two, focus mainly on such activities.

Forms of participation which permit a more direct role in decision-making and those which take place outside regular channels will be examined briefly at the end of this chapter. These less common forms of participation are beyond the will and beyond the reach of most citizens most of the time in modern democracies. We may regret this and may seek to expand the body of citizens who engage in these neglected forms of participation, as some citizenship theorists wish to do. But we must not therefore fail to recognize the crucial importance of ordinary electoral activity. Although citizens are for much of the time only spectators in the drama of political decision-making, the extent and quality of this audience is a matter of great concern in a democracy. If this audience is to have a favorable influence on the course of political action, its size and the character of its members must achieve the standards of citizenship. We cannot prove that if citizens achieve these standards, they will have such influence, but we can assume that if citizens fall short, they will usually fail to have influence. Participation, like other aspects of citizenship, is a necessary but not a sufficient condition for democratic politics.

LOW PARTICIPATION

Nothing is more evident from empirical studies than the fact that at present even ordinary electoral participation by citizens is not, whatever the causes, very impressive. Even the turnout in American Presidential contests or British General Elections—which average less than two-thirds and four-fifths of the respective electorates—is for citizenship theorists no cause for pride. And turnout in off-year national elections is much lower; by-elections in Britain, for example, seldom bring out more than half the electorate. Only about 45 per cent of the American electorate are regular or 'core' voters, and about 40 per cent are completely outside 'the political universe'. Furthermore, the situation has probably deteriorated through the years. In this century the rate of turnout of citizens eligible to vote declined until 1930 and, despite a moderate resurgence, has never returned to pre-1900 levels.[1]

Turnout figures by themselves do not tell the whole story. Citizenship theorists often urge not only that citizens vote but that they vote with a feeling that their vote really matters. Yet far fewer people care about the outcome of an election and have a sense of political efficacy than vote.[2] The picture looks still more gloomy if we consider other forms of electoral participation, such as taking part in party and campaign activities, contributing money to parties of candidates, displaying campaign buttons or stickers, or trying to persuade others to vote in a certain way. Arranging these forms of participation in a hierarchy with descending numbers of people involved at each level, one political scientist classifies about 60 per cent of the electorate as 'spectators'—persons who do no more (and usually less) than display buttons or stickers. About one-third do not qualify for any place in the hierarchy.[3] Local politics and community political action, where some theorists have expected to find more extensive interest, evidently enlist no more citizens than national politics.[4] If anything, the estimates of participation based on surveys exaggerate the extent of participation that actually occurs. This is partly because many respondents probably answer so that they appear to be more responsible citizens than they are. Also, in any sample, the persons who cannot be located for interviews are more likely to be less politically involved and interested than those who can be interviewed.

It has often been claimed that evidence such as this undermines the views of citizen participation held by democratic theorists like the citizenship theorists. But a closer analysis will show that this claim, if directed against citizenship theory, is not warranted. In the first mode in the schema, let us consider six functions specified by the condition for participation. Different sorts and different degrees of participation are required depending on which particular function of participation is under consideration. We shall see that the condition can be virtually satisfied, if we are prepared to accept weak or minimal criteria for some functions.

SINISTER INTERESTS

A primary function of participation is to help ensure that what some nineteenth-century democrats called the 'sinister interests' of the rulers do not prevail over the interests of most of the citizens. Twentieth-century citizenship theorists make the same point, sometimes using the same phrase, sometimes writing about the 'abuse of power', or the danger of the 'one or a few' identifying 'their private good with the good of the community'.[5]

This function refers to a deliberate disregard of most citizens' interests, not to well-intentioned mistakes. It might seem, therefore, that regular elections, by which rulers could be discouraged from deliberately violating citizens' interest on pain of losing their jobs, would be sufficient to fulfill this function. But that it is not so easily fulfilled becomes clear when we try to decide what constitutes a violation of the interests of most citizens (even if we count what a citizen wants as an expression of what is in his interest).

A minimal criterion of whether citizens are protected against such a violation is the existence of adequate opportunities (e.g. elections) which would allow citizens to object effectively to what rulers do. On this criterion, a level of regular participation by citizens in elections great enough to force rulers to take elections seriously would be required. But for this purpose a rate of turnout in elections even lower than that which now occurs would be satisfactory. As long as the citizens who do vote are informed about what the rulers do and are not controlled by rulers, a majority of *any* number of voters are a threat to rulers if an electoral result can remove rulers from power. Under such circumstances, therefore, we might be tempted to say that if the minimal criterion of adequate opportunities to object is satisfied, and if no majority of voters disapprove in a given time period, then no violation of the interests of most citizens has occurred in this period.

At best, the absence of disapproval or protest is merely a negative indicator. It tells us only that the rulers are refraining from doing what most people do not want, not whether the rulers are doing what most people *do* want. But the existence of opportunities to express effective disapproval is not sufficient even as a 'negative' protection against violation of majority interests. Many political scientists often fail to notice this since they concentrate on specifying the characteristics which the processes and institutions of a political system must possess to provide adequate opportunities for expression of disapproval. Even when these opportunities exist and are used, two possibilities may develop which would prevent a majority from recognizing what they do not want. First, if not all interests are represented in the formation of public opinion and in elections, the absence of protest or disapproval is an unsatisfactory indicator even of majority interests. Failure to register a complaint in the political processes may be the result not of satisfaction or lack of concern but rather the result of a disability, such as not having enough money to get a proper hearing or being completely alienated from the political system. Second, acceptance of a proposal or a candidate may have undesirable consequences which would be apparent to knowledgeable citizens but not to citizens with little political interest or experience. These two possibilities make it necessary for the participation condition to specify two further functions of participation. Fulfilling the first function requires fulfilling these two additional functions.

EXCLUDED INTERESTS

Citizenship theorists assert that extensive participation is necessary so that all interests are considered and expressed by those who know them best. The assertion is supported by the presupposition that as a general rule each individual (or group of individuals) knows his own interest better than any well-intentioned ruler. This function of participation is most often presented in the form of the 'shoes-pinching' argument, the best known version of which is Lindsay's. 'Only . . . the ordinary man can tell whether the shoes pinch and where; and without that knowledge the wisest statesman cannot make good laws.'[6] Even if this argument is accepted, it does not,

Lindsay thinks, necessarily imply that participation by all in the control of government is necessary since benign rulers could discover what the people want by conscientiously soliciting the grievances of ordinary citizens. But unless people have power behind their grievances, the rulers will not listen: 'Experts do not like being told that the shoes they so beautifully make do not fit'.[7] In Lindsay's theory, then, the second function of participation in effect collapses into the first; it is really the possibility of the rulers having 'sinister interests' that requires extensive participation. Laski, too, sometimes telescopes these two functions. But actually the 'shoes-pinching' argument is stronger than Lindsay or Laski implies. For citizens often do not come to recognize their interests until they actually come to express them in political processes. Wants and dissatisfactions do not carry labels ready to be read off by rulers. That recognizing one's political interests is at least aided by participation is shown by the evidence considered in the next section that the more a person participates, the more politically knowledgeable he is.

To decide whether this function of participation is fulfilled is not a straightforward task. It would not be appropriate to test the presupposition that underlies the function—that individuals be treated as the best judges of their own interest—against empirical evidence. The presupposition, as we have seen, is not an empirical generalization or hypothesis, but rather it is a declaration of intention to treat individuals' claims about their own interest with respect. It serves notice that a theorist who accepts the presupposition will be more prepared than a theorist who does not to admit that what an individual claims is in his own interest actually is.

How can we decide whether this second function of participation is fulfilled? Clearly, participation by all citizens is not required. In the case of this function, the participation condition would be satisfied if all interests or preferences were represented in the processes by which a decision is adopted. This indirect expression of interests, many citizenship theorists have argued, can be accomplished by pressure groups and other associations, in spite of the fact that some earlier democratic theorists condemned them.[8] (Parties, too, share the role of the indirect expression of interests, but since parties aim more to influence the results of elections than the content of public policy, they are discussed in Chapter 5.)

Can pressure groups and other associations perform this role adequately? A full answer to this question is not possible here, partly because the evidence in the field is, as one authority has remarked, 'scant', but mainly because to attempt such an answer would transform this study of citizens into a study of institutions.[9] However, we should notice that some of the defects of pressure groups which are alleged to undermine their role as vehicles of indirect representation do not necessarily do so. It is true that a minority of the electorate belong to organizations that sometimes take stands on political issues, that of those who do belong few can be counted as active members, that the ratio of actual members to potential members of groups which associations represent is small, and that leadership of associations does not usually reflect the opinions of the rank-and-file.[10] If we are prepared to adopt a concept of symbolic representation, however, none of these facts undermines the function under consideration here.[11] A citizen need not be a member to be represented symbolically by a group or an organization. An organized group could be said to represent symbolically citizens who endorse its aims and identify themselves with it though they do not belong to the group. It would be possible to discover by surveys the extent of such endorsement and identification. At present the evidence is insufficient to establish the seemingly reasonable hypothesis that most interests in society are at least symbolically represented by groups and associations of some kind.

The main objection to introducing a concept of symbolic representation into democratic theory stems from the fact that the concept is satisfied when citizens merely *feel* represented. This feeling, it is feared, may be manipulated by leaders. Is not a concept of symbolic representation the basis of the fascist theory of representation?[12] This objection does not hold, if we can assume what the next chapter seeks to demonstrate, that citizens in the countries we consider are not likely to be manipulated in this way. If citizens are not manipulated, symbolic representation may be assumed to reflect real needs or wants, even though it may issue from affective responses of citizens to a group or to leaders. Even when a group fails to represent adequately the material interests of citizens who identify with the group, we should not infer that these citizens are not being represented as they wish to be. There probably is some point at which citizens would no longer identify with a group which failed to satisfy their material interests—perhaps at the point where a group causes more harm to their material interests than they receive from the satisfaction of feeling identified with it. If symbolic representation sometimes permits citizens to satisfy their psychic interest in identifying with a group at the expense of their material interests, the presupposition of autonomy instructs us to presume that such a choice is in their interest. This presumption could be rebutted if evidence showed that citizens do not know that their material interests are being sacrificed by the group which symbolically represents them; *and* that citizens do not consider the sacrifice worth the value of identifying with the group. A necessary condition of establishing the second point would be to show that citizens cease to identify with the group. Hence, as long as citizens continue to consider a group to represent them in this symbolic way, we must presume that the group expresses their interests (again provided manipulation does not take place). In the absence of the evidence that would be required to rebut the presumption, we may tentatively conclude that groups and other associations represent the interests of most citizens at least symbolically.

Still, the problem remains that some interests may not be represented, whether directly or symbolically, with the strength that their numbers deserve. Consumers, for example, are at a disadvantage because they do not meet together in their ordinary activities as do workers and managers. So are the unemployed, who have insufficient resources to mount a political protest or perhaps even to develop political identifications. Such disadvantaged interests are not easily organized so that they can be directly represented, and therefore probably cannot be represented symbolically as easily as other interests. If no effective organization at all exists to represent interests, symbolic representation cannot take place. Indeed, in such cases, the illusion of symbolic representation could lull persons with these unorganized interests into quiescence in a manner that is unacceptable even on a minimal interpretation of democratic theory.[13]

But this problem of unorganized interests can be satisfactorily handled if we adopt a concept of equality which can accommodate some limited amount of discrimination. In Chapter 6, such a concept will be proposed. In any case, if pressure groups derive their political leverage not from threats but from 'standing alliances' with parties, the fact that some interests are not organized, or not so well organized as other interests, may not matter so much as is usually thought—if parties give expression to these unorganized interests.[14] In Chapter 5, we shall see in what sense parties may be said to do just this. Thus, the failure of some citizens to vote or to belong to groups does not prove that these citizens' interests are excluded in a way that would violate the second function of participation.

POLITICAL KNOWLEDGE

Many citizenship theorists believe that participation increases citizens' political awareness and knowledge. This is the third function of participation.

Dewey maintains that all genuine knowledge, including political knowledge, can be acquired only by 'acting upon the world'; it cannot be passively absorbed. 'Men have to *do* something; they have to alter conditions'.[15] An activist epistemology such as this, reminiscent of Marx's theory of knowledge, has not been the dominant theory in philosophy. The most common philosophical theories of knowledge do not emphasize acting upon the world (beyond shaping phenomena by mental categories or interpretations) as an essential ingredient in knowledge. Yet for understanding knowledge of political interests, an activist epistemology seems a more appropriate approach than other more common theories of knowledge. For if a citizen does not try to influence his political environment in some way (at least by voting), he may not discover that he has political interests. Without 'acting upon' the political world, he cannot be said to have very good grounds for assurance that he has correctly interpreted his personal interests in political terms. Knowing your political interests implies not merely that you have wants and desires with respect to objects that a political system may allocate; but also that you can translate those wants and desires into *political* demands, such as support for a candidate, party or policy.

When individuals begin to participate in politics for the first time, they often assert new demands, reflecting new political interests. These new demands arise not simply because a new group of individuals have attained some political power with which political leaders must reckon. Frequently, individuals themselves had not conceived of their interests in terms of these political demands until they began to participate in politics. Until black Americans began to try to influence political decisions about school policy, many did not recognize that they had an interest in political decentralization. Political participation, then, can create political knowledge.

One consequence of the activist view of political knowledge is that we cannot justify regular non-participation by a citizen on the ground that he knows his own interest best. For a citizen cannot be said to know what his interests are until he participates to some degree. The presupposition of autonomy itself assumes at least some minimal degree of participation as a condition of having knowledge of political interests. Thus, we refuse to count as political knowledge claims which are not based on some fairly regular participation for some period of time, even if it is only voting.

A second consequence of the activist view of political knowledge is that the more that a citizen participates, the more knowledgeable he should become. In fact, voting and other forms of participation are highly correlated with the level of political information. One study found, for example, that 64 per cent of voters had adequate knowledge of candidates and only 11 per cent of non-voters did.[16] Voters also tend to have more opinions than non-voters, be more informed about politics, and to be better able to perceive differences between parties and candidates.[17] Even if the education level were held constant in arriving at these correlations (as it often is not) so that we could be sure that the higher level of information of more active persons is not entirely the result of better education, we could not safely conclude that participation is the cause of increased

61

political awareness and information. But it does seem as reasonable to assume that participation fosters political knowledgeability as to assume the converse, as do some political scientists.[18] It is most likely that the two factors mutually reinforce one another. The more a citizen participates, the more he is exposed to political ideas, the more political experience and self-confidence he acquires—and hence the more politically knowledgeable he becomes. At the same time, the more knowledgeable he becomes, the easier it is for him to participate. Thus, although the evidence is not entirely satisfactory, we can say that participation does, as citizenship theorists hope, contribute to the awareness and information which would help citizens to identify their political interests. But to decide whether a sufficient number of people are in fact knowledgeable enough to fulfill this function, we must know more about how political opinions are formed, a subject treated in the next chapter.

LEGITIMACY

Rousseau most eloquently described how participation can make citizens feel that the laws and decisions of a system are their own and can encourage citizens to obey and support even acts they initially opposed. But twentieth-century citizenship theorists also consider it an important function of participation to help make acts of the government legitimate in this sense—to give citizens what Merriam calls 'a sense of proprietorship' about them. Such a sense contributes, as Simon points out, to the creation of citizens' consent. Other theorists have focused instead on the deprivation of this sense—the alienation felt by citizens who do not or cannot participate. Dewey, for example, often deplored the 'meaninglessness' of politics for the politically inactive.[19] In all these forms, this sense of 'proprietorship' (or its absence) does not exhaust the content of the idea of legitimacy (or its contrary). The idea of legitimacy implies that a system is not only *felt* to be right or just but actually *is* so according to certain rational principles. One such principle would require that a system satisfy all the standards of citizenship. In fact, unless the system is legitimate according to such standards, most citizenship theorists would consider a subjective sense of legitimacy to be quite undesirable. A sense of legitimacy is not meant to imply complete approval of all aspects of a political system or to exclude a desire for significant reforms of a system.

Yet the subjective element of legitimacy which a sense of proprietorship expresses does represent a vital function of participation. It contributes indirectly to the democratic objective by supporting a stable system in which processes required by other functions of participation and other aspects of citizenship can operate. More importantly, citizenship theorists consider it a good to be sought for its own sake.

Two types of satisfaction, which have been investigated by several studies, serve as fairly good indicators of the extent to which this sense of proprietorship exists. The first is what Almond and Verba call 'satisfaction with the role of participant'. People who claim to have a feeling of satisfaction when they vote, for example, are said to be satisfied in this role. Such satisfaction is related to subjective political competence, i.e. the extent to which citizens believe they can participate in political decisions. Subjective political competence in turn is associated with actual participation.[20] Hence, there is some reason to believe that participation promotes many citizens' sense of satisfaction with their role in the political system (although the causal relationship may be reciprocal and other factors may contribute too).

The second type of satisfaction is general approval of, or attachment to, the system. This is no doubt often part of what leads a citizen to be satisfied with his role in the system. However, the two should be distinguished because some studies have found that satisfaction with one's role is the result more of long-standing personal and social traits while satisfaction with a system is due more to the immediate political environment.[21] For this reason, satisfaction with the system is probably more responsive to political participation than satisfaction with one's political role. Neither of these kinds of satisfaction should be confused with satisfaction with the outcome of an election, which is significant for legitimacy only insofar as it affects the first two kinds of satisfaction. A citizen *could* disapprove of the outcome of every election without ever being dissatisfied with the system or even with his role in it.

It is not certain that participation is necessary to create satisfaction with the system, for some studies appear to have shown that non-participation may be a sign of general satisfaction. Furthermore, high levels of participation, especially in unstable conditions, may be the result of general dissatisfaction and hence could hardly be said to foster satisfaction, at least not in any direct way.[22] Nonetheless, a number of studies conducted at the community level under fairly stable conditions have found that higher levels of participation are strongly associated with higher levels of satisfaction with local politics or with the community generally, and lower levels with dissatisfaction. Considering the available evidence, Campbell concludes that in the short-term general satisfaction is associated with non-participation but that in the long-term deep frustration and dissatisfaction are linked to non-participation too.[23] Presumably we may therefore say that citizenship theorists are not mistaken in associating participation and satisfaction with the system at the level of more fundamental long-term phenomena, although the evidence is not adequate to say for sure that participation actually produces satisfaction.

If satisfaction is associated with participation, can we say further that satisfaction contributes to the stability of a system? We can find some indication that this is so from comparative data. A much higher level of satisfaction (as measured by pride in institutions and government) is found to exist in the United States and Britain than in Germany, Italy and Mexico, which probably would be considered less stable.[24] It should be noted, however, that the differences in satisfaction among these countries are not due entirely to differences in rates of participation. Other factors, such as the age and performance of the political systems, may be even more important. The assertion that participation contributes to satisfaction probably is better established by studies within one system than by comparative studies.

SELF-REALIZATION

In holding that participation helps citizens discover and 'develop their capacities' and give them a sense of being 'in control of their destinies', Thomas Vernor Smith expresses a view commonly held by citizenship theorists about another function of participation—the promotion of self-realization.[25] Undoubtedly no purely empirical description can ever exhaust the content of the idea of self-realization, which is for many citizenship theorists closely linked to the idea of positive freedom. Whether an action promotes positive freedom usually depends on whether it meets certain criteria based on a prescriptive conception of what a worthwhile life is. Nonetheless, there are several ways in which the empirical content of the idea can be explored. One attempt to do this is suggested by Christian Bay. However, he is more concerned to establish that self-realization or psychological freedom derives chiefly from 'childhood circumstances' than he is to discover what political circumstances (such as participation) may affect it, though he does not deny that political circumstances may very well have an important effect.[26] Robert Lane's contention that the politically active man is psychologically strong and happy supports the traditional belief about the beneficial function of participation, provided such psychological benefits are partly the result rather than wholly the cause of participation, and provided that these benefits can be taken as part of the meaning of self-realization.[27] Even so, participation can easily be detrimental to psychological needs, as Lane is aware: While participation may enhance self-esteem, for example, by allowing one to appear to be an 'inside dopester', it may also land one in political controversies where an attack on one's principles could be a blow to self-esteem.

More clearly political is the 'sense of political efficacy'—the feeling that one's 'vote counts in the operation of government' and that 'there are other reasonable ways in which [one] can influence the progress of the system'.[28] This feeling, extensively investigated in empirical studies, is also part of what is meant by self-realization. Although the sense of political efficacy no doubt originates partly in basic personality factors, these factors probably do not completely determine the sense of political efficacy. Within the limits set by a citizen's personality, political activity may have an important independent effect on this sense. Such an effect is suggested by the numerous studies which find that various forms of political involvement are highly correlated with the sense of efficacy, even when many other variables are held constant. The sense of efficacy and participation probably reinforce each other. A citizen with a high sense of efficacy is more likely to participate. And as he becomes more familiar with the system and develops ties, he becomes more and more confident of his ability to achieve political results.²⁹

Participation is also thought by citizenship theorists to develop social virtues, such as a sense of cooperation and community—virtues which are usually assumed to be part of self-realization too.³⁰ Civic cooperation ('the propensity to work with others in attempting to influence government') does seem to be more prevalent in countries such as the U.S. and U.K. which have higher levels of participation than it is in countries with lower levels.³¹ But there is no particular reason why participation should lead necessarily to more cooperation and better communal relations. Political activity may just as easily create social antagonisms as facilitate social relations. Moreover, there appears to be no correlation between various indices of community well-being (such as Angell's indices of a community's moral integration) and levels of participation.³² The belief that participation fosters social virtues is therefore not very well established.

So far in the first mode in the schema we cannot tell whether the condition for participation is satisfied simply by examining levels and kinds of participation. The three functions of participation which are most directly related to the democratic objective depend in various ways on other conditions yet to be examined. To make sure 'sinister interests' do not prevail (the first function), a theory must stipulate that no interests are excluded (the second function) and that the citizenry is not politically ignorant (the third). The second function depends on whether groups have equal opportunities to organize (an element of the equality condition) and on whether an electoral choice for a party can be said to express interests (part of the rational voting condition). The third function depends on the nature and extent of political discussion in the electorate (the discussion condition). However, it is already evident that participation does *contribute* in significant ways toward fulfilling each one of the functions which citizenship theory posits, including the promotion of legitimacy and self-realization on which the democratic objective does not directly depend.

Even if the condition for participation is satisfied, other standards of participation remain to be examined—the constructive ideal, which urges more participation within existing structures, and the reconstructive ideal, which urges an increase in participation beyond what could be achieved within existing structures. The reconstructive ideal can be justified by showing that much more participation than exists at present would not be undesirable. Even if the highest level of participation implied by the reconstructive ideal would not be realizable or even desirable, the ideal remains valid. It performs, as we have seen, a vital dialectical role in citizenship theory. The constructive ideal, however, requires further justification: we must show that participation *can* be encouraged by non-radical changes.

THE DESIRABILITY OF MORE PARTICIPATION

Citizenship theorists, because of the important functions they assign to participation, do not usually doubt that more participation, either in the sense of more intensive or extensive citizen activity, is desirable. But a number of other recent writers do. And, as we saw in Chapter 1, some elitist democratic theorists do too, though not specifically on the basis of the empirical studies considered here. Using these studies, recent writers level four principal arguments against the demand for greater political participation.

The first argument—the argument from instability—is that political indifference is necessary and desirable because it serves as a 'cushion' against the actions of highly motivated partisans, who might otherwise disrupt the equilibrium of the political system and prevent sensible leaders from effecting the compromises required to maintain the system.[33] The trouble with this argument is that it is tautological. No one denies that a system needs enough indifference to hold it together and enough involvement to make it move. The question is: how much is enough? Without a criterion for how much participation would actually disrupt the system the argument amounts to this: Too much (i.e. whatever is disruptive) will be too much (i.e. will disrupt the system). The methodological objection that the variables these theorists use in their concept of equilibrium are not quantified has substantive implications. It is only because the concept is not more precise that existing levels of participation can be represented as falling within the limits supposedly required for equilibrium, and by implication any higher levels can be represented as exceeding the limits.

Since some systems admittedly less stable than the U.S. and the U.K. have either higher or lower levels of participation than the U.S. and the U.K.,[34] it might be possible that the range of equilibrium levels of participation lies between the levels of participation that exist in the unstable systems. But even if we assume that levels of participation are significant causes of the differences in stability among the countries (an assumption which is by no means established), it does not follow that greater participation in systems such as the U.S. and the U.K. would disrupt these systems to an undesirable degree. Even on this assumption, the alternative to the present situation in the U.S. and the U.K. is not total collapse but merely the instability that characterizes, say, present-day Germany or Italy. Moreover, the costs of some instability appear acceptable when we consider that the resolution of some of the major problems, such as racial discrimination, in the 'stable' democracies seems to require greater political participation. The increased activity bred by the civil rights movement in the U.S. has undoubtedly exacerbated social cleavages and tensions in American society, but from the perspective of citizenship theory it would be difficult to deny that these consequences are on balance acceptable.

To be sure, a 'sudden intrusion' by masses who are greatly dissatisfied with the whole political system, as in Germany, 1930–3, and Austria 1923–30, may represent 'a danger to the democratic system', as Herbert Tingsten observed.[35] But these and other examples of high participation are not applicable to systems such as the U.S. and Britain where such utter disaffection from the system is not so widespread. (Tingsten concedes that his observation probably does not apply to the U.S. and Britain, but only because he mistakenly believes that not many people identify with parties in these countries.) Participation by itself does not disrupt the democratic processes; the stability of a system is surely not that fragile. In any case, to try to explain stability in terms of degrees of participation is far too simple and superficial.[36] Actually, unusually high rates of participation may in some circumstances simply reflect higher levels of education and status, as in the suburbs of the Eastern United States. *Low* levels of participation may be a threat to stability, since politically inactive individuals are more susceptible to quasi-totalitarian appeals and more easily mobilized into anti-democratic movements.[37]

A second argument—the argument from incompetence—is that an increase in participation would involve persons who have undesirable attitudes or personalities. Since at present non-participants are relatively less stable in their partisan inclinations, less informed, less interested, and more vulnerable to manipulation by extremist appeals, this argument is partly based also on the fear of the instability that greater participation might produce. But non-participants are also thought to be incompetent from a liberal point of view, because compared to participants, they are more opposed to change, more likely to be against civil liberties and generally less tolerant. (On the other hand, non-participants are also more likely than participants to be in favor of welfare measures and, in certain cases, more internationalist in foreign policy.)[38]

Another trait that non-participants are supposed to exhibit more than participants is authoritarianism, the inclination to issue orders and demand unquestioning obedience as well as to accept orders and give such obedience to others in positions of authority. It may be that a moderate amount of authoritarianism is actually desirable in a democratic personality since some psychologists feel that it encourages more effective personal relations. But since authoritarianism is thought to have contributed to the acceptance of Nazism in Germany, no one wants more participation if it would draw extremely authoritarian persons into political life. Most attempts to pin down political authoritarianism have been beset with difficulties in devising a questionnaire free of the tendency to evoke set responses from interviewees. The authors of *The American Voter* were able to overcome some of these difficulties but could find a relationship between authoritarian personality and attitude toward political issues only in the college-educated segment of the population. They discovered very few authoritarians in this group, though they speculated that there are more in lower educational groups (where non-participants are more likely to be found).[39]

In any case, the presence of undesirable traits among persons who are at present non-participants is no argument against encouraging them to take part in politics. For we do not know that these traits could not be ameliorated or even eliminated by active and regular political participation, especially since many investigators and citizenship theorists believe that participation would be likely to enhance social bonds and give these citizens a real stake in society.[40] This belief is supported by evidence cited earlier, showing that participation may increase citizens' sense of efficacy and may improve their level of political information. It is quite likely, in other words, that the lack of power corrupts.

Admittedly, there is some risk in increasing participation, since we cannot be sure that some unacceptable instability would not result or some undesirable attitudes and traits would not be introduced into politics. If no further values were involved, perhaps we would be justified in deciding not to take the risk. But since it is lower-status groups who are excluded, a further value *is* involved. The democratic objective, as well as the standards of equality and the presuppositions of citizenship, would suffer if we decided to avoid the risk of increased participation.

'To campaign for . . . more general participation', writes a proponent of the third argument against more participation, is 'to press for a more regimented democracy'—an idea which is 'alien to the spirit of liberal democracy'. Another advocate of the argument holds that 'many of the ideas connected with the general theme of a duty to vote belong properly to the totalitarian camp and are out of place in the vocabulary of liberal democracy'. A low level of participation is supposed to indicate that life in a society is not governed by 'total politics'.[41]

This argument from the bogey of totalitarianism derives what little plausibility it might have from a failure to make important distinctions. A 'duty to vote' in citizenship theory rests on a moral imperative. It is, therefore, of a logically different order from a duty to vote in a totalitarian society, which is based on a coercive injunction.[42] The truth of this is evident from the difference between the functions which elections (and other forms of citizen participation) perform in totalitarian and liberal democratic systems. In the former, elections are primarily to mobilize and demonstrate support for a regime; in the latter they often also effectively express disapproval and can result in a change in political leadership. As for the fear of 'total politics', it is not sufficient to assert, as MacIver does, that the fact that totalitarians demand maximum participation indicates that their purposes are closer to those of liberal democracy than are the purposes of fascism.[43] There are important differences between on the one hand taking an active, informed interest in politics (as the democratic citizen should), or even devoting one's working life to it (as the democratic politician might), and on the other hand feeling that one's every activity has political implications (as the totalitarian citizen should). If these distinctions are made, the argument from the bogey of totalitarianism is not very plausible.

A fourth argument—the argument from satisfaction—is that apathy or non-participation is a sign of satisfaction with the politics of the system and that, therefore, it is pointless to demand more participation.[44] We have already seen that non-participation is not necessarily a sign of satisfaction. Even among those citizens who do participate to a limited degree, satisfaction with their current role is no argument against encouraging them to expand their political activity. For the expression of dissatisfaction, as I have already pointed out, is not the only important function which citizenship theory assigns to political participation.

Similar objections apply against a variation of the argument from satisfaction. The variation holds that it is irrational for an individual to participate in politics in most instances since his influence on the outcome of (say) an election will be negligible and hence will not make any difference as to whether his interests are satisfied.[45] But citizens do, and according to citizenship theory should, participate for reasons besides the intention to influence political outcomes. Moreover, a stronger concept of rationality, which refers to the general interest, requires participation by each citizen where it would be undesirable if everyone failed to participate and desirable if everyone did participate.

In the second mode in the schema, the central question is whether more participation can be expected as a result either of certain social and political trends or as a result of moderate reforms. Elitist democratic theory, as I have indicated, is inclined to pay relatively less attention to whether participation can be increased in this way. Citizenship theorists view the prospects for greater participation more sanguinely and see the need for greater participation as more important. Let us examine first the trends and then the moderate reforms which citizenship theorists most commonly mention.

Graham Wallas predicted a 'large extension of electoral interest' as opportunities for education widen, as more people move into urban environments, and as more people are exposed to media.[46] Present evidence suggests that these trends may very well contribute toward participation, as Wallas and other citizenship theorists hoped.

Most measures of level of education in available studies distinguish only among two or three levels of formal education and hence exclude altogether the self-education that many citizenship theorists consider to be equally important. Even so, almost all studies suggest, Campbell notes, that 'perhaps the surest single predictor of political involvement is number of years of formal education'.[47] Although people with better education participate more partly because they are also in higher socio-economic groups, education seems to have an effect on participation which is independent of these status variables. Since by most indicators the level of education is increasing in the U.S. and Britain,[48] we should expect that participation will tend to increase gradually, *ceteris paribus*. There are certainly limits to the effect that education alone can have. It cannot eliminate non-voting which is the result of depressed social conditions that drain the meaning from all aspects of life, including politics. Further indications that other factors besides education are at work are the fact that the historical trends of participation and education do not coincide very closely, and the fact that the much lower general level of education in nineteenth-century America did not prevent a much more intense and uniform mass participation.[49]

It is not obvious that urbanization should increase participation. Indeed, as newcomers move into a community, participation often declines, since newcomers may not easily meet residence requirements for voting, may not be familiar with politics or groups there, and may feel no sense of belonging to the community. But more generally these effects of geographical mobility probably are cancelled out by other factors. For other evidence indicates that people who live in urban environments are generally much more likely to vote than those who live in rural environments, and that people in metropolitan areas vote more than those in smaller towns. These relationships are not always found, but the exceptions usually involve special circumstances. The absence of any significant relationship with turnout rates when states are ranked according to proportions of people in urban residences or urban employments is probably due to the fact that such rankings do not take into account the 'cancelling-out' effect in the variables. The same is true of the negative correlation between percentage increases in urban population and participation.[50]

The chief explanation for the generally favorable effect of urban living on participation is, according to Campbell, the fact that 'the urban citizen is in constant contact with groups of people whom he may identify with and be influenced by, his neighbors, his work group, his union, his local party organization, and the like. Some of these groups have political relevance and they stimulate him politically'.[51] However, once nearly all of the population of a country is concentrated in urban areas, the effects of urban living itself may not contribute to further *increases* in participation. If not, we cannot look to urbanization alone to sustain a trend toward greater participation.

Increased exposure to political stimuli from mass media also shows a marked association with participation. If an increase in the political content of the media accompanies the continuing expansion of communication activity, we can expect a favorable effect on participation. There is no evidence yet that a saturation point has been reached that would numb people to any further effect of media exposure.[52]

G. D. H. and Margaret Cole suggest that the widening of the scope of governmental activity which occurs in the modern welfare state will tend to increase political activity among ordinary citizens.[53] The assumption is that as government impinges more and more on the everyday affairs of all citizens, they will be inclined to participate more. Some support for this assumption is found in the studies which show that groups whose interests are at present more affected by governmental policies tend to be more active politically. (This is probably not true of groups, such as the unemployed, who suffer from severe economic need.)[54]

If these were the only trends in modern life, many citizenship theorists might be content to let nature take its course. But trends exist which may discourage participation. The fact that the issues of politics, as well as the process of political decision-making, are becoming more specialized and technical means that it may seem less worth the effort to participate in politics. A similar specialization in industrial life may make it more difficult to acquire the social and political skills and awareness which would encourage political activity. It might be thought that the continuing decrease in the working week, by providing more time for politics, would facilitate participation, but in fact people prefer to use their leisure for other activities. Only 2 per cent of those questioned in the U.S. and Britain mentioned politics or civic activity as their preferred leisure activities.[55] It is possible that as their leisure time expands, people will be able to pursue more time-consuming activities (such as travel) which might cut still further into the time they could devote to politics. Finally, the continuing assimilation of ethnic groups into the mainstream of social life, however desirable in itself, could have a negative effect on participation. Where such groups are concentrated now, turnout is higher, the sense of political efficacy greater and political organization better. These beneficial effects of concentration will be lost as members of those groups become dispersed throughout the population.[56] However, these effects may be offset by the effects of upward mobility on the individuals who are being assimilated.

THE CONSTRUCTIVE IDEAL: REFORMS

Since present trends alone evidently cannot very soon bring about the increase in participation that citizenship theorists desire, the theorists also propose a number of moderate reforms which could have this effect. It may be true that the fundamental sources of non-participation are deep-seated social and psychological forces which can be effected only by radical changes. But to argue therefore that these should be the 'target' for reform, as many social scientists imply, is to discourage constructive political reform.[57] Social conditions such as family life and child development are not yet a central concern of politics. If these conditions are assigned the blame, politicians and political scientists are absolved from doing anything about apathy. It is better to treat the symptoms than to do nothing, and in politics, as in medicine, this is often the only feasible treatment. Furthermore, the interrelationships between society and politics are so complex that treating the symptoms may help cure the disease. Yet it must be conceded that what can be accomplished by moderate reform is probably more limited than many citizenship theorists suppose.

No doubt turnout in elections could be facilitated, as some citizenship theorists hope, by simplifing voting procedures—for example by instituting automatic or simpler registration, standardizing ballot forms, and reducing the number of offices which appear on the ballot, as well as changing the frequency of elections. Anything which makes voting less mysterious and forbidding would also have a similar effect on other forms of participation by suggesting to citizens that politics is an activity with which they can cope. A survey using a U.S. national sample showed that two-thirds of non-voters considered themselves ineligible to vote because of registration requirements or the complexities of voting requirements.[58] In an important study of 104 American cities over 100,000 population, Stanley Kelley and his associates found that at least in Presidential elections registration requirements are a more effective deterrent to voting than anything else that normally would discourage citizens from voting.[59] Of the variables they examined which affect registration, one of the most important is simply the date at which registration rolls are closed; the closer that date is to the date of the election, the greater is the number of citizens who register. Where motivation is low and formal restrictions on voting are great, as in the South, the effect of loosening or removing restrictions on voting is of course even greater. The strong impact of voting arrangements on participation should give pause to those social scientists who maintain that significant expansion of participation can be attained only by social, psychological and educational reforms. Besides registration requirements, many other political restraints on participation need to be reexamined. It is not plausible to defend long ballots and frequent elections, as some democratic theorists have been inclined to do, as means for giving the public more control of its government—if these devices actually reduce participation.

Merriam holds that another way to overcome the 'ignorance and timidity' about voting which discourage many citizens from casting a ballot is to organize campaigns 'for greater familiarity with the mechanism of voting, with the form of the ballot and with voting and registration procedure'. Presumably this could be done most effectively as part of 'get-out-the-vote' campaigns. Studies in Ann Arbor, though it is hardly a typical city, give some weak support to the belief that such campaigns are effective, although because so many stimuli affect a citizen's motivation to vote any conclusion about the effect of one factor must be treated with caution.[60] It might be assumed that since the feeling of citizen duty is highly correlated with participation an appeal to the duty to vote might be good strategy for a 'get-out-the-vote' campaign. Such appeals may have some effect, but they will be more likely to succeed with white, urban, and higher-status citizens, whose participation is already the least unsatisfactory.[61] Much more promising is canvassing by party workers, which tends to activate a substantial number of citizens who might otherwise have failed to vote. Admittedly, parties do not canvass as much as citizenship theorists might wish, and party workers do not always have an incentive to persuade people to vote if they believe that non-voters are disproportionately likely to favor the other party. Yet in campaigns to increase turnout, party workers are usually more highly motivated and therefore perhaps more effective than members of civic organizations.[62]

Another suggestion urged by many citizenship theorists is to strengthen and encourage organized groups, such as trade unions and educational associations, which could help citizens develop political skills and awareness, and thereby facilitate general political participation.[63] Strengthening group activity is seen as a way to overcome the unfavorable effects of specialization of labor in a modern industrial society. Evidence indeed suggests that this diagnosis is correct: persons with lower-status occupations, which are generally the more routine, participate less than those with higher-status occupations (even when education and income levels are the same). In a study of a shipyard workers' housing project where workers were forced to take all community positions of authority because workers were the only residents, one result was an unusually high voting turnout.[64] Strengthening groups would also alleviate one important source of non-participation—the feeling that a citizen must ' "save up" his irritations, desires or enthusiasms until the next election'.[65] The proposal thus goes beyond trying simply to increase voting turnout.

Is there any reason to believe that if this reform could be carried out it would succeed? People of all classes who belong to groups do participate more actively in politics. And the more groups they belong to, the more likely they are to participate in politics. Since non-voting and other forms of non-participation tend to be shared behavior, active membership in a group which is politically aware would almost certainly cause a citizen to become more politically involved, or at least more interested in politics. Furthermore, group membership, several studies suggest, has the greatest potential to stimulate activity among less interested citizens.[66]

However, we should not expect too much from strengthening groups in this way, since the factors which affect participation are largely the same that at present determine enrolment in organizations. Unless a special effort is made to enlist lower-status citizens into groups, participation will continue to be unequally distributed even if membership in groups is extended and activity intensified. Also, if this reform were too successful, group intransigence and conflict, which make compromise much more difficult, would possibly be more prevalent. And since increase in group activity might mean that more citizens would have multiple memberships which might subject them to cross-pressures, a negative effect on participation could be produced.[67]

A common complaint of citizenship theorists is that participation is so low because elections are dull. There are no real issues in campaigns, they argue, and no real differences between major parties.[68] If this charge has some truth in it, does it really affect participation? Can anything be done to make elections more interesting to more citizens? Three kinds of stimulation must be distinguished in answering these questions: partisanship, competitiveness, and importance of alternatives.

The more strongly a citizen identifies with a party, the more likely he is to vote.[69] But since party identification is for most voters a fairly stable characteristic, not much could be done to intensify such identification even if it were desirable to do so. More significantly related to participation are two other forms of partisanship—how strongly one supports (or opposes) a partisan position on issues and how strongly one feels about a candidate.[70] Significantly sharpening partisan positions on issues is probably not possible without seriously weakening the two-party system in which each party can win only by securing support from the middle of the ideological spectrum. Adopting more attractive candidates is a more feasible alternative, although its consequences may sometimes be repugnant to liberals (for example, Eisenhower was to most voters personally much more attractive than Stevenson). The impact of television on political life may make it more important for parties to seek attractive candidates.

Competitiveness, as measured by the closeness of a vote rather than the perceived closeness or the strength of partisan identifications, appears in some local elections in the U.S. and Britain to foster more participation, though quite a few studies have failed to find this effect.[71] The key to greater competitiveness seems to be strong party organization at all levels and the absence of one-party dominance and non-partisan elections in some electoral units.

The importance which citizens attach to alternatives presented to them in an election (a factor which is to some extent distinguishable from partisanship and competitiveness) constitutes the essential difference between what have been called 'high-stimulus' and 'low-stimulus' elections. Besides attractiveness of candidates and differences between the party positions, the importance of an election to a citizen is affected by how significant he thinks the office to be filled is, and how crucial he believes the problems are with which the winner will have to deal. 'Psychological involvement' (usually defined as interest in an election and concern about the outcome) is a closely related factor which also tends to encourage participation.[72] Of course, to manufacture 'crisis' elections would not be desirable, but to convey the idea that in our time the foreign and domestic responsibilities of politicians vitally affect all citizens would be, and might also be more feasible than it used to be. Making sure that all offices which are subject to election do actually have the potential for real power would also help, as would combining elections of chief executives with elections of lesser officials. The mass media, the next chapter will show, can play an important part in all of these tasks.

Insofar as any of the constructive changes to increase participation take place, a further reason exists for being cautiously optimistic about their success. Some evidence indicates that there exists a large reservoir of citizens who are willing to participate in various ways but have not yet done so, in some cases possibly because they have not been asked.[73]

Thus, some support for the constructive ideal of participation can be found. It is easy enough to find reasons why these proposals to stimulate participation would not work or could not be implemented, but until they are tried under various conditions for reasonable periods of time it would be a mistake to reject this constructive ideal of citizenship theory. Contrary to the assumptions of elitist democratic theorists, Dewey's plea to 'experiment' is still compelling.

DEMONSTRATIONS

In the past decade or so, the most prominent form of citizen participation has not been electoral activity but demonstrations against particular injustices and particular policies, especially racial discrimination and the Vietnam War. To prod public officials into meeting their demands, demonstrators choose tactics such as sit-ins, marches, rent strikes and job blockades that are intended to arouse public conscience, as well as to penalize those persons most directly responsible for the injustices. Many of these activities should be accepted as legitimate forms of participation, provided demonstrators do not infringe upon other persons' rights, or refuse to accept legal penalties when they do. And in many cases, demonstrations have been more effective than electoral activity would have been in attaining the goals of citizens. But the issue here is whether demonstrations help fulfill the standards of participation. Even though these sorts of demonstrations are often intended to change social and political structures, they take place within existing structures and are directed at officials who hold authority within those structures. They therefore should be considered as a means of realizing the functions specified by the participation condition and the constructive ideal of participation.

Those citizenship theorists who mention demonstrations as a form of participation give qualified approval to them.[74] However, very few say anything at all about this form of participation. Nor is reliable behavioral evidence on this subject plentiful. This is partly because demonstrations are too sporadic and transitory to permit sustained investigation with the quantitative techniques of social science. Even if the movement which spawns a demonstration does not vanish before social scientists can study it, it often changes its character before any study can be finished. Nevertheless, some evidence prompts a few observations.

Demonstrations activate some groups of citizens who, compared to other groups, were previously less involved in politics—especially youth and blacks, whose electoral participation lags behind other groups. However, within these groups, it is the better educated and more ambitious persons that are most likely to join demonstrations and protest movements. Since these persons soon move on to careers and family responsibilities, the movements which they support are very unstable. Consequently, unless the injustices against which the activists protest are quickly and completely corrected (which of course rarely happens), the organizational skills and sustained pressure that are required to effect permanent change are never developed. This consequence partly accounts for the failure of the civil rights movement to match its initial successes. A movement whose principal instrument is demonstrations cannot count on succeeding generations for a steady supply of the youth on whom it must rely. Each new generation is likely to have different concerns from its predecessors. The generation that devoted itself to civil rights gives way to the generation that concerns itself with the Vietnam War. And there is the persistent possibility that in any generation the 'reserve army' of activists will drop out of political life altogether.[75]

But however unstable are demonstrations and the movements that nourish them, they do undoubtedly have a political impact that other forms of participation do not. More importantly for our purposes, they probably do give expression to political interests that might not otherwise be heard, and probably do foster political knowledgeability, a sense of legitimacy and self-realization to degrees not otherwise attainable at any given time. Furthermore, demonstrations may contribute to the goal of the constructive ideal which urges greater participation in the future. As an increasing number of leisure-time activities compete with politics for citizens' attention, the more dramatic and exciting forms of political participation, such as demonstrations, are likely to fare better in this competition. Further, demonstrations are more likely than electoral forms of participation to be stimulated by the mass media, which play an increasingly large role in political life.

It would be unfortunate if demonstrations detracted from the significance of electoral activity. Actually, they may complement it. It is likely (though there is no evidence about this) that the political skills and consciousness developed by demonstrators will enable them later to participate more actively and effectively in less demanding political activities than they would have otherwise done when the demands of their careers and families discourage them from being serious demonstrators.

The sort of demonstrations which I have been discussing must be distinguished from those which aim at or succeed in disrupting

81

the whole political system indefinitely or permanently. The latter kinds of demonstrations are not endorsed by citizenship theorists (except by Laski in a few of his writings). Such demonstrations, it would be argued, violate the presupposition of autonomy. They would destroy the only mechanisms that most citizens have for expressing and satisfying their own political interests. Perhaps the only way to fully realize some of the standards that derive from the presuppositions of citizenship is by radical change, which would in the short-term violate the presuppositions. But, as Chapter 2 indicated, evidence from social science is not of much help in establishing to what extent such radical change is necessary. In any case, the whole problem of demonstrations is so inadequately treated by citizenship theorists and requires so much further development that it unfortunately must be relegated to those overcrowded halls of further research.

THE RECONSTRUCTIVE IDEAL OF PARTICIPATION

Dispersal of political decision-making—for example, by decentralization, devolution, or regionalism—is sometimes offered by citizenship theorists as another cure for the low levels of participation. Such proposals are most frequently made by theorists, such as Cole, Hobhouse and Laski, writing mainly from British experience where political authority is more concentrated and the need for dispersal greater. But the logic of their arguments is equally applicable to the U.S.[76]

Clearly, major redistributions of power would require changes in the structure of the social and political system, and to prescribe such change is thus the role of a reconstructive ideal of participation. Such an ideal is similar to the reconstructive ideal of equality, since both picture a decentralized political structure that would encourage all citizens to engage in effective political participation, not only electoral activity but also activities to influence governmental and other political decisions more directly. The ideal of equality, however, further urges equal participation; that goal implies additional structural reforms which will be discussed in Chapter 6. Here I concentrate on the possible effects of dispersal of power on the level of participation, rather than its distribution. This subjec obviously raises a host of complex problems; I can make only a few general remarks about some of them.[77]

Citizenship theorists do not long for a Rousseauesque rural community, however much they admire some of the virtues of life in such a community. They accept the urban, industrial environment as a fact of life, but not without hope that radical change might give citizens a greater chance for meaningful participation. As with all reconstructive ideals, behavioral evidence is of limited utility in assessing this ideal. The problem is complicated further by the fact that theorists (perhaps deliberately) do not specify exactly the powers that are to be dispersed, the size of the sub-units to which they are to be dispersed, or the relationship of these sub-units to the central authority and to each other.

However, the basic assumption is clear enough: smaller units will stimulate citizens to participate by making access to power easier and issues more comprehensible. Some evidence about present societies might be relevant to this assumption even though citizenship theorists expect a restructuring of society to have effects which may not be apparent in any present society. Some limited support for the basic assumption can be found in the fact that even now local politics in the U.S. elicit more of certain kinds of participation (such as contacting a public official) and more concern and self-confidence than do national politics. Although turnout for city elections is generally lower than for Presidential and General Elections, it is probably not lower than turnout for off-year Congressional elections and by-elections. In general, there appears to be no *consistent* relationship between turnout and the *size* of a political unit (measured by population, area, or density).[78]

Proponents of the reconstructive ideal of participation also assume that the smaller units to which power is to be dispersed will have greater responsibilities than at present. If so, it is possible that lower levels of turnout in city compared to national elections (as well as some other manifestations of less local involvement) could be improved. If the problems with which the political unit deals are significant, participation is likely to be much greater. One of the causes of some of the present low levels of involvement in local politics is the fact that many of the functions of local government are routine.

The reconstructive ideal of participation, then, actually makes two mutually opposed demands, both largely for the purposes of promoting participation. The size of political units should be as *small* as possible so that power is accessible and issues comprehensible but as *large* as possible so that many of the significant problems which face modern society come within the jurisdiction of the local units. The problem therefore is to discover the size of the unit which would give the optimum mix of these two demands. Dahl has tentatively suggested that such an optimum size may be a city between 50,000 and 200,000 population. Certainly, the American state would not be a satisfactory model for an ideal political unit, since most states suffer from the disadvantages of bigness with few of its advantages.[79]

Many of the traditional objections to the decentralization implied by the reconstructive ideal are not supported by evidence. Dahl and Tufte suggest that relatively small units may not be less successful than larger units in providing for welfare and cultural life of the citizens. Although smaller units generally have less diversity and less political competition than larger units, this probably is not only the consequence of smallness but also of the lesser degree of urbanization, and is an argument against dispersing power to local units, as they are now constituted, not an argument against the restructured society envisaged by radical reformers.[80] Finally, the argument that a central or federal authority is needed, for example, to redistribute resources and maintain basic legal rights can be accepted without giving up the reconstructive ideal, although it must be admitted that too little thought has been given to the role of such a central authority in the reforms pictured by the ideal.

Despite the importance of empirical evidence for clarifying and suggesting approaches for dispersal of power, the justification of the reconstructive ideal of participation does not depend completely upon such evidence. It is sustained ultimately by a vision of all citizens engaged in effective participation in political units of a magnitude that invites their understanding and loyalty. It is a vision of a political life which has yet to flourish in the twentieth century.

CONCLUSION

The standards of participation in citizenship theory are intimately connected with the other standards to be analyzed in the chapters that follow. In the first mode in the schema, we cannot determine whether the functions specified by the condition for participation are fulfilled until we examine the functions of discussion, rational voting and equality. In the second mode, many of the same trends and reforms which tend to realize the constructive ideal of participation also contribute toward other constructive ideals of citizenship. Also, the reconstructive ideal of participation pictures a political structure which underlies the prescriptions of other reconstructive ideals of citizenship. While a complete view of the standards of participation must therefore await consideration of other standards, it should already be evident that participation does contribute toward fulfilling the functions set forth by citizenship theory, that some important arguments against the desirability of greater participation are not tenable, and that some trends and moderate reforms implied by the constructive ideal of participation can increase participation. Furthermore, the evidence from social science which is pertinent to the reconstructive ideal of participation is not inconsistent with it.

4 Discussion

Political discussion helps make other forms of participation meaningful. All citizenship theorists emphasize the importance of discussion; Lindsay, Dewey and Ross see discussion among ordinary citizens as *the* essential of democracy.[1] Acts such as voting, which are meant to express preferences or interests, are meaningless unless preceded by discussion. Discussion also adds a social dimension that otherwise might be absent in more individualistic forms of participation. Hence, the standards of discussion need some attention beyond that given to those of other forms of participation.

In the first mode in the schema, three functions of discussion will be examined. Discussion is supposed to help citizens to recognize their own political interests; to create and reveal common interests; and to maintain peace and stability.

THE PROCESS OF DISCUSSION

The first function of discussion—to help citizens recognize their political interests—is especially significant in citizenship theories, since the satisfaction of the condition for participation, as we have seen, depends partly on discussion fulfilling this function.[2] The evidence cited in the previous chapter which indicated that participation promotes such political competence also suggests that discussion may have the same effect. The effect should be even more marked than for other forms of participation since discussion is a more active form. Some studies have shown that compared to passive reception of information (as in a lecture), discussion is more effective in changing attitudes, in influencing action and in stimulating problem-solving types of thought. These studies, however, were conducted in special settings, typically in factories, classrooms or laboratories. The discussion usually concerned the best means to attain goals about which there was no fundamental disagreement. The goals were either taken for granted, or were set by a person or organization outside the group which was

86

engaged in discussion. Therefore, the findings of this research on small group behavior is, as Sidney Verba cautions, not immediately applicable to processes of political discussion in a whole society. Small group discussion in settings studied by social psychologists is bound to be more successful than discussion in groups which seek to make decisions about basic social and political alternatives.[3] Nevertheless, much political discussion among ordinary citizens approximates the conditions that characterize the discussion of small groups in the special settings. Citizens often engage in discussion with persons with whom they share basic values, and about alternatives which are posed by persons and institutions outside their group.

But even in the special settings investigated in the studies by social psychologists, discussion may have unfavorable effects. Discussion sometimes increases motivation of members of the group at the expense of greater information which a lecture would provide. Also, the extent to which a person perceives himself as having participated in a group discussion appears to be more important to his satisfaction with a decision made by the group than is the extent to which he actually did participate in the discussion. He may in this way deceive himself about his contribution to a group conclusion.[4] However, on these points, the difference between discussion in special settings and political discussion in society works to the advantage of the latter. Political discussion does not take place in an isolated context but rather in one in which many other communications filter into members of the group. The fact that lectures convey more information than discussion therefore may not matter so much in political contexts. Also, since political discussion is an ongoing activity, the fact that some citizens exaggerate their actual participation in any one discussion may give them greater self-confidence and sense of importance in the group—which could increase their actual participation in the next discussion. It seems fair to conclude that the evidence from research on small groups does not undermine citizenship theorists' hopes for political discussion and in certain respects gives some support to the view that discussion sometimes helps citizens to recognize their interests more fully.

But to say that discussion sometimes has this effect leaves unexamined the extent and impact of discussion in the lives of citizens in a democracy. Specifically, we must ask: are the people who actively discuss politics influential in discussions in which the bulk of the electorate engage? and is the discussion which takes place likely to help citizens to recognize their interests? If so, the discussion may be said to be rational at least in a minimal sense.

Over 80 per cent of the electorate discuss politics at some time during a campaign, and about 70 to 80 per cent do so between elections. Nearly 65 per cent follow campaign discussion 'quite a lot' through the media, and nearly everyone is exposed to some discussion through at least one of the media.[5] Much of this exposure and discussion is of questionable value in helping to enlighten citizens since it is very uninformed and irregular. But some of this discussion—the most influential—is with 'opinion leaders', persons who are better informed, more interested in politics, more attentive to the media, and generally more persuasive. The most commonly used definition of 'opinion leader' or 'active discussant' is a person who answers 'yes' to the questions 'Have you tried to convince anyone of your political ideas recently?' and 'Has anyone asked your advice on a political question recently?' These opinion leaders are not members of a social or economic elite; they are scattered through all status groups. Opinion leaders, it has been observed, are 'so thoroughly *ordinary citizens* that they are in fact models or proto-types for the others whom they inform, argue with, and influence in politics'. Earlier studies of personal influence (for example, in *The People's Choice*) did not rule out the possibility that opinion leaders talk only to each other. But subsequent research indicates that even though opinion leaders comprise a minority of the electorate (not more than 30 per cent and perhaps as little as 15 per cent), they do affect, through the process of personal influence, the preferences of citizens who discuss politics less actively.[6]

Since for the purposes of this study the best criterion of whether this process of personal influence helps citizens to recognize their interests is whether it results in rational voting, a final appraisal of the process must await the conclusions of the next chapter. However, two characteristics of the process can be mentioned which indicate that it is likely to be rational in the sense of encouraging citizens to recognize their own political interests.

Admittedly, this has to be a weak form of rationality. In the transmission of information and opinions by personal influence, distortion occurs (although evidence about this process is very scant). Ideological concepts and patterns of thinking which are displayed in the media or even among opinion leaders do not show up in the mass public. The content of personal discussion is even more stereotyped than that which appears in the mass media. The problem is not simply that most citizens are unable to articulate an ideological basis for their preferences. Their preferences usually do not fit any internally coherent belief system at all. Even the link between partisan preference and objective social class is much less strong than it would be if opinion leadership worked perfectly. Hence, much of what opinion leaders know and believe never registers with the less active citizens. The reason is not that citizens form their opinions under some other influence (for example, the mass media). Nor is it that they hold idiosyncratic opinions in spite of what opinion leaders tell them. On many issues, many citizens' preferences show no consistency over time; indeed, the best model for explanation of changes in their preferences seems to be one which would predict random change. The trouble is that many citizens simply have no structured and consistent opinions at all on many political issues (though most do have moderately stable partisan attachments).[7]

Insofar as personal influence is effective, one characteristic of the process which justifies considering discussion as rational is that an individual's opinions or attitudes are usually formed and maintained by reference to the groups with which he associates. The impact of social groups on opinions and attitudes—a phenomenon well studied by social psychologists—has political consequences. Individuals consistently bring their political opinions and attitudes into line with those of the groups to which they belong (or in some cases groups with which they merely identify). 'People who work or live or play together are likely to vote for the same candidates'. Although primary groups such as families and work associates are more important in this process, secondary groups seem to have some effect too. It should be noted, however, that although the impact of groups on opinions is very significant, the political effects may be exaggerated somewhat by survey data. Since the data depend on respondents' reports of the political preferences of their associates, these reports are likely to be distorted in favor of the respondents' own preferences.[8]

The process of personal influence is one which was described and praised by many citizenship theorists before it was investigated thoroughly by modern social scientists. Dewey's 'face-to-face intercourse', Friedrich's 'personal authority of the common man', Wallas' 'oral interchange of ideas', and Lindsay's 'centers of discussion' all closely correspond to aspects of the process of personal influence.[9] Giving the idea of this process a place in democratic theory, therefore, is quite compatible with most citizenship theories. Furthermore, this process is likely to generate preferences and opinions which reflect the most important values and interests of an individual as he perceives them. The process of discussion in this way contributes to citizens' recognition of their interests and is in this sense rational.

It might be objected that this portrait of the ordinary citizen being molded by the groups and opinion leaders with whom he associates is no more flattering than that of a citizen being manipulated by elites. In either case, the citizen appears to be deprived of the individuality that earlier democratic theorists valued so highly. None of the twentieth-century theorists considered here, however, is so radically individualist as earlier theorists are commonly believed to be. In fact, many of these twentieth-century theorists devote much effort to dispelling the spirit of nineteenth-century individualism from which, they think, emanate the doctrines of isolated, egoistic man and *laissez-faire* politics and economics. Most twentieth-century citizenship theorists would agree with Dewey that the consequences of 'combined or conjoint action . . . differ in kind from those of isolated behavior', and that the content of social judgment is not purely personal.[10]

Nevertheless, the theories of Laski and Dewey as well as those of most other citizenship theorists remain individualist in two important ways, though some of the theorists prefer to call their doctrines 'neo-individualism' (Merriam), 'personalism' (Simon), or theories of 'individuality' (MacIver). For all of these theorists, individuals are the objects upon whom the benefits of democracy are to be conferred. Finding out what individuals aspire to is a chief purpose—not the realization of some collective will, as in Idealist theories. (In a very early work Dewey did espouse a quasi-Idealist theory in which individuals were depicted as organs of a collective will, but in his mature work he repudiated this view.) Also for all these theorists, individuals are the units from which opinions must be solicited. The opinion of the individual is the most significant unit—not the opinion of his group leader, as for example in some of the villages of India. Two social scientists who have studied public opinion in India report that many of their respondents did not know what their own opinions were until 'they had spoken to the individuals who ordinarily participated in or led the process of finding or making opinions'. This total deference, these investigators observe, is quite different from the attitude toward opinion leaders and group opinions in more developed countries.[11]

The process by which an individual acquires and maintains his opinions and attitudes by reference to groups could not accurately be described as conformity—except in the sense of conformity which would have us say that even non-conformists are conforming to the standards of their group. Many students of opinion formation prefer to describe it as a learning process in which an *individual* acquires 'fresh viewpoints' from others. An individual's making up his mind involves the selecting of 'values from the many group identifications of the individual—a process which, while it may be non-cognitive, is certainly not necessarily irrational'.[12]

A second characteristic of the process of personal influence is that the groups in which the process occurs serve as insulators against the manipulative potential of the media. If the opinions of a citizen were manipulated by the mass media, they would be less likely to be rational in the sense of reflecting his own view of his interests. Elitist democratic theorists who fear such manipulation would be partially vindicated. However, groups do protect the ordinary citizen, as Lindsay hoped, against 'the molders of mass opinion'.[13]

4 Discussion

Studies suggest the existence of a 'two-step flow of communications': 'ideas flow often *from* radio and print [and other media] *to* the opinion leaders and *from* them to the less active sections of the population'.[14] The media are thus not so potent as theorists of mass society have feared; the media do not act directly upon an atomized mass of individuals. Personal influence is much more effective with most people than the media because compared to media, personal influence is more adaptable to the interests and aversions of particular individuals, appears to come from more trustworthy sources, and offers more immediate rewards and punishments for responses to the influence. Berelson and associates write:

> In this process [of opinion formation] the principal agencies are not Machiavellian manipulators, as is commonly supposed when bloc votes are delivered at the polls, but the ordinary family, friends, co-workers, and fellow organization members with whom we are all surrounded. In short, the influences to which voters are most susceptible are opinions of trusted people expressed to one another.[15]

Indeed, the potency of personal influence compared to other forms of influence is so great that the real danger is the possible use of face-to-face communication for political indoctrination.[16] Although its use by Western democratic governments is not a serious threat to citizens, its use by extremist groups in these countries may very well be.

Thus, discussion encourages a citizen to see his interest in terms of the persons who are most like him and is in this way rational. This comes closer to being his own view of his interest, and according to the presupposition of autonomy closer to being in his own interest, than a view determined by the media. To say that the process is rational in this limited sense is not to say anything about the individual citizen's process of thought. In that process, habitual and emotional responses are probably more common than reasoned and informed thinking.

MASS MEDIA AND MANIPULATION

Even if personal influence insulates most citizens from the manipulative potential of the mass media, the dangers of the media cannot be ignored. For opinion leaders, who are quite attentive to the media, might be vulnerable to manipulation by the media. Media, after all, are the most effective way of stimulating personal influence.[17]

Manipulation refers to the skillful management or control of citizens' opinions. But not all such control would count as manipulation. The object of the control must be in the interest of the manipulators or persons whom they are serving. It must also be against the interest and without the knowledge of the persons being manipulated. Media communication in the U.S. and the U.K. does not satisfy all of these conditions in the way that would be necessary to establish that manipulation of political attitudes and opinions occurs to a significant extent.

First, the presentation of much political propaganda is not skillful. Decisions about what political communications to issue and how to present them are not made strictly according to criteria of effectiveness for persuasion. The advice of the most skillful media experts is often ignored for the sake of satisfying other interests and values of the organizations that sponsor the communications. Sometimes it is moral scruple which leads politicians to reject a potentially persuasive but manipulative piece of propaganda. More often, it is the difficulty of securing agreement and coordinating plans in the large organizations that can afford to mount massive propaganda campaigns. Occasionally, politicians fail to follow expert advice because, as one member of a British party publicity group observed:

The politicians taking part [in planning campaign broadcasts] just weren't interested in disinterested advice. They just knew they were right ... The meetings of the group concerned with television were devoted to a discussion as to whose turn it was to appear on a TV program. Once chosen, the politician regarded it as 'his' program. He was the principal performer, and he was also acting as producer.[18]

Hence, the skillful control of opinion implied in the idea of manipulation is probably much less common or likely than is popularly believed.

Even if would-be manipulators were always skillful, it would be difficult for any one political organization to control opinion through the media to further its own interest at the expense of other groups. Competition among media and their users, citizenship theorists such as MacIver, Cole, Simon and Merriam hope, acts as a constraint on manipulation.[19] It prevents the domination of the channels of communication by only a few sources. The monopolistic patterns in British and American newspaper ownership and the newspaper editorial favoritism of the Republican party in the U.S. do not mean that competition of political ideas in the media as a whole is entirely absent.[20] There are other sources of influence besides support of a newspaper publisher; connections with key editors and especially reporters are often more important. For reasons of economy, most newspapers must rely on the wire services, which by tradition are impartial—almost to the point of dullness. The danger is not too much but too little bias. Moreover, most citizens now rely chiefly on television for their political information, and several British and American studies indicate that television is 'as near[ly] impartial as could be'.[21] Considering the media as a whole, another study concludes that during at least one campaign a 'competitive situation' existed in which the efforts of both parties were 'counterbalanced'.[22]

However, the degree of competition which exists in the U.S. and Britain at present certainly does not ensure that *all* opinions and facts which deserve to be heard will receive equal expression. It is often observed that communications which challenge the status quo are much less likely to be promulgated than those which defend or at least do not criticize it in any fundamental way. But if this means that the mass media can never influence significant and desirable change, it is false. The impact which the media have had on racial segregation suggests that a regional status quo is not immune from effective attack by national media. Even attacks on more widely accepted structures are not ignored in the media. Demonstrators and radical reformers receive increasingly greater attention in the media, especially television (although quantitative evidence about the relative amount of attention they receive is lacking). They certainly are not always presented in an unfavourable light; indeed, they often speak for themselves. Demonstrations and their perpetrators are particularly exciting news which media find difficult to resist. It wins audiences and increases circulation. Yet insofar as users of the media share a common interest in maintaining present structures against radical reform (and many probably think they do), competition as it now exists would not by itself prevent manipulation for the sake of this common interest of the users.

But, finally, even if aspiring manipulators were skillful and were able to dominate the mass media for their purposes, two further checks prevent control of citizens' opinions against their own interests in a manner that would count as manipulation.

In the first place, the people who are more attentive to the media are also those who are more likely to compare information and opinions they receive from the mass media with that from other sources. They are also more likely to be self-confident and psychologically stable, and to have firm partisan commitments.[23] In short, they will be much more likely to resist external pressures designed to enlist their support against their own interests.

In the second place, citizenship theorists, such as Wallas, Laski, MacIver and Friedrich, who argue that human nature or some fundamental character or instinct of ordinary citizens serves as a barrier to manipulative propaganda, were on the right track.[24] Not only does lack of interest and information about a subject disincline people to pay attention to communications which are aimed at changing their minds, but also a general resistance to information and persuasion coming from media appears to exist even among the interested, active readers and viewers. Trenaman and McQuail, concluding a careful study of two British constituencies in the General Election of 1959, write:

Political attitudes have some protective device which, once the elector has recognized an election campaign as propaganda aimed at persuading him, can apparently screen off and, at least temporarily, suppress any direct effect . . . behind this protective screen there seems to be an element of independent judgment and free choice of work.

These writers attribute about one-third of the changes in attitudes during a campaign to such 'specific acts of judgment', which cannot be accounted for by other influences, including influence of groups.[25]

The mass media of course are not impotent. Their influence on politicians and other elites is significant. And the media in many cases determine for everyone what becomes a political issue and what does not. But for most citizens, including most opinion leaders, the greatest effect of the media is to reinforce existing opinions, beliefs and attitudes.[26] This effect makes desirable change more difficult, but it should not count as manipulation since it need not be influence against the interests of citizens. If then we wish to change citizens' views of their interests, we should not imagine our task to be easier than it is by supposing that the media and the political elite which uses them are the main source of resistance to change. The target must be citizens themselves. Indeed, the mass media, though initially magnifying citizens' resistance to new attitudes, become the supporters of new attitudes once they are accepted.

The conclusion that the mass media normally do not change most citizens' political attitudes has been questioned by some investigators on the ground that the data on which it is based were collected *during campaigns* when most people are most firmly fixed in their attitudes and beliefs. Many people have made up their minds about candidates before a campaign begins—from one-half to three-quarters of the American electorate and more than four-fifths of the British electorate. These critics suggest, therefore, that *between campaigns* the media may be much more potent.[27] But no evidence has been offered to support this speculation, and the political effects which media are supposed to have between campaigns are so vaguely described that to identify them would be extremely difficult. It is said that a 'dissemination of distrust' of politics, for example, results from the emphasis in the media on crises and complexities of politics, but it is not clear how such an effect could be proved.[28] The media's power to influence opinion on policy matters between campaigns is probably slight. Key found, for example, that although the press overwhelmingly opposed governmental action in the field of medical care in the U.S. during the period 1948–56, 44 per cent of a national sample of citizens agreed 'strongly' that the government ought to act in this field, and another 17 per cent agreed though less strongly.[29]

Studies conducted in classrooms and other experimental situations find that people's opinions are more vulnerable to influence by various kinds of communications than the studies based on survey research suggest. However, as Carl Hovland, a leading experimental researcher in this field, admits, 'the real life communication situation is better described in terms of the survey type of model' (though he insists that survey research neglects crucial variables in the communication process).[30]

Thus, because of deficiencies in skill in the use of mass media, the variety of sources of opinion within the media, and more importantly because of the general resistance of citizens to media persuasion, the claim that opinion leaders or other citizens are manipulated by communications in the mass media cannot be sustained.

It may still be objected that a more pervasive kind of manipulation occurs which eludes not only social scientists but nearly everybody in a society. From childhood, we learn ways of thinking, ideologies and beliefs which, it is argued, support the prevailing social and political structure and with it the interests of the dominant groups and elites over the interests of the rest of the citizens. Here the mass media are not the only culprits; the entire process of socialization is to blame. However, this doctrine of pervasive manipulation is self-defeating. It is logically possible for a few individuals to escape such manipulation and to qualify as the best judges of interests of all the citizens still restrained by their manipulated perspectives. But if the manipulated citizens are to identify correctly those individuals who are not manipulated, they need criteria of identification which are not products of the prevailing ways of thinking in their manipulated society. But on the doctrine of pervasive manipulation, it would be unlikely, if not impossible, for citizens to accept or understand such criteria. A view based on the presupposition of autonomy, which the doctrine of pervasive manipulation must reject, at least has the advantage of identifying the judges of citizens' interests without such self-defeating consequences.

However, the mere absence of manipulation, though significant, is not in the view of most citizenship theorists sufficient for democratic discussion in the full sense. Reflecting a view held by many other citizenship theorists, Dewey writes that 'the essential need is . . . the improvement of the methods and conditions of debate'.[31] Genuine debate which would inform people of opposing views and offer possibilities for desirable change does not occur very often in the media. When it is available, most people ignore it.

4 Discussion

The content of both public and private campaign discussion, British and American students of elections have often pointed out, is not very informative. Candidates and citizens tend to talk past each other, emphasize symbols of consensus, emotional appeals and generalities about ends on which everyone can agree. All these tendencies are reflected in and reinforced by the media.[32]

Furthermore, the same factors which help people to resist manipulation have the consequence of stifling exposure to controversy and debate when it *is* available. Most people, whether or not intentionally, listen to what they want to hear and read messages in support of what they already believe. This 'selective exposure' usually undermines the possibility of debate that would inform citizens.[33] Thus, if the condition for discussion is to be satisfied, we cannot require that the media foster genuine debate. However, these factors discouraging such debate are not completely intractable and scope for improvement, as called for by a constructive ideal, does exist. The evidence against the possibility of debate is conclusive only if one rejects the presupposition of improvability.

If debate is a possibility, so admittedly is manipulation. If democratic reformers can, for example, overcome selective exposure, aspiring manipulators can too. Yet since on balance the pressures are against manipulation and debate, only a large effort by many people at all levels of society could make either debate or manipulation work. And manipulators would be less likely to command the support required for such an effort. Furthermore, some of the factors which discourage manipulation, for example competition among media, would encourage, or at least not discourage, debate. The possibilities for debate will be examined in detail when we look at discussion in the second mode in the schema below.

In the first mode, the case for saying that the first function of discussion, to help people recognize their interests, is fulfilled now looks adequate. Active discussants seem to be influential in the formation of preferences or opinions, though in an indirect and imperfect way. Two characteristics of the discussion process have been shown to help citizens to recognize their own interests. Discussion is rational in this limited sense. Whether discussion yields rational voting decisions will be considered in the next chapter.

SENSE OF COMMUNITY

For most citizenship theorists, the purpose of discussion is not only to help citizens recognize what is in their own interest, but also to help them to see that their interests are partly identified with those of a larger community of which they are members. A 'spirit of the common life', in Lindsay's words, is supposed to emerge which is superior to the opinions of any particular individual because it is the product of diverse experiences and interests.[34]

One sociologist, a student of group discussion, concludes that the collective judgment of a group is often superior to the judgment of the individuals in it. This is not only because discussion brings together the skills and views of many individuals, but also because discussion 'leads to the improvement of individual judgments'.[35] There is some empirical support for the belief that the result of group discussion transcends the opinions of its individual members, though it must be conceded that the collective result is shown by these studies to be technically superior, not necessarily superior in any moral sense. The studies mentioned earlier which show a tendency toward homogeneity of opinions within groups of all kinds suggest that a group interest does in fact emerge from discussion and activity.

But such group interests arise in collectivities less inclusive than the whole community. Does the process which occurs in primary and secondary groups extend to the community as a whole? Is there community-wide discussion, as Dewey for example hoped, which helps to 'break . . . down the barriers of social stratification which make individuals impervious to the interests of others'?[36] The broad conclusion usually reported about research on political discussion across status lines—that discussion is mostly with like-minded people—suggests that such community-wide discussion is unlikely. If people are left to arrange their own discussions, most will talk to people with whom they agree and whose socio-economic status is the same as theirs.[37] However, the broad conclusion is misleading in several respects. There are reasons to believe that quite a lot of discussion does occur which might generate, if not a community-wide common interest, then at least an awareness of the interests of other groups besides one's own.

4 Discussion

In the first place, the status barriers to discussion are not so rigid as the broad conclusion mentioned above would suggest. In one of the principal studies on which the conclusion is based, more than half of the white-collar workers had political discussions with persons in the professional and managerial category; nearly three-quarters of the semi-skilled and unskilled workers talked politics with persons in other occupational groups. In the second place, when cross-status conversations do occur, they are generally tolerant, two-way exchanges; people who discuss politics with persons with whom they disagree are more likely to change their minds. In the third place, the data on which the pessimistic conclusion is based are drawn from campaign periods. There is some indication that *between* campaigns political discussion is more likely than during campaigns to occur among people who disagree. Finally, indirect links do exist among various groups: each group's opinion leaders introduce ideas into their groups from outside sources. Whatever the cause, some evidence suggests that after a campaign citizens are more likely to see themselves 'as sharing the problems of a much larger community than [their] immediate family or neighborhood'.[38]

PEACE AND STABILITY

Apart from its usefulness in creating and sustaining opinions and preferences, discussion itself is valued as an alternative to violence and coercion. Commitment to discussion, Merriam writes, represents the 'disposition to find a solution through peaceful consent rather than through division and violence'. For citizenship theorists, especially Dewey, MacIver, Ross and Kelsen, this commitment is explicitly part of the meaning and justification of democracy. Laski is no doubt correct to observe that successful use of discussion in society presupposes some convergence of the ultimate interests of those who take part in the discussion. But Laski is exceptional among citizenship theorists in his readiness to deny such convergence and to predict and (in some writings) to recommend violence instead of discussion.[39]

The commitment to discussion relies on a fundamental preference for non-violent politics—and may be held even at the cost of delaying what are considered to be the right solutions. This preference is not simply a Hobbesian fear of disorder and desire for security. It represents a belief in the morality of discussion; only through accommodation, compromise, and reasonable persuasion which are the hallmarks of democratic discussion should men *qua* moral and rational creatures be moved to action. This respect for the autonomy of individuals means that coercion is in principle to be avoided, no matter how worthwhile the cause.[40] Resting on an overriding respect for a citizen's right to form his own opinions, the commitment to discussion is a further reflection of the presupposition of autonomy. Therefore, acceptance or rejection of the commitment does not depend completely on evidence from social science.

Some evidence can be mentioned which partially supports this commitment to discussion, however. Some studies indicate that regular opportunities for expressing and compromising opinions, as provided by discussion, reduce the chance of violence. Another effect of discussion, as I have pointed out, can be to expose people to new ideas. This effect, coupled with the tendency of the media to serve as 'tutors of tolerance', contributes to a sense of mutual forebearance which preserves peace and stability. Finally, the fact that people who discuss politics are more likely to have stable political preferences suggests that discussion may help maintain political stability by making people less vulnerable to sudden, disruptive appeals of extremist groups.[41]

QUESTIONABLE REFORMS

Much of what was said about the constructive ideal of participation is germane to the ideal of discussion as well. However, the most crucial question concerning political discussion in the second as well as the third modes in the schema is how to improve the quality of discussion to which citizens are exposed and in which they engage. The most promising avenue for constructive improvement in the quality of discussion appears to be the promotion of what I shall call rational propaganda. Before examining this possibility, however, I shall consider three other proposed reforms which are of questionable value.

4 Discussion

First, dissemination of scientifically established social and political information, for example by a governmental or independent non-partisan commission, is not likely to have so great an effect on most citizens as Dewey and other theorists believe.[42] Since the perception or interpretation of information is, as we have seen, subject to selective exposure, individuals in most situations can 'protect' themselves against facts they do not wish to believe, especially if they are presented in a neutral way.

Another proposal made by Ross and others—that the sponsor or source of all political communications be required to be identified clearly—is also unlikely to be very helpful. Experimental studies have shown that the initial resistance to a message from an unfavorable source fades within a few weeks; people fail to associate the source with the message any longer.[43]

Finally, Laski's lament that 'only a clash of great principles produces widespread public attention' offers no guide to desirable reform of democratic discussion.[44] It would be foolish to revive the great nineteenth-century debates on religious toleration that Laski praises if it were possible to do so (and even Laski does not recommend that). But if political discussion in our time is cast in terms of 'great principles' rather than concrete policies and personalities, most citizens will not be very interested. People notice and remember specific, concrete ideas which are relevant to their experience. One survey found that in the Kennedy-Nixon debates the discussion of medical care for the aged, for example, actually changed some older people's voting intentions; it was an issue which people could 'translate into their own personal and even selfish calculations'.[45]

All these reforms are based on an unsatisfactory model of how a democratic citizen should respond to political communications if he is to be rational. The model implies that only if a citizen responds cognitively to communications can he be said to engage in rational discussion or make rational decisions. It should be clear from my earlier argument that rational discussion in a weak sense can take place without much cognitive information; and it will be suggested in the next chapter that the same is true for voting decisions. But even for a constructive ideal which would posit a stronger form of rationality, the model is misleading.[46] By limiting rationality to cognitive responses of citizens, the model ignores affective responses which are, I shall argue below, equally important if citizens are to absorb and act on political communications. (Proponents of this model are correct insofar as they wish only to emphasize that cognitive responses are now less common in political propaganda and therefore deserve greater attention from reformers.)

Yet to reject this model we need not fall into the opposite error of treating citizens as irrational creatures who never respond to cognitive appeals. This is the error that underlies many contemporary approaches to the study of propaganda. Similarly, models of campaign strategy often assume that candidates must use mostly irrational propaganda.[47] What is needed for a satisfactory constructive ideal of discussion in citizenship theory is a concept of propaganda which avoids both the rationalist and irrationalist exaggerations. The idea of rational propaganda provides such a concept.

RATIONAL PROPAGANDA

Although no citizenship theorist specifically develops a concept of rational propaganda, the concept would not be out of place in the thought of some citizenship theorists. To strike a balance between the excessively rationalist and irrationalist models of the democratic citizen is equally an aim of citizenship theorists and the concept of rational propaganda. It is an ancient aim in the study of political communication, pursued in Aristotle's *Rhetoric*, which presents a theory of argumentation intended to avoid the extreme of a syllogistic logic on the one hand and that of a forensic art of stirring emotions on the other.[48]

Rational propaganda may be described as communication which contains a balance of cognitive and affective appeals and which has the objectives of influencing opinion and eliciting action. The 'objectives' referred to in the definition are supposed to distinguish propaganda from other kinds of communication. 'Balance' is what makes the propaganda rational. So long as men are not pure intellects, a rational response to propaganda requires an affective response as well as a cognitive response. Some social scientists have recognized the need for a balance between these elements.[49]

4 Discussion

A constructive ideal which involves promoting rational propaganda can be formulated without developing a criterion for balance, provided that two assumptions about the character of actual political propaganda are made. The first assumption is that political communications usually do not contain a proper balance of the two kinds of appeals; the second is that the deficiency is in cognitive appeal. Thus to approach a balance, a constructive ideal prescribes an increase in cognitive appeal. But besides a balance, the objectives of rational propaganda should be better realized, and for this, as I shall explain below, both kinds of appeal are important. Therefore, the constructive ideal of discussion which recommends that we promote better rational propaganda should be interpreted to urge that we increase the cognitive appeal of propaganda; and increase the affective appeal as much as is consistent with the increase in cognitive appeal.

Cognitive appeals are those which are primarily intended to evoke responses such as *reasoning* about facts and about values. Affective appeals are those which are primarily intended to evoke responses such as *feeling* approval and disapproval. Such definitions by example, though the traditional way of characterizing these and similar terms, may not seem very satisfactory even when they are fully elaborated. Yet with terms as comprehensive as these, no better alternative is available, so far as I can see. If we were willing to restrict 'cognitive', as some philosophers and linguists propose, to statements which can be true or false, the problem of definition might be easier. But such a restriction is misleading for analysis of political communications. For most kinds of utterance (questions and exclamations as well as statements) can elicit a cognitive response and can be used to make a cognitive appeal.[50]

One piece of rational propaganda will be said to be *more cognitive* than another to the extent that it uses evidence which is more factual than intuitive; better reveals differences among opposing views; is more specific; and employs a greater variety of arguments. These criteria do not reveal much about the validity of the arguments used in a political communication. Nor do they guarantee that a communication will be more cognitive than affective. However, if one piece of propaganda better satisfies the criteria than does another, the first is likely to produce a more cognitive response than the second. One piece of rational propaganda will be said to be *more affective* than another to the extent that it is designed to better arouse and retain the interest and attention of listeners; and evoke stronger sentiment or emotions favorable or unfavorable to the message.

Although these two sets of criteria are not mutually exclusive, an attempt to make a communication more cognitive will sometimes reduce its affective appeal. For example, an argument cannot be too elaborately specific without becoming too dull to hold an audience's interest. In cases where the two sets of criteria conflict, a compromise or balance between them will have to be found. Where it is struck for any particular piece of propaganda will depend on the context in which the propaganda is issued and on the form in which it is expressed.

Both cognitive and affective appeals, under certain conditions, are necessary if a communication is to influence opinion and elicit action. Affective appeals may contribute to these objectives in at least three ways.[51] First, most people can be moved to action more readily by affective appeals. Second, the size and attention of the audience can be increased by catering to people's dislike of long and uninteresting presentations and by avoiding unnecessary offense to their more intense prejudices. No matter how good an argument, it is politically worthless if few listen to it. A third way is by means of the personality of the speaker—a kind of affective appeal sometimes overlooked, though it was stressed by Aristotle. A listener is more likely to be persuaded if the listener feels that the speaker shares his general social values and if the listener feels that the speaker is trustworthy. Actually, in political systems where few important issues are really timely at the moment of the election and especially in the American system where party discipline is weak, a candidate's personality may be a better guide to his future behavior than what he says he will do, or what his party stands for.[52]

Cognitive appeals may help to influence opinion or elicit action in at least four ways. First, in many political contexts the elite and opinion-leaders are part of the same audience to which the mass propaganda is directed. From evidence cited earlier we might infer that they may be more likely to be influenced by cognitive appeals than by mostly affective ones.[53] This provides an incentive for mass propaganda to be more cognitive. Second, even the members of the audience who cannot follow the reasoning in a communication are likely to be impressed by the fact that a discussion is intended to evoke a cognitive response. As pessimistic an observer of public opinion as Walter Lippmann feels that reasoning in a public discussion is worthwhile because it allows the public to judge whether participants in the controversy are following 'a settled rule of behavior or their own arbitrary desires'.[54] Attempts to observe the 'settled rule' of 'reasonable discussion' are probably helpful in influencing opinion and eliciting action. A third way in which cognitive appeals may contribute toward these objectives is to ensure that the affective appeal is not counterproductive. Psychologists have found that to be influential, affective appeals must be accompanied by a certain amount of cognitive content, at least giving information about alternative courses of action. This provides a partial check on the abuse of affective appeals.[55] Finally, I have mentioned studies which suggest that more specific and explicit communications are more likely to be influential.[56] Greater cognitive appeal is not *always* necessary to elicit action or to influence opinion. Only under certain conditions will more cognitive appeal be needed to achieve the propagandist's objectives; even under such conditions the need for affective appeal will not be eliminated. What some of these conditions are can be discovered by looking at some empirical studies.

Three sets of findings suggest some strategies to foster rational propaganda in the way that the constructive ideal recommends. First, to the extent that opinions can be influenced, presenting both sides of an issue is more influential than presenting one side. (The actual findings of laboratory experiments are somewhat more complicated than this generalization indicates, but for the circumstances in which political discussion takes place, the generalization is sufficiently accurate.)[57] This generalization suggests that public confrontations or debates would be suitable for promoting better rational propaganda. Not only would confrontations further propagandists' objectives, but they would also be likely, as we shall see in the next section, to generate the interest and response conducive to more affective appeal, and to provide the incentives to give propaganda more cognitive appeal.

Many citizenship theorists, it will be recalled, stress the importance of debate in political discussion. But 'debate' must be understood to include other types of confrontations than those to which it is most commonly applied. In this wider sense, a debate would not rule out audience participation or the use of independent questioners. Furthermore, 'debate' need not imply, as Dewey believed it did, that the speakers are already in possession of a truth or a belief and that the only problem is to convince the audience.[58] The speakers in a debate may *act as if* persuasion is their only objective, but the debate as an institution can be a means for seeking truth as much as for advertising it.

A second set of findings suggests that television is an appropriate medium for the promotion of rational propaganda in the manner urged by the constructive ideal. Admittedly, television has not proved to be a great catalyst of political interest, as some writers originally expected, though it does not induce passivity either. Moreover, evidence about the effects of television compared to other media is not entirely satisfactory. No comparative study of an adequate sample of listeners and viewers in an actual political situation could be conducted now because television impinges on everyone. The 1952 campaign was perhaps the last chance for such a study, and very few were carried out then.[59] Nevertheless, television probably holds more promise than other media for improving political discussion in a democracy.

Selective exposure among television audiences occurs less often than in any other mass medium of communication. Not only does a partisan message on TV reach more people on the other side, but it also reaches more uninformed citizens than a message in any other medium. Thus, it strengthens cognitive appeal on at least one count by exposing more people to a greater variety of views.[60]

Television is more trusted than other media and is regarded as more authentic—an important aspect of affective appeal. It is sometimes charged that the very presentation of an event on a television screen distorts the 'reality' of the event. The authors of studies of television coverage of the MacArthur Day ceremony in Chicago and the 1952 party conventions attempted to document such a charge by showing the radical differences between what viewers and spectators saw. However, most of the spectators and many of the participants could not see what was going on during the ceremony and the conventions. Surely in such cases the television presentation has as much claim to be called the 'real event' as what most spectators saw. It is often the television presentation that is remembered and referred to by most people and which therefore has the greater impact on future politics.[61]

Of all sources, television is probably the most informative for the largest number of people, and therefore has the greatest potential for making rational propaganda more cognitive. This is so, even though the proportion of its total content devoted to political information is low, and even though there is no evidence to show that material presented over TV is better retained than that presented by lecture, print or radio. It is also no doubt true, as critics claim, that television, unlike newspapers, has no 'long tradition of political enlightenment'.[62] But the responsibility for such enlightenment is now assigned to broadcasters by the government. It should be relatively easy at least to discover whether broadcasters fulfill the responsibility since the networks are more in the glare of publicity than are most newspapers. The content of broadcasts is more closely controlled by advertisers than is that of the press, but some sponsors are coming to prefer the drama of controversy to the blandness of absolute impartiality. If so, this would improve the affective as well as the cognitive appeal of televised rational propaganda.

A third set of findings—that active participation in the communication process improves the chances of a participant's being persuaded—suggests that the televised debate or confrontation could be supplemented by small discussion groups consisting of people with mixed opinions. A similar technique was used with some apparent success in St Louis to educate the public about metropolitan reform, and could be readily adapted to other types of political discussions. The Civic Education Center and Station KETC in St

Louis sponsored the television presentation and group discussions at four hundred 'viewing posts' in private homes. A trained leader presided over a group of about ten people in a one-hour discussion of a program which they had just seen. Afterwards, the program's participants returned to the air to answer questions phoned in from the viewing posts. Again, in such situations, cognitive and affective appeals are probably strengthened.[63]

All these efforts to make rational propaganda more cognitive and more affective would be fruitless if the media were completely without influence on citizens' opinions. However, several findings in communication research suggest that people's resistance to the media described in the first part of this chapter is not total and hence some hope exists for using the media to promote rational propaganda as the constructive ideal urges. Resistance to the media, while great enough to discourage manipulation, may not be so great as to prevent better discussion. From the perspective of citizenship theory, one is inclined to emphasize the possibilities for debate implicit in these findings. The presuppositions of citizenship encourage attempts to improve the quality of political discussion in this way.

One study found that nearly two-thirds of those who follow their own party's campaign propaganda also follow the other party's—and pay attention to it. For many other people accidental exposure —watching 'because it's there'—counteracts selective exposure.[64] A number of other studies have found that the media can be effective in changing attitudes and conveying information about new ideas, the personalities of public figures, and the relative importance of issues. Also, the media can successfully communicate information in many instances where people resist the change of opinion the communicator intends. This suggests that even messages from 'the other side' can be informative. Finally, when a mechanism exists for carrying out the recommendation of a media message, the message is more likely to be effective; presumably the ballot could be such a mechanism.[65]

TELEVISED CAMPAIGN DEBATES

An examination of the most celebrated political confrontation in recent years—the televised Kennedy-Nixon exchanges of 1960—

illustrates the advantages and disadvantages of attempting to foster rational propaganda in the way the previous section suggested. Three features of the debates will be treated here: confrontation between opponents, projection of candidates' images, and the size of the audience.

A confrontation between political opponents affects the speakers as well as the audience in a manner that can make propaganda more cognitive. The audiences for the debates included an almost equal proportion of Republicans and Democrats.[66] Because of selective exposure, this was probably not true of the audiences before which each candidate appeared alone. Hence, more people heard views opposed to their own in the debates than they did in other campaign propaganda. Debates can also improve the quality of what the speakers say by reducing the temptation to resort to tactics of evasion and distortion. These tactics often succeed when an opponent is not present, as in a typical campaign oration, but are less likely to do so in a debate.

A comparison of the debates with single appearances of Nixon and Kennedy during the campaign supports the hypothesis that a confrontation is more conducive to cognitive appeals, as judged by the criteria listed above.[67]

1. Compared to the speeches, the debates encouraged the candidates to refer to more factual evidence to meet challenges to statements they would normally offer as self-evident. For example, the debate discussion of the costs of each party's program and the dangers of inflation forced the candidates to relate factual evidence to their arguments in a manner that was not matched in typical campaign speeches.[68]

2. The candidates more clearly revealed their differences by acknowledging agreement on many points. Nixon kept stressing that he agreed with Kennedy on the ends of certain policies but differed on the means. The candidates expressed agreement on internal security, the defense of Berlin, economic assistance to underdeveloped countries, and the unimportance of religious affiliation for political office. That they could agree on these issues in general terms would not be noteworthy but for the fact that in

their non-debate appearances they each expressed genuine agreement on only one issue.[69]

3. Both candidates were also more specific about their programs in the debates than in their single appearances. An illustration is the medical-care issue. Kennedy in his speeches implied that the Republicans did not have any program for medical care. In the debates, he was forced to recognize that they did, but he was also able to point out the differences in the plans. A very specific discussion of how the candidates planned to get their programs through a hostile Congress was not matched in any of the solo appearances.[70]

4. The discussions of the education issue illustrate the greater variety of arguments which the debate encouraged. In his single appearances, Nixon usually used only two arguments to state his position on federal aid to education—most often either asserting that America has the best schools in the world or warning that the Democrats would bring federal control. Kennedy repeatedly rested his case on either the assertion that too few high school graduates go on to college or the accusation that Nixon voted against federal aid for teachers' salaries. In the debates, all of these arguments were developed more fully, and others were presented.[71]

The debates possibly had an indirect effect on the quality of political propaganda in other parts of the campaign. Stanley Kelley suggests that in other campaign appearances the candidates, aware that most of their listeners had been exposed to opposing views in the debates, therefore less often attacked straw men than candidates had in speeches in previous years. By showing that 'it is possible to disagree without being disagreeable', the debates also probably encouraged more good-tempered discussion among the public generally and reduced the fear of discussing politics.[72]

The second feature of the debates—the projection of images—is part of the source of the affective appeal of the debates. Many investigators claimed that people paid more attention to how the candidates performed and to what kind of persons they seemed to be than to what they said. Katz and Feldman, summing up the results of twenty-two different surveys conducted during and after the debates, concluded that the 'debates were more effective in presenting the candidates than the issues'.[73] This conclusion certainly is questionable since very few of these surveys actually asked viewers about the issues in detail. But even if the debates were more successful in projecting images, this would not justify the outrage that many critics displayed.[74] The projection of images was probably necessary to arouse and hold the interest of so large an audience. Furthermore, images are by no means an irrelevant consideration in making a proper choice between candidates. Voters have a legitimate interest in what kind of person the candidate is, since if elected he will represent them not only in what he does but by what he is. Several citizenship theorists, as we shall discover in the next chapter, are prepared to approve of choices made in this way.

Television may put a premium on personality, but compared to speeches before a large crowd, television improves the accuracy of a candidate's image. By means of television, Eisenhower's public image in 1952 was altered from that of a 'powerful decisive warrior' to that of a 'less overawing' and 'good-natured man'. Similarly, by filling in Kennedy's image in 1960, the media made voters less likely to see Kennedy only in terms of a Catholic stereotype. Of course, deliberate fraud is quite possible on television, as the quiz show hoaxes demonstrated. But a political candidate will be unlikely to be able to rig all his television performances. He will frequently face newsmen and others who have a strong interest in exposing deception, were he to try it. Moreover, most British viewers, Trenamen and McQuail conclude, are more influenced by a competent television presentation by political candidates than by a 'slick' one.[75]

Another aspect of a candidate's television image (not wholly distinguishable from his personality) is his performance under stress before an audience. This too may enhance affective appeal, as well as being a legitimate fact for voters to consider. In a manner reminiscent of the Roman Senate or of the Teutonic tribal assemblies in Tacitus' accounts, the debates gave voters a 'living portrait of two men under stress' and let voters decide which style and pattern of behavior they preferred in their leaders. More than this, the performance before the camera may very well be a partial indication of performance in office. The debates required the candidates to think clearly and quickly under stress, to be well informed, and to be able to clarify 'public opinion regarding the ends and the instruments of policy'. All of these abilities are important skills for leaders in popular government.[76]

More than 115 million people saw at least one of the four debates. The enormous size of the audience meant that benefits from any improvement in rational propaganda were magnified many more times than they could have been in any other context. One critic of the debates, who cherishes the Lincoln-Douglas debates as his model of political discussion, concedes that the enormous audience for the television debates gave the Kennedy-Nixon debates an advantage over the Lincoln-Douglas debates.[77] But this critic and others who complained about the short period of time in which the television debaters had to answer questions appear not to realize that the advantage of a large audience cannot be had without some costs.

Many of the criticisms of the debates could be met in the future by adjustments of the format. It may be desirable, for example, to stage some debates without questioners or with a panel of ordinary voters as questioners. The formats could then be compared to see which is more successful in promoting rational propaganda as the constructive ideal recommends. Another criticism is that too many issues were included and some major ones such as civil rights were excluded. This shortcoming could be overcome in the future by more careful allotment of time, as suggested by the American Political Science Association's Commission on Presidential Debates. Finally, in view of the fact that the debates presented too many complex and remote issues, some effort should be made to emphasize issues which involve people's more immediate interests rather than problems with which they have little experience or concern.[78]

Several legal reforms which would help in staging debates should be mentioned. First, candidates for at least the highest offices might be required by law to engage in a certain number of debates. However, it would not be desirable to require, as British law did until recently, that even interviews and regular newscasts present spokesmen from each of the major parties, when a spokesman from one appears. Since an offer of time is not sufficient, one party could veto the presentation of the other parties' views on some issues. Second, better legislation should be enacted regarding campaign expenditures so that 'equal access' to audiences can become more of a reality.[79] Third, certain legal restrictions on broadcasters might be eased. In the U.S. the equal-time provision of Section 315 of the Communications Act should be repealed, at least as applied to national campaigns. That provision requires broadcasters to provide equal time for all bona fide candidates for public office, once time has been given to any one candidate. The chief objection to the provision is that it has the effect of preventing broadcasters from offering free time to *any* candidate because to do so would mean that the same offer would have to be extended to dozens of other candidates from minor parties. In view of the performance of the networks during the temporary suspension of Section 315 (as applied to Presidential and Vice-Presidential candidates), the suspension could be made permanent. In Britain, Section 63 of the Representation of the People Act of 1949 has hampered political broadcasting during campaigns. Broadcasters have rightly argued that the provision has handicapped their ability to provide adequate coverage especially of constituency races. More latitude should be given to broadcasters during campaign periods.[80]

This generally favorable analysis of the debates should not be taken as a recommendation for making the debates the only form of political propaganda during a campaign. Even though the debates have been compared here favorably with speeches, the latter may sometimes produce better rational propaganda than the former. Theodore White insists that Kennedy's New York campaign speech about Quemoy-Matsu was 'as fine a campaign discussion' of the issue as he heard—much better than the discussion of the issue during the debates.[81] On the other hand, the speech was provoked and largely shaped by what had been said by both candidates on the issue during the *debates*. In this way these two forms of propaganda can be complementary.

Confrontations need not be limited to opponents in a campaign. Press conferences under certain conditions can be appropriate forums for better rational propaganda. Nor need confrontations be limited to Presidents and Prime Ministers. Granada Television's marathons in northern Britain in 1959 were a fairly effective quasi-debate between all the candidates in the Northern constituencies, and the New York Senatorial campaign in 1956 generated better rational propaganda partly because the candidates debated. The benefits of confrontations do not derive entirely from being broadcast. State-supported voters' pamphlets, as used in California, Oregon and North Dakota, are a written form of confrontation and are thought to be effective by many political campaign managers.[82]

The press can report campaigns and political news as confrontations more than they now do—for example, by using bracketed material and cross-references to indicate an opposing view which might be reported elsewhere, and by encouraging more interpretative reporting. Checks against unfair or sensationalist reporting could be provided by a press council, as in Britain but with authority to compel testimony and retractions.[83] Finally, in view of the finding that many citizens have made up their minds *before* the campaign, confrontations should also be held *between* campaigns.[84]

RECONSTRUCTIVE IDEALS OF DISCUSSION

Laski and Dewey argue that the quality of discussion in democracies cannot be improved significantly until present social and economic conditions are radically altered. As long as the media are run for profit by a capitalist class, they maintain, information is bound to be distorted in favor of that class. Even if fair and accurate information were available, it would be of little use as long as class divisions make agreement on ideas of social justice impossible. (At times, both Laski and Dewey nevertheless concede that a great deal can be done within present systems to improve discussion.)[85]

Insofar as this radical reform rests on a vision of a society unencumbered by conflicts among various interests and blessed with completely disinterested exchange of ideas, it seeks discussion that could hardly be called political. The vision is therefore not very suitable for a political theory of democracy—not even as an ideal. The disinterested exchange of ideas would probably rapidly degenerate into an uninterested exchange. But Laski, Dewey and others who urge this sort of reform are motivated also (perhaps more so) by their aversion to the inequality that prevails in access to the media under present conditions. Even if these theorists were to concede that totally disinterested political discussion is undesirable, they would protest that the dominance by only a few interests is still more undesirable. Such dominance limits the points of view to which citizens are exposed. More importantly, dominance by groups which have the strongest interest in maintaining the status quo restricts the expression of proposals for radical change. Furthermore, since the objective of commercial interests which control the media is to expand audiences and circulation, information is slighted for the sake of entertainment. Hence, they would propose a reconstructive ideal which (coupled with economic and social reform) would imply public control of all the media.

These theorists' diagnosis of the present state of the media no doubt contains much truth, though content analyses that would adequately support it do not exist. However, evidence about the internal processes of the media would probably show that other factors besides the profit motive (for example, the pressures of time) are more important in accounting for biases and the quality of media presentations. In any case, the consequences of the profit motive are not, as we have seen, unambiguous. Some of the news that is most dramatic and most likely to expand audiences and circulations is that generated by radical ideas and activities.

What about the proposal for public control of the media implied by the ideal? Evidence gathered under present social conditions cannot be conclusive. To implement the proposal fully would eliminate the conditions under which any present investigations were conducted and the conditions on which the reliability of any conclusion would depend. But if the performance of non-commercial media under present conditions is any guide at all, the consequences of public control, would not be without disadvantages. Present non-commercial media, such as the BBC, are so sensitive to charges that they might be biased that they often eschew controversy. For many years, the BBC avoided reporting elections in their news broadcasts. And American broadcasting networks, which are subject to control in the 'public interest' to a greater degree than newspapers, have often been so cautious that viewers and listeners may find it difficult to discover that any fundamental differences of opinion exist in American politics.

Certainly there is a case for *some* increase in non-commercial instruments of communication, for instance as proposed in the Carnegie Commission's admirable report on Public Television. In Britain, the Pilkington Report argued that commercial competition had the effect of lowering the standards of BBC television presentations (although BBC officials denied this). A content analysis comparing the BBC and independent television programming found that the BBC devoted considerably more of its time to programs of an 'informational type'.[86]

Whatever the merits in the radical reforms implied by this reconstructive ideal, they are too conservative in two respects. A more promising and more visionary reconstructive ideal of discussion would not accept, as the proposals for public control do, that television and the press must remain only *mass* and *one-way* media of communication. This second reconstructive ideal pictures a broadcast system in which multiple channels to every home would allow programming specially tailored for the smallest political unit (even the ward) as well as the largest; and control devices and two-way channels which would permit interaction among viewers and between viewers and speakers. Most of the elements in such a system are already technologically (though not yet economically) feasible. With multiple channels and neighborhood hook-ups (by means of UHF, microwave and satellite relays), every representative and important administrator at every level of government would be able to talk to citizens in his district. If coaxial cables can be constructed with appropriate feedback capacities, citizens could actually participate in discussions with local political leaders. Even in the case of national presentations, a more interactive kind of participation than now occurs could be arranged. For example, while watching a brief summary presenting the essence of each item in the news, each viewer would by pressing a button select those items about which he wished to learn more. During the rest of the broadcast, when fuller accounts would be given of each of the various items, each viewer's TV receiver would automatically select for him from the multiple channels a program tailored for his own interests. All these proposals could be adapted for the newspapers of the future, which would be transmitted as 'hard-copy' television.[87]

Such a system would not only improve political discussion by generating a greater amount of more active discussion about problems of greater interest to each citizen. It would also sustain and strengthen the local political units to which power would be dispersed in line with the reconstructive ideals of participation and equality.

CONCLUSION

The confidence which citizenship theorists express in the capacity of citizens to engage in political discussion that contributes toward democratic objectives is not based entirely on presuppositions. Some findings of social science also support it.

In the first mode in the schema, discussion through the process of personal influence is shown to be likely to be rational in the sense of encouraging citizens to recognize their own interests; opinions and preferences are formed by reference to groups and are not manipulated by mass media. Hence, the first function of discussion appears to be fulfilled, as far as we can tell by examining the process of discussion. Whether discussion can be said to result in rational voting depends on the analysis of the next chapter. Discussion also helps many citizens to become aware of the interests of people who have different interests from theirs, thus contributing to a sense of community, and it encourages peace and stability to some extent.

In the second mode in the schema, the constructive ideal which was treated in detail in this chapter posits a stronger form of rationality than that which normally occurs in the process of personal influence. That ideal urges that we strengthen the cognitive appeal in rational propaganda, and, as far as is consistent with this, the affective appeal also. Televised confrontations or debates would be most likely to help realize this ideal. (A second constructive ideal, which was not analyzed here, would correspond to the constructive ideal of participation, and would urge more discussion of all kinds by all citizens by means of changes which could take place within existing social and political frameworks.)

In the third mode, one reconstructive ideal, which implies public control of the media, could be adopted only with reservations. A second ideal, picturing a multi-level, multi-directional broadcast system, is more satisfactory.

5 *Voting*

The ways in which citizens do, could and might vote rationally are the principal concern of this chapter. Thus the standards of rational voting will be examined in all three modes in the schema for citizenship. However, it is the first mode which requires the most analysis because the question of whether voters are rational has been most disputed and because the conditions for participation and discussion partly depend on the condition for rational voting.

Unless citizens in some sense vote rationally, participation and discussion cannot be said to achieve the democratic objective. Whether participation fulfills the function of helping citizens to develop political interests depends on the nature of political discussion. In the previous chapter discussion was shown to be rational at least in a weak sense. But a crucial test of discussion is whether it results in rational voting. As far as most citizens are concerned, it is in voting that the results of discussion are most readily manifested. The ballot, despite its limitations, is the single most important mechanism for most citizens to express their interests to their leaders. Thus citizenship theory emphasizes voting.

Although this chapter thus deals mainly with voting as the expression of choices, this aspect of voting is not the only reason citizenship theorists consider voting significant. The act of voting, as a form of participation, contributes toward fulfilling all of the functions set out in the chapter on participation, including the promotion of legitimacy and self-realization.[1]

Two broad kinds of rational choices have been distinguished: a choice made in accordance with self-interest; and a choice made in accordance with the general interest.[2] Both kinds of rationality will be applied here primarily to individual voters (considered in aggregates), though the rationality of the collective result of an election will also be examined briefly. The rationality of self-interest is the more important kind in the first mode in the schema, since the democratic objective has been defined in terms of self-interest. Examining this kind of rationality, I shall argue that in a theory of citizenship rational choice should be treated from the perspective of voters' action, not their calculations or their behavior alone. Although citizenship theorists do not explicitly develop an argument for treating voting in this way, the perspective of rational action is more favorable to citizenship theory than are the perspectives of calculation or behavior. Evidence from social science will be used in giving 'rational explanations' of voters' actions, but such explanations should be framed not in the causal langue of social science but in the language of reasons.

RATIONAL CALCULATION

According to a common model of rational decision, an individual would on the basis of an accurate assessment of all relevant information weigh alternative means to his goals and choose the means which most efficiently realize those goals. This model postulates rational calculation as the standard by which to appraise a decision and by implication voters' behavior.[3] Sometimes a further requirement is added: the individual's decision must be connected with his other decisions and goals in a consistent and coherent way. In politics, this requirement would usually mean that a voter's decision would have to fit his ideology.

Citizenship theorists—in particular Hobhouse, Ross, Wallas, Friedrich and Dewey—object to applying this model to citizens not only because citizens do not satisfy it, but also because, according to these theorists, citizens do not need to satisfy it for democracy to function in at least a minimally satisfactory way.[4] (Nearly all citizenship theorists, however, retain *part* of the model as an ideal, as will be explained below.)

It would indeed be surprising if voters did calculate according to this model. Compared to situations where men might be more likely to seek information and to weigh alternatives in this way (for example, in buying a new house), citizens are little involved in the voting decision and expect from it no immediate, personal consequences for which they feel responsible.

5 Voting

Some elitist democratic theorists, notably Schumpeter and Lasswell, believe that because many of the cues and responsibilities of everyday life are missing in the voting situation, voters will be more likely to give in to the 'dark urges' of their unconsciouses.[5] But the fact that voting and politics remain a relatively minor concern for most citizens in the United States and Britain suggests the opposite. People are too casually involved in politics, one social psychologist writes, for 'choices to be connected to high-key personality dynamics which make or break marriages, and raise or ruin careers'.[6] Evidence indicates, for example, that partisan choice does not appear to be generally determined by deeper personality factors such as authoritarianism. Also, very few voters were attracted to Eisenhower because he represented a 'father figure'.[7] Thus for some of the same reasons that careful rational calculation is rare among voters, so is deeply irrational choice. But if citizens were gradually to become involved in political activity much more than they are at present, such irrational choices would probably be no more common. The more active a citizen is, as we have seen, the more psychologically stable he is likely to be.

How can we find out if voters do calculate to any extent at all? Some writers suggest that we simply ask voters to explain their votes and opinions to see what sort of reasoning, if any, they display.[8] The trouble with such an approach is not only that the responses may be rationalizations but also that voters may have forgotten how they arrived at the decision, or without realizing it they may not yet have gone through the reasoning that will be decisive for them. Using survey questionnaires which are relatively open-ended, Campbell and his associates have tried to find out how voters reason. Typical responses ('I was born a Democrat and just stay with it', or 'I trust Ike because he saw the horrors of war') display few signs of reasoning that would connect the choice with the individual's interests.[9] Responses such as 'I just like him' are preferences, which some philosophers would be willing to count as reasons in a very minimal sense.[10] But such reasons cannot be said to satisfy the model of rational calculation. In any case, since we want to know if a choice is in the voter's interest, we require further information beyond simply that it is his preference.

Rational Calculation

Almost no matter how the requirement that an individual consider all relevant information is interpreted, the political information possessed by American and British voters seems quite inadequate for any rational calculation. More than a majority are ignorant of some basic political facts (such as which party controls Congress) and cannot correctly identify which party supports which position on some controversial issues. A majority have no consistent opinions on many (though certainly not all) important issues.[11] Furthermore, many citizens appear not to be capable of accurately assessing what information they might have. Not more than a third of the electorate are 'highly accurate' in their perception of where a candidate stands on an issue. The Elmira study indicated that people who favor a candidate whose opinions differ from theirs tend not to know where he stands on the issues. Given a minimum of ambiguity, they tend to think even that he agrees with them about the issues. If a candidate tries to distinguish sharply his position on a highly controversial issue such as civil rights, he may succeed, as Goldwater did to some extent in 1964.[12] But in pluralist societies where a candidate for national office needs to secure support from diverse and often antagonistic groups, clarity on issues is not to be expected very often (nor perhaps always welcomed).

If rational calculation implies that voters think in an ideological framework, then most voters also fail on this count to be rational. Views which are conventionally liberal on domestic policies are held by many people who are conservative in their views about international affairs—and vice versa. Many lower-status voters, who are more likely to be liberal on welfare issues than are higher-status voters, are more conservative in their attitudes toward innovation than higher-status voters. In a British study only two-fifths of the electors had *any* sense at all of the meaning of 'left' and 'right' in politics. Even in a campaign with relatively high ideological content such as the American Presidential race in 1964, nearly half the electorate remain ideologically unaware. A large proportion of voters do consistently favor social welfare policies and government intervention. But many of these same voters also object to the taxation needed to finance such policies more than do the voters who oppose welfare policies and government intervention.

All of this leads some investigators to conclude that not ideology but 'immediate self-interest' is at the root of most voting. About 60 per cent of the electorate (including ideologues) usually attain levels of conceptualization sufficient to comprehend politics at least in terms of short-term, group interests. Anyhow, it is surely doubtful whether all voters should think ideologically, as intellectuals and journalists are prone to do. Ideology may help one relate and order the confused data of politics, but it also creates rigid categories of thought and sustains resistance to some new information.[13]

RATIONAL EXPLANATION OF ACTION

Instead of postulating unrealistic standards of rationality, we should, at least, in the first mode in the schema, seek to understand voters' actions on their own terms. Not only may voters' calculations take place without being detectable, but more importantly voters may be rational without doing any calculation at all. They may, for example, simply accept the advice of opinion leaders. In other words, voters may act rationally without thinking rationally.

To make use of an important philosophical distinction, we can say that many voters know *how* to vote in accordance with their interest though they may not know *that* the vote is in accordance with their interest. The criterion for 'knowing how' is actually performing an action (or having the ability to do it); the criterion for 'knowing that' is stating propositions which give the rules or canons for a proper performance of an action (or having the ability to do so).[14] 'Knowing how' is sufficient to make a choice rational, I shall maintain, if plausible reasons can be suggested which the chooser *could have* given for making his choice, whether or not he does in fact give them.

Quite a few citizenship theorists propose a somewhat similar concept of rational action. Dewey suggests a distinction—between rational action and rational thinking—which seems very close to the distinction between 'knowing how' and 'knowing that'. He favors rational thinking over rational action, however. Lindsay also elaborates a distinction between rational action and rational thinking; the former he identifies with 'goodness' and the latter with 'cleverness', which is ethically neutral. Friedrich explains rational action in terms of 'character', which is a 'consistent loyalty to believed-in standards'. In addition, MacIver, Wallas, Simon and Laski mention concepts of rational action which could be used in understanding citizens' action.[15]

Although citizenship theorists suggest the general approach for explaining the rationality of voters' action, none of the theorists develops a concept of rational explanation or understanding to use in such an approach. (MacIver, in works not concerned with democratic theory, comes closest.) For a concept of rational explanation more nearly adequate for the purposes of this inquiry, we must turn to work in the philosophy of history.

Giving reasons which a person could in principle have given constitutes for some philosophers of history a 'rational explanation'.[16] Such an explanation may take the form of a process of calculation through which a voter could have gone. But on my interpretation a rational explanation of voters' actions requires only that the reasons attributed to the voters in the explanation should be compatible with empirical evidence about voting behavior; should be translatable into terms which the voter could understand; and should express why the voter's choice is in his interest. ('Interests', as I argued in Chapter 1, should be understood as wants or desires which the voter would claim now or which he could be expected to claim in the near future. Interests thus include not only material interests but also the desire that certain values be realized even if they produce only psychic satisfaction.)

The first two requirements specify the limited sense in which a rational explanation assumes that a voter *could* have given reasons. Clearly these requirements are weaker than those usually postulated or implied for rational action, for example in the model of rational calculation. A rational explanation does not assume that a voter did in fact calculate. Furthermore, since such an explanation is given from the voter's point of view, inadequate information and inaccurate perception are no bar to the voter's action being explained rationally. Nor must a voter reach conclusions in a way in which we would approve—for example, in accordance with any ideology. The justification for using these weaker standards for rationality is the presupposition of autonomy. Compared to elitist democratic theory, which does not share this presupposition, citizenship theory is not so likely to brand irrational a citizen's choice when it does not conform to what elites or activists would choose.

The third requirement more explicitly specifies how the presupposition is to be observed. In constructing a rational explanation, we seek reasons that will exhibit voters' action as being in their interest from their perspective. Like a Kantian regulative principle, the presupposition enjoins us to keep looking for reasons to support a rational explanation, even in the face of apparent counter-examples. This does not mean that all voters' choices can be rationally explained. It is possible to imagine instances which would count as irrational. An example would be a Welsh miner who voted Conservative but claimed that he thought the Conservatives provided neither inspiring leadership nor government which would be better for him and the country than the Labour party could provide. Here we probably cannot find any plausible connection between the voter's choice and any desire or want he may have. The failure to do so would make it impossible to satisfy the third requirement for a rational explanation.

It might be objected that even if voters' action can be shown to be rational by means of rational explanations, no new facts have been established. Since on this view nearly all voters could turn out to be rational in a sense, rational explanations, it may be said, merely redescribe voting behavior which others, including elitist theorists and critics of democracy, have considered irrational or non-rational. Yet redescribing, or more accurately re-conceptualizing, voters' behavior can have significant consequences, as I shall point out. Moreover, it is a mistake to treat rational explanations simply as empirical hypotheses or propositions, since such explanations reflect the presupposition of autonomy. A rational explanation does not purport to prove new facts about voters, but rather proposes new ways of looking at old facts. It can show that, given the presuppositions of citizenship, empirical evidence is not incompatible with seeing a voter's action as in his interest.

Although findings of social science are an essential ingredient in the rational explanation of voters' action, we adopt a different approach in a rational explanation from the approach we would adopt in a strictly empirical or scientific inquiry. First, unlike scientific explanations, rational explanations do not aim to show that an account of a particular action is in accord with, or deducible from, statements of general laws and conditions.[17] For this reason, rational explanations do not explain and predict in the fully scientific sense of the term. But they do explain human action in the sense of making it more understandable or intelligible.

Second, in rational explanations we use the evidence from voting studies not to establish causal hypotheses but to formulate principles of action. The explanation is framed in the languge of reasons, not solely in the language of causes or empirical associations as in social science.[18] The assertion, for example, that a citizen's lower status is a reason for his voting 'left', though supported partly by the same evidence as the hypothesis that status may be a cause, is expressed in a language which carries different implications from the language of a causal hypothesis. The language of reasons implies that the conduct being explained is meaningful to the agent; it is the product of an agent *capable* of choosing freely. Causal language does not imply these ideas, though it need not deny them.

This contrast between the two kinds of explanations does not depend on the doctrine, revived by some contemporary philosophers, that actions cannot have causes, or can never be properly explained by causes.[19] Although the philosophical issues involved here remain controversial and puzzling, we can say, I think, that this doctrine does not take account of the many instances in which we properly refer to causes in explaining human actions. Nevertheless, it seems to be the case that when we do use the language of reasons to explain an action, we imply that the agent is capable of deliberating, choosing and acting as a rational human being. A causal explanation need not be incompatible with a rational explanation; indeed the very possibility of acting differently in the future requires causal knowledge.[20]

Much of the voting behavior of democratic citizens certainly deserves criticism. The ideals of voting to be mentioned later will specify some grounds for criticism. But nothing is gained and something important, as I have suggested, is lost if we refuse to consider voters' action at any present time as rationally explainable.

Moreover, if we conceptualize voters' conduct in terms of reasons they could have given, we are more inclined, when we disapprove of their choices, to expect to present citizens with reasons to change their minds. We are perhaps less inclined to try to change their attitudes by manipulating their behavior and their habitual responses. Thus, the portrait of voters we accept in the first mode in the schema affects the approach we take toward reform in the second and third modes.

Let us now draw on the leading studies of voting behavior to see how several kinds of rational explanations of voters' action can be given. These will be only sketches for rational explanations.

VOTING BY STATUS

From a sociological perspective the 'most impressive single fact about political party support', Lipset writes, 'is that in virtually every economically developed country, the lower-income groups vote mainly for parties of the left, while higher-income groups vote mainly for parties of the right'.[21] In Britain, this pattern is clearest in the upper-middle and lower-status groups; in the United States in the higher-status groups. Because religious and regional differences cut across status groupings more in the United States than in Britain, status voting in the United States (except in some urban areas) is less pronounced than in Britain, though American voting is far from classless.[22]

Even though many citizenship theorists also hope that voters would consider the general interest when they vote, the theorists take it for granted that voting by status is in most voters' self-interest. (Voting studies usually take income, occupation, education or some combination of these as indicators of status, uneasily evading some controversies in the theory of social stratification.) Given the fact that voters have only two or perhaps three choices, voting by status is so evidently in voters' material interest that the rational explanation of their action is straightforward. The fact that subjective status (the class to which the voter assigns himself) is more strongly associated with the direction of voting than is objective status does not undermine this conclusion. This fact could mean simply that for some voters the satisfaction derived from voting with the class with which they identify outweighs the material benefits which they might associate with voting with their objective class.[23]

Voting by status is not usually grounded in consciousness of class conflict. By several measures, not very much class consciousness of this sort underlies voting decisions either in the United States or Britain. Where it exists, a British study recently indicated, it is probably declining. The status basis of voting is largely developed before adulthood—before any sophisticated consciousness of class conflict could arise. However, some primitive form of class consciousness is probably developed at an early age in working-class families—what Richard Hoggart has characterized as a sense of division between 'them' and 'us'. Moreover, among many adults, especially working-class citizens, voting is supported by at least an awareness of class interests. In a study by Butler and Stokes, seven out of eight working-class Labour supporters gave clear indications of seeing politics as representation of class interests, though not mainly as representation of opposed class interests.[24]

Neither should it be thought that status is the only kind of motivation based on material interests. Attitudes towards unemployment, recessions and general 'economic outlook' have effects on voting which cut across status lines, though lower-income groups are usually more responsive to such economic factors. Voters of both classes tend to reward the governing party when they perceive that they are economically better off than before and tend to punish it when they are worse off. There is, furthermore, a correspondence between perceptions of economic well-being and economic indicators such as levels of prices and employment.[25]

In both the United States and Britain significant numbers of voters deviate from the broad patterns of voting by status. Rational explanations probably can be provided for deviations, but they will need to be somewhat more complex. Two important deviations illustrate this.

In Britain about one-third to two-fifths of manual workers who vote cast their ballot for the Conservatives. Although a significant working-class Republican vote exists in the United States, in Britain the phenomenon has been a preoccupation of almost all studies of voting behavior. No single explanation accounts for the difference between Conservative and Labour manual workers, but according to Jean Blondel, the 'most satisfactory element of explanation is trade union membership'. Manual workers who are members of trade unions are at least three times more likely to vote Labour than Conservative; manual workers who are not trade unionists are much closer to being evenly divided.[26] Why should non-unionists be more likely to vote Conservative? Perhaps because they are less influenced by traditions of union distrust of the Tories and therefore more ready to accept the Conservatives' claim to be able to manage the economy and to maintain prosperity better. Or perhaps because non-unionists are less frequently reminded of the impact of politics on their material interests and therefore more likely to find satisfaction in the strong government and aristocratic style associated with the Tories. Even if this second speculation is true, voting on the basis of such reasoning could be rational. Not all voters need put their material interests ahead of other satisfactions. In any case, strong leadership might in the mind of some of these voters be linked with greater material welfare. Some evidence indicates that this is so, but more is needed before we are warranted in having much confidence in rational explanations here.[27]

Another deviation from status voting is found in differences in voting between younger and older members of the same status group—for example, the tendency of the generation of new voters in 1948 and 1952 to be more Republican than their elders in the same group. The difference between the age groups can probably be accounted for by the fact that the older generation experienced the depression at the time when their party attachments were formed, and the younger did not.[28] Hence, a historical approach becomes relevant to any rational explanation of this sort of voting behavior. The failure of the Republicans to deal with an economic crisis and the Democrats' efforts to meet it led many voters to feel that the Democratic party would be more likely to act in their interest in the future. Without the personal experience of Republican failure, the younger voters were not so inclined to be anti-Republican.

Political Attitudes

Some allegiances formed in this way persist even *through genera-tions*, long after the initial reason for the attachment to a party has disappeared.[29] Yet it is quite rational to penalize a party even after it has mended its ways. To do so serves notice to parties that their failures (and perhaps also successes) will have consequences beyond the next election. Historical attachments in any case do not usually persist indefinitely if they are contrary to status groups' interests. In the long term, 'most shifts by groups from one party to another occur as reactions to a rational contradiction, in which the interests or social position of a group and the program of its traditional party are at a variance'.[30]

POLITICAL ATTITUDES

Voting by status cannot by itself account for all patterns of electoral behavior—probably not more than 40 per cent. This is not only because deviations occur within classes but also because in some elections (e.g. 1952) significant shifts toward the victorious party occur in all classes. Although such shifts do not imply that the status basis of voting is permanently weakened, they do suggest that more 'immediate determinants of an individual's voting behavior' than his (relatively permanent) status must be invoked in some situations to explain his voting. Consequently, many investigators— most notably those at the Michigan Survey Research Center—focus on voters' attitudes toward issues, candidates and parties. Each of these three kinds of attitudes exerts an independent influence on voting.[31]

For most voters most of the time, attitudes toward issues do not play a very great role in how they vote. One British study estimated (on the basis of reasons for voting given by voters) that the 'maximum proportion of voters whose vote was primarily decided by an issue or issues' was not more than 10 per cent. An American study put the figure at 17 per cent. Comparing voters' attitudes toward issues with their party's positions on issues, we find as many as three-fourths of voters choosing a party with whose position on issues they significantly disagreed.[32] The reasons that issues seem to matter little is that few voters are familiar with many issues; or have strong opinions on them; or see any difference between the parties. Most of those voters who satisfy all three of these conditions (a minority of the electorate) do tend to support the party whose positions on issues they regard most favorably, especially on domestic welfare issues they consider most important. Even in this group, however, some voters do not follow this pattern; their behavior must be attributed to other influences such as attitudes toward party and candidate.[33]

Attitudes toward issues probably do influence voters in 'crisis' or 'critical' elections, such as in the American elections of 1860, 1896, and 1932, when, Campbell speculates, 'great issues have divided the nation and realigned the underlying political balance for years to come'.[34] And such elections after all are a crucial test of voters' judgment. Furthermore, in ordinary elections voters' positions on very broad issues (such as who will keep the peace better, or who is less corrupt) divide fairly clearly the Republicans from the Democrats.[35] Issues are probably also expressed in voters' images of parties, and they may be important in interpreting the meaning of the collective result of an electoral decision (as will be explained below). Nevertheless, the independent influence of issues most of the time must be considered slight. That voting on the basis of issues has always been considered rational does not mean, however, that voting for a candidate or a party, irrespective of one's opinion of the candidate's or party's position on current issues, cannot be rationally explained. Many citizenship theorists, as we shall see, assert or imply that such voting is quite rational.

If leaders were always chosen solely on the basis of their personal appeal, the risk of incompetent but attractive leadership would not be negligible. However, most of the time for most voters candidates' appeal is not sufficiently strong to outweigh party loyalty and perhaps even attitudes toward issues. (This is even more likely to be true in Britain than in the United States.) In elections when this does occur, only a minority of the voters are so affected, even though the outcome of the election may be determined by their attitude toward a candidate (as in Eisenhower's victories in 1952 and 1956). 'Candidate orientation' has received less study in Britain, and some writers (e.g. R. S. Milne) assume that the concept does not apply to the British electorate. But although the appeal of the candidate for whom people actually vote in the constituency may not be important to them, the appeal of the party leader (the aspiring Prime Minister) may in fact be the basis of their voting decision.[36]

While we sometimes wish to condemn voters for being swayed by a candidate's personal appeal, we should not deny that such behavior can be explained rationally. Some citizenship theorists (notably Hobhouse, Friedrich and Lindsay) approve of voters' taking the candidate's personal appeal into account in reaching a decision.[37] Voters who decide primarily or partly on the basis of a candidate's personal appeal may reasonably believe that such a choice is in their interest in at least two ways. In the first place, I suggested in the previous chapter that leaders represent candidates not only in what they do but in what they are. Voters have a legitimate interest in the kinds of persons their leaders are, especially in the case of ethnic groups for whom the election of 'one of their own' implies, through a symbolic recognition of the group, an 'estimation of the group's worth and dignity'.[38] In the second place, a candidate's personality may be, for voters with imperfect political information, as reliable a guide to his future behavior as party platforms, and views on issues. Thus, voters may be sensible to choose the candidate with whom they identify, as many were attracted to Truman because of his image as the 'plain man's candidate'. The appeal of Roosevelt reminds us that such identification does not always require that the candidate actually mirror the qualities of the citizens who identify with him. Voters may express what they would wish to be like, were they political leaders. A candidate's personal appeal may be an indication of his competence as a leader, but it is not always perceived that way. In 1956, Eisenhower was 'honored not so much for his performance as President as for the quality of his person'. In 1948, voters of both parties were more likely to think of Dewey as more 'capable' and 'competent' than Truman. Truman was 'honest', 'sincere', 'spunky', and 'down-to-earth'.[39]

For most voters the party with which they identify themselves (party identification) usually seems to be the most significant *single* influence on their voting decision in most elections, though in some elections other factors may overcome party identification for a decisive number of voters. Party identification generally accounts for the voting behavior of more than 80 per cent of voters with party affiliation and more than 60 per cent of all voters in the United States. Voters tend to change opinions to fit their party rather than switch parties; and if the party changes its positions, so do its supporters. In one British survey, 80 per cent of the supporters of both parties said they would continue to support their own party even if its policies were always the same as the other party's. Although status is important in explaining voting decisions, party identification is more closely linked with vote than any status or population variables.[40]

Party identification, though often originating in childhood, may be interpreted as an expression of self-interest. Voters, according to a British social scientist, consider their party choice to be an 'expression of group loyalty, or an assertion of the material interests of the group to which they think they belong'. Many voters hold images of the major parties as dedicated to the interests of particular groups within society (e.g. working class, or businessmen) or as committed to a broad range of policy objectives (e.g. extension of welfare services). Most voters actually vote for the party whose general image they prefer. They thus base their vote decision on what they believe to be the 'general superiority' of their party—not necessarily on any specific issue or candidate but on an 'over-all impression of competence' and a 'total policy'.[41] Parties also seem to be representative of their supporters, however, in the limited sense that a party's leaders are more likely to be more similar in socio-economic status to their own supporters than to the supporters of the opposition party. However, leaders' views on many policy issues do not always resemble their followers' in this way.[42]

Considering that most voters do not understand the complexities of many issues and that parties often are unable to carry out their specific promises because of unforeseen developments and internal disagreements, we should conclude that voting by party identification is no less rational than voting for specific issues and in some cases may be more rational. To be sure, voters must assume that parties and elected officials generally live up to their images. But it seems reasonable to believe that if parties and officials do not, their images will eventually alter.[43]

Although parties generally differ enough to give most voters a genuine choice, the choice is limited in at least three respects. Voters are, first, restricted to only two or three alternatives. The 'package' a voter finally chooses may contain many items he does not like—not only specific issues, but broad positions too if, for example, he is a domestic liberal and an international conservative. Second, some significant political problems never become issues between the parties. Slavery, school integration, income tax, and child labor laws, for example, were in the United States handled mainly outside party politics. While other procedures may be more effective at times, placing some issues beyond party conflict does restrict the area of voters' choice. Third, voters play only a very minor role in the selection of the choices which are finally presented to them on election day. By means of primaries in the United States and previous General Elections in Britain, voters can exert some influence on which candidates the parties will put up and what broad positions they will take on some issues. But mostly these decisions are made outside voters' view and beyond their control in organizations which are not internally democratic.

Citizenship theorists, realizing that voters' choices cannot be interpreted as anything so specific as a mandate for particular policies, describe the voters' role as limited to passing on 'broad' alternatives—policies as well as candidates.[44] The term 'broad' appears in many of these theorists' discussions, but it is seldom analyzed. I suggest that voting according to what empirical investigators have called 'partisan attitude' is an appropriate interpretation of choosing a 'broad alternative'. Party identification probably shapes much of partisan attitude, but the latter is better specified by a composite measure of attitudes toward the personal attributes of candidates, issues, and the comparative record of parties as managers of government. Partisan attitude is probably the best currently available predictor of voting behavior of the largest number of citizens. It is better than party identification, and usually better than voters' own predictions of how they will vote.[45] Prediction is not the main objective of rational explanation, but partisan attitude has the advantage of bringing together a number of important factors which a voter could take into account in reaching a decision in his interest. Partisan attitude, then, provides one of the most fruitful foundations for a rational explanation of voters' action. If voters' behavior reflects a blend of influences from his attitudes toward issues, candidates and the past performances of parties, his action can be understood as founded on reasons reflecting his interest.

The attitudinal approach to voting behavior, drawn on in this section, is often seen as a rival to the sociological approach, emphasized in the previous section.[46] However, in constructing rational explanations we are not limited to a single approach. The fact that the attitudinal approach often accounts for more of the variance in voting behavior (i.e. explains more in an important scientific sense) is not sufficient reason to adopt it as the sole empirical basis for rational explanations. Party identification, for example, may often account for more behavior than status does, but party identification may also suggest less fertile connections than status explanations do between some voters' actions and their interests. Rational explanations are thus usually less systematic and parsimonious than scientific explanations but nevertheless more useful in citizenship democratic theory. In this and the preceding section, I have sketched some ways in which rational explanations might be given, no matter which approach or which variables are thought to be most illuminating.

THE GENERAL INTEREST

In citizenship theory, voting in the general interest is at least as important as voting in one's self-interest, although voting in the general interest remains imperfectly realized.

Conflicts between self-interest and the general interest are played down by some theorists. Lindsay, for example, believes that citizens develop a sense of the general interest from devotion to smaller groups such as the family, neighborhood and trade union—groups which, I have maintained, reflect self-interest.[47] Nevertheless, to discover to what extent voting in the general interest actually occurs, we must find a concept which is empirically distinguishable from voting in one's self-interest.

Of the many senses of the 'general interest' (and related terms, 'common interest' and 'public interest') which are used in political analysis, one seems to be the most relevant to voting.[48] A policy, decision, or rule would be in the general interest if, compared to other alternatives, it benefits the public at least as much as any special group. A special group is to be understood to be any (logical) class of citizens defined by social, economic or political characteristics which exclude other individuals. A public is that class defined by such characteristics which do not exclude any citizens. Thus the class comprising all consumers is an example of a public, since any citizen can belong to it. So is the class of all citizens. That group of individuals of lower socio-economic status is a special group since citizens of upper socio-economic groups cannot belong. The general interest is thus not necessarily the same as an aggregation of individual or group interests. The concept of the general interest is relevant to a conflict between public and group or individual interests, not to a conflict among group or individual interests. This broad concept of the general interest may be expressed in two ways in voting: substantively—by voters choosing an electoral alternative which benefits a public as specified above; and procedurally—by accepting aspects of the electoral process which benefit a public.

In most elections, it is difficult to tell if voters are considering a substantive general interest because the choices they face between candidates or between parties cannot be said to be choices clearly between self-interest and the general interest. Most people *say* that they believe that their party or candidate will be best for the country as a whole as well as for their own group or for themselves. But this may be simply a reflection of that human habit of seeing what is good for you as good for everyone. Some evidence indicates that at least a minority of the electorate will support expenditure for public projects (such as parks), even though it may cost them more than it will probably benefit them.[49] The final test of the inclinations of citizens and leaders to consider the general interest must be sought not in voting behavior but in the provision of adequate common benefits, such as mass transportation, recreation and clean air. Evidence from social science need not be invoked to evaluate efforts toward providing for the general interest. Obviously, such efforts have not been very impressive. Voting in the general interest in the substantive sense, therefore, must remain an ideal. It must be assigned to the second and third modes in the schema for citizenship theory.

It is easier to find evidence to show that voters display a concern for the general interest in a procedural sense. The acceptance of the procedures of the system, especially the electoral verdict, is taken by some citizenship theorists to be a sign of the existence of this form of the general interest.[50] Underlying the reconciliation to the defeat of one's candidate are such factors as the comparative absence of enmity toward opposition parties and groups, the absence of extreme partisan division between the supporters of the major parties on most important issues, a widespread belief in the desirability of turnover in office, and some rough agreement on which issues are important and which are beyond discussion, and on what criteria for leaders are relevant.[51]

The consensus which these factors underlie probably should not be interpreted as an agreement on a set of principles or beliefs.[52] Some evidence indicates that while ordinary citizens do endorse some fundamental principles of liberal democracy (such as free speech), they do not, when asked about concrete applications of those principles, give responses which square with the principles. While nearly all Americans agree in principle that everyone should be able to speak, teach and read whatever views he wishes, more than half of the electorate believe that 'freedom does not give anyone the right to teach foreign ideas in our schools' and that 'a book that contains wrong political views cannot be a good book and does not deserve to be published'.

However, these conclusions, though broadly sound, are not so clear as they are often assumed to be. One of the major studies on which they are based (that by Samuel Stouffer) was conducted in the aftermath of McCarthyism. It is hardly surprising that at that time ordinary citizens would not support civil liberties for Communists. In fact, very few *leaders* were willing to agree that an admitted Communist teacher should not be fired. On a few issues, citizens actually responded quite admirably. A substantial majority of citizens as well as leaders (70 and 87 per cent respectively) said they would support civil liberties for a man whose loyalty has been questioned but who swears that he is not a Communist. And citizens were *more* likely than leaders to be lenient toward a man who took the Fifth Amendment to avoid testifying against his friends. In another study, conducted by Prothro and Grigg, some of the responses which the investigators assume to be inconsistent with the general democratic principles are not. For example, the principle that 'public officials should be chosen by majority vote' is supposed to be inconsistent with 'if a Communist were legally elected mayor of this city, the people should not allow him to take office'. Citizens who agreed with both propositions should not be accused of failing to understand the principle or of being extremely illiberal. Some liberal democratic theorists have argued that the general principle of accepting decisions reached by majority vote must in a democratic system be understood to exclude accepting a decision which would give power to someone who is committed to overthrowing the system.

The poor showing of ordinary citizens is frequently contrasted with the greater commitment to democratic principles and practices expressed by political leaders and influentials. Elitist democratic theorists take comfort in this difference and pin their hopes for democracy on the leaders. But on a number of critical issues—for example, social and ethnic equality—the elite do not do significantly better than ordinary citizens. Moreover, the relative superiority of the elite where it does exist does not help democracy much, even on an elitist interpretation, if as is the case on some issues a majority of the *elite* hold undemocratic or illiberal views. Finally, we should remember that the better educated elite is more likely to know the proper, acceptable responses to give to survey interviewers. Some of the difference between the elite and ordinary citizens may simply be the result of the greater honesty or naïveté of the ordinary citizens.

Despite the weaknesses of some of these studies and the implications sometimes drawn from them, the consensus that exists among most citizens is better interpreted not as agreement on a set of well understood principles and beliefs but rather as a pattern of behavior or perhaps as a reflection of a certain culture. Several citizenship theorists in fact propose the latter interpretations.[53]

If a procedural general interest exists in that the electoral verdict is widely accepted, it gives the act of voting a significance beyond the expression of interests. In casting their votes, citizens who accept the electoral procedure actively renew their commitment to the legitimacy of the whole system. Voting thus is not exclusively a matter of exercising a choice but is also an activity which helps sustain the feeling that the system is legitimate. We have already seen that voting, like other forms of participation, does have this effect. Of course, a false sense of legitimacy may be generated in this way in a system that ought to be regarded more critically by its citizens. But if other aspects of citizenship are adequately emphasized, this danger will be lessened. Short of violent revolution, almost any challenge to a democracy should be compatible with a commitment to its legitimacy.

As significant as concern for the general interest in the procedural sense is for the stability and smooth operation of the political system, it is not for citizenship theorists as important as the substantive form of the general interest.[54] That a procedural general interest exists implies very little about the quality of citizenship. Criminals can accept most of the 'rules of the game'. We must conclude then that only in a weaker sense can voting in the general interest be said to be expressed by most voters in the United States and Britain.

THE COLLECTIVE DECISION

Some writers argue that while most voters are rational only in weaker senses, the voters who determine the outcome of the election are rational in stronger senses. In this way the collective result of an election is supposed to be more rational than the sum of its parts. However, it is by no means clear exactly which voters are to be considered as determining the outcome of an election. In an important sense, all citizens who voted for the winning candidate determine the outcome since *any one* (though not all) logically could be included among those voters who make up the winning margin. In a more conventional sense, the outcome of an election is determined by the voters who change from voting for one party in the past election (or not voting at all) to voting for the opposition (or the winner) in the present election. If these voters are assumed to form a constant bloc of 'floaters' from election to election, and if they are more competent voters than others, we might be able to say that the outcome of an election in a sense is determined by voters who are more rational than most voters. Some nineteenth-century democrats relied on this line of argument to defend the rationality of voting, and some twentieth-century theorists have repeated it.[55] However, twentieth-century citizenship theorists, in their greater egalitarian concern for all citizens, do not employ a defense which ignores all but a minority of citizens.

In any case, presently available evidence does not support the claim that changers (those who change either during or between campaigns) are *more* interested, informed, or educated about politics than other voters. Indeed, changers are probably *less* competent than non-changers. The earlier studies which purported to prove that changers are less competent have been challenged, especially on the ground that they relied on voters' ability to remember their own vote at the previous election. A more recent study by Philip Converse, which does not rely on the recall ability of voters, finds that voters who switch between elections are more likely to be less informed than those who do not.[56]

Whatever the weaknesses or strengths of the changers, the broad meaning of the collective result of an election is in large part what most citizenship theorists assert it to be—in Lindsay's phrase 'an expression of approval or disapproval of what has happened'.[57] Summing up empirical studies of elections, Key writes: 'Popular action takes place mainly in retrospect rather than in prospect'. The now classic case of disapproval is 1952. Popular disapproval of Truman's handling of foreign policy (the 'loss' of China and frustration about Korea) was a distinctive characteristic of the 1948 Democrats who switched to Eisenhower in 1952. Moreover, in the electorate as a whole the single most striking factor appeared to be an unfavorable attitude toward the Democratic party as a 'manager of government', which presumably included foreign policy as well as domestic administration. In contrast, the 1956 election has been interpreted as an expression of approval of the performance of the Eisenhower administration, probably again mainly in the field of foreign affairs.[58]

Beyond the expression of retrospective approval and disapproval, elections can be taken to a limited degree as a statement about goals and policies since switchers' and new voters' policy views, as Key has shown, resemble the party for which they vote more than the other party. The authors of *The American Voter* see electoral results as expressions of 'broad goals of governmental actions' (for example, economic prosperity) and 'very generalized means of achieving such goals' (for example, federal responsibility for the national economy).[59] Plainly the policy content of an electoral verdict provides no clear mandate for any specific policy; to know which of the issues (if any) was most decisive is usually impossible. The policy content of an election is important, however, for politicians, who from the flow of issues through the years may develop a sense of what courses of action will not incur the disapprobation of the electorate. The issue or policy content of an election thus is important chiefly for helping collective electoral decisions to function as broad expressions of approval and disapproval. That this should be the chief role of elections seems reasonable; voters, like most mortals, are much less likely to be deceived by the past than by the future. Undoubtedly, political leaders can in some instances defer controversial decisions until after an election so as to avoid voters' disapproval. But leaders cannot count on major problems accommodating themselves to the time schedules of elections. In any case, voters may condemn a leader for indecisiveness as well as for making a decision which they do not like.

It might be objected that the electoral system sometimes has the consequence of punishing or rewarding leaders for events over which they have little or no control. To credit leaders for (say) economic prosperity, which may prevail even in spite of their policies, it would be said, is an instance of the fallacy of *post hoc ergo propter hoc*. Yet the electoral system could hardly be designed to apportion credit and blame as a social scientist would wish to do (if he could). How extremely difficult it is for anyone, let alone most citizens, to decide in a short time how far a government is responsible for broad social consequences. But elections can serve to stimulate the best efforts of leaders to maintain such conditions as economic prosperity, even though they know that if they fail and are defeated, it may not be their fault. If elections are sometimes illogical and unfair in their attribution of responsibility, they are nevertheless useful in their effects on the behavior of leaders.

VOTING IDEALS

This and the previous chapter should suggest that the standard of rational voting in the first mode in the schema is satisfied in various ways. The process of discussion contributes toward rational voting by discouraging manipulation and by encouraging formation of opinions and preferences by reference to the opinions of one's groups. The voting decision itself is rational in the sense that citizens express their self-interest by voting, for example, according to their status or their partisan attitude; and in that voters express the general interest in a procedural sense by accepting the electoral verdict.

Citizenship theorists do not stress encouraging more of these forms of rationality for their own sake, however. Thus, in framing the ideals of rational voting in the second and third modes in the schema, we should use a stronger concept of rationality than status and partisan voting—just as the discussion ideals in Chapter 4 dealt with the idea of debate, not just with non-manipulation and group reference. The main element in a stronger concept of (self-interested) rational voting is the idea of choice.[60] Voters can be said to be voting more rationally in their own interest to the extent that they understand better the meaning of their choices; and have a greater range of genuine alternatives from which to choose. The first objective is that of a constructive ideal, since moderate reforms and trends can contribute to it; it can also be an objective of a reconstructive ideal. The second would require radical changes and is therefore the objective of only a reconstructive ideal. In addition to the stronger concept of self-interested rational voting, I suggested a stronger concept of voting in the general interest which is the basis of two other ideals—a constructive ideal that urges more voting in the general interest; and a reconstructive ideal that urges that all voting be in the general interest.

None of these ideals have any significant role to play in elitist democratic theories. Not accepting the presuppositions of citizenship theory, elitist theorists are disposed neither to have much confidence in citizens' abilities to make rational choices nor to expect much improvement in their abilities to understand the basis of their choices.

My treatment of the voting ideals can be briefer than that of other ideals since the voting ideals are realized in many of the same ways as the other ideals of citizenship theory. Realization of some of the other ideals also directly contributes toward realization of rational voting. For example, the promotion of better rational propaganda is an important way to further more meaningful choice. Also, the realization of the ideals of equality would extend the benefits of greater political information and skill to many more citizens, and may help make people vote more often in the general interest, assuming that as a lower-status person acquires higher status, he behaves more like a higher-status person with respect to the general interest. For at present upper- and middle-income voters are more likely to be 'public-regarding' on many issues than lower-income voters. So are voters compared to non-voters.[61]

The principal way to improve voters' understanding of their choices is to make voters better informed about politics. To urge that voting be more rational in this stronger sense is not necessarily to urge that voters be freed from the 'restraints of party voting' or status voting.[62] We do not want to eliminate party and status voting or even necessarily to weaken it—just to make it better founded when it occurs.

Most of the same trends which promote participation also contribute to rational voting. Certainly education, which is extolled in citizenship theory, enhances voters' ability to choose, as Merriam, Dewey and Wallas particularly stress.[63] It does so both by making voters more informed about political alternatives and also by improving their level of conceptualization. Education appears to erode unthinking adherence to parental political views. Further, the exposure to a wider range of ideas by means of education makes it more likely that a citizen will consider the general interest in form-ing his political opinions. Obviously some kinds of education are better than others; educational *reform* is always essential. 'Pouring "civics" into the electorate won't help much . . . teaching men how to use knowledge, how to conceptualize, appraise evidence, infer causality' should be the goal. Further, citizens must be taught not only to consider intelligently what political alternatives are in their own interest but also to consider what alternatives are in the public interest.[64]

The increasing impact of the media, of urbanization, and of governmental services should also have a favorable effect on citizens' levels of political information and their willingness to consider the general interest. Trends in media and urbanization increase people's awareness of the significance of politics and of other people's interests. Urbanization may increase status voting, but probably not to the point that harmful effects would be felt on voters' concern for the general interest.[65] Expansion of governmental services means that more people are brought into closer contact with more political problems; the more concrete and immediate political issues and policies are, the more likely citizens are to understand them. An unfavorable influence on rational voting is specialization of labor and politics—just as it was an unfavorable influence on participation. People whose jobs do not help them to develop political skills and awareness will be baffled in a society which is highly technical and specialized. Assimilation of ethnic groups in society may remove impediments to a concern for the general interest, but it may also eliminate the points of reference for self-interested rational voting for some citizens.

In neither the United States nor in Britain does there appear to be a general erosion of class voting which would suggest the disappearance of these points of reference for voters. At the same time, this moderate sort of class voting, especially since it is limited by the consensual influences of party voting, may provide a foundation for concern for the general interest. Compared to religious and regional loyalties which rest on values rather than material interests, class divisions are probably more easily com-promised and more likely to be compatible with the political consensus upon which a concern for the general interest is built.[66]

Many of the reforms which a constructive ideal prescribes to generate more meaningful choice in voting are the same as those which citizenship theorists propose to increase participation. Simplifyng registration and voting procedures, for example, would allow citizens to concentrate on the substance rather than the form of voting. Dispersing political decision-making within present structures and making parties more competitive in some regions should make it easier for voters to see what is at stake in their electoral choices. Strengthening group activity also should improve voters' awareness of what an election means to them. So that voting does not become entirely group- or self-interested, such reforms should be accomplished by attempts to encourage discussion *among groups*—for example, by making sure that the discussion groups and forums mentioned in Chapter 4 embrace citizens from different social and cultural backgrounds.

The frequent suggestion to make American parties more responsible might seem to be a way to make voters' choices more meaningful.[67] If parties were more cohesive and more centralized, voters could perhaps more often expect to see policies which a party advocated actually carried out. Voters' choices would seem more meaningful because the consequences of the choices would in fact be more significant. But as far as rational voting is concerned, such a reform would be of little value. As we have noticed, most voters do not choose a party because they endorse all of its policies. Furthermore, such a reform is incompatible with other reforms, such as the dispersal of decision-making, which have been shown to help increase participation and to help improve voters' understanding of political choices.

Reconstructive ideals of (self-interested) rational voting would emphasize increasing the range of choices available to voters, as well as enhancing the meaning of choices. No citizenship theorist would urge referenda on every major policy, but several have advocated changes in electoral or party systems so that the electorate would have more alternatives. A common objection to the multiplication of parties and representatives is that the consequence of such changes would be weak and unstable governments, as in the Third and Fourth French Republics. That multi-party systems are not the only cause of such instability is shown by the stability of the Scandinavian multi-party systems.[68] The most serious objection is that the expanded range of choice which multi-party systems give is illusory since the parties ultimately have to compromise their ideological differences to get a majority to make the government operate. The only improvement is that more of the compromises occur more publicly at the governmental level rather than privately in the party caucuses as in a two-party system. Similar difficulties arise with functional representation, but there is a further objection as well: Why should occupational and economic interests be the only ones to be represented?

Whether or not we decide against proposals that would expand the range of choice for the electorate, a reconstructive ideal serves as a reminder that the element of choice in a voter's decision is restricted; and as a warning that we should not reject reforms on the ground that voters have all the choice they could legitimately expect or exercise. But a reconstructive ideal of self-interested rational voting can do more than this. It should imply much the same radical reform that the reconstructive ideal of participation prescribes—major redistributions of power in a structure of relatively small political units. As we have seen, such a structure could make citizens' choices more meaningful. While such reform would not necessarily increase the number of alternatives for voters, the alternatives actually posed would be more closely tailored to more citizens' interests. In a structure brought about by such a reform, citizens would have more opportunity to influence the menu of alternatives presented in elections. And the local units in which this influence would be exercised would have more impact on citizens' lives than local units do at present.

A reconstructive ideal which prescribes that voters always vote in the general interest in the substantive sense, if fully realized, might not have desirable consequences. Only if all the fundamental interests in society were identical or in complete harmony would a politics of pure public interest be acceptable. The reconstructive ideal in this sense remains valid as a challenge, however, simply because the general interest is so easily neglected in favor of self-interests and group interests.

CONCLUSION

Most voters are rational in the sense that a rational explanation of their action can be given. Thus, in the first mode in the schema for citizenship, the condition for rational voting can probably be satisfied. Further, the conditions for participation and discussion also can be considered fulfilled, insofar as they depend on citizens' voting rationally.

The idea of rational explanation is not only compatible with citizenship theories. It is implicit in citizenship theorists' suggestion that action rather than calculation is what counts in assessing voters' performances. Much of the content of any rational explanation must be drawn from the findings of social science. But the language and perspective of a rational explanation in citizenship theory differ significantly from those of social science. Also in the first mode in the schema, the condition for voting in the general interest can be satisfied in a weak, procedural sense. In the second mode we noticed possibilities for encouraging stronger forms of rationality in voting. Finally, in the third mode, reconstructive ideals urge reform to permit much greater choice.

So far we have considered three aspects of citizenship—participation, discussion and rational voting. The analysis has shown that weak conditions involving each are probably satisfied, and that constructive ideals corresponding to the conditions may be realizable. However, the distribution of these aspects or activities of citizenship among individuals and groups in a society is yet to be analyzed. This distribution must be examined to determine to what extent and in what ways it can be said to be equal and can be made more equal. For in citizenship theory, the standards of equality are cardinal.

6   Equality

Citizenship theorists do not always agree about their interpretations of the standards of equality, but they do agree that democracy without some significant form of equality is unacceptable. For democratic socialists such as Laski and Cole, equality is the essence of democracy. For all citizenship theorists, the principle that men are, or should be allowed to become, equal in the exercise of citizenship is paramount.

This chapter focuses primarily on equality and inequality in participation, discussion and rational voting, and in the opportunities to engage in these activities. The chief concerns, then, are the distribution of citizenship and the distribution of the opportunities for citizenship. Standards of equality in all three modes in the schema for citizenship deal with both of these kinds of distributions. Of the many possible categories of persons who might be discriminated against in the distribution of citizenship, two overlapping groups have in our time raised the most critical problems—lower-status persons and black persons.

The question of equality in the exercise of more direct forms of power, such as the making of decisions in political organizations, will be considered at the end of the chapter. Such equality, which goes beyond citizenship concerned with electoral politics but which contributes to all forms of citizenship, provides the basis for one reconstructive ideal of equality in the third mode in the schema.

The ideal of equality, more often than most other ideas discussed in this essay, has been recruited for political combat by all manner of ideologues. Both a cause and an effect of being engaged in ideological warfare is that the idea expresses not one but several concepts. Although the analysis here begins with a single formal concept of equality which appears to underlie all the standards of equality, several other concepts must be introduced in applying the formal concept to the substantive problems of the distribution of citizenship.

6 Equality

The formula which expresses what is usually assumed to characterize all substantive ideas of equality is: Treat all persons equally (in whatever respect is under consideration) unless a relevant reason can be given.[1] The point of the term 'relevant' is that not any reason is to count as a legitimate excuse for inequality. The reason must show the relation between the grounds for inequalities in the distribution of a benefit on the one hand, and the primary purpose of the benefit on the other. If, for example, the primary purpose of medical care is to cure the ill, ability to pay cannot be used as a legitimate reason for unequal distribution. On the other hand, ability to pass an appropriate examination may be a relevant reason for discriminating among applicants for a civil service post since the primary purpose of the civil service—competent administration—is furthered by the appointment of more qualified persons. The formula, as interpreted here, does not by itself provide an answer to whether a particular instance of unequal treatment is legitimate. Any particular benefit will have to be considered in the context of other benefits and values in society. Inequalities in civil service appointments, for example, in favor of certain racial groups may be justified to compensate for past inequalities and to contribute toward greater equality in society as a whole. Even when one benefit is considered alone, the formula may not yield a determinate answer. What is to count as the primary purpose of a benefit is often ambiguous or controversial. However, the formula does remind us that unequal treatment must be justified and does suggest what sort of considerations have to be advanced to justify it.

CITIZENS AND EXPERTS

Can any relevant reason be given for unequal treatment with respect to citizenship? Citizenship theorists do not think so. The most common general argument against equal citizenship has been that certain persons because of their expertise in politics are more competent than others to take part in *all* aspects of the political processes. Elitist democratic theorists, not sharing the presuppositions of citizenship theory, tend to adopt such an argument, as Chapter 1 suggested. Citizenship theorists reply to this argument that on the subject of the ends of political action there can be no experts—just as Kant maintained that there can be no experts in morals. Citizenship theorists do not assert that there can be no experts in political administration. They mean that on questions of the broad direction politics should take, such as those decisions presented to voters, all men should be treated as equally able (or unable) to judge. (As I shall suggest later, some theorists also imply that, given the proper opportunities, all or most men can become qualified to exercise more demanding forms of political power.) Citizenship theorists support their belief with two main arguments, only one of which is partially adequate.

An argument from the nature of the political judgment which citizens are called upon to make is the least inadequate. There are two versions of this argument. The first version is usually presented in the form of analogy, such as Merriam's: A man 'may not be able to build a house but he can tell when the roof leaks'. Or because men know a leak when they see it, they are, according to MacIver, able to tell a good plumber from a bad one though they know nothing about the techniques of plumbing.[2] Even if we accept the doubtful assumption that no knowledge of a technique is necessary for assessing the application of the technique, we must still question the relevance of the analogy for the political choices a citizen must make. Such choices are not usually between technical success or failure in solving specific problems. The citizen's decisions concern which problems he thinks deserve more attention. He chooses, for example, between men and parties that would emphasize civil rights over property values, and those that would reverse the emphasis. His choice is more like that between architects than between plumbers. Such a choice requires an evaluation which at least partly must be made independently of any criteria of technical expertise.

The second version of the argument from the nature of political judgment, stressing that citizen's choices are based on values, is thus more to the point. On this view, set forth by Laski, MacIver and Friedrich, no degree of expertise would qualify one man over another to make these fundamental choices of value since the choices imply an assessment of what a citizen thinks is in his own interest.[3] That this choice can finally be made only by an individual is not an empirical assertion, but expresses, as we have seen, a presupposition that the individual should be autonomous in such ultimate choices. That is part of what is meant by saying it is *his* interest. In selecting the alternatives which seem more likely to further his interest, the citizen is well-advised to make use of expert knowledge not only on the means to achieve what he values but also on the ends that persons in situations like his own have found to be most satisfying. Men who reflect about values more than others should be heard with respect, but their role must be to try to persuade others, by rational argument, not to decide for them.

A second argument designed to support the belief that there can be no experts on political ends is more an attack on experts than a defense of citizens. Experts, it is said, are not as capable as ordinary citizens in these matters because experts lack the balanced perspective that comes, in Lindsay's words, from participation in 'the ordinary rough-and-tumble of life'. Experts, according to Dewey, lead a 'cloistered life' shut off from the knowledge of the needs of the masses, and according to Laski, inevitably see their own specialities as most important.[4] But experts can, and in this age of the academic consultant often do, become involved in the 'rough-and-tumble' of practical affairs. Indeed, in some instances they become so involved that a traditional role of the academic as the disinterested critic of practical affairs has been compromised. In any case, experts surely are no more prone to overemphasize their specialities than are ordinary citizens, who in an industrial society are in many respects equally the victims of specialization.

Empirical evidence is not offered by proponents of the anti-expert argument. Explaining why an expert simply cannot 'co-ordinate his specialism with the total sum of human knowledge', Laski unintentionally reveals why almost no empirical evidence is considered. An expert who could 'coordinate his specialism' ceases, by definition, to be an expert.[5] Thus, proponents of this argument fail to show whether *actual* experts suffer the defects of their *a priori* experts. Fortunately, the argument is not successful, since if it were it would prove too much. Intended to support the case for equality, it would in effect justify inequality: experts would not be entitled to equal treatment with respect to citizenship.

The case for equality would not collapse even if citizenship theorists' reply to the argument against equal citizenship could not be sustained. Independently of this reply, it can be shown that no relevant reason can be given for justifying the exclusion of any person from the activities of citizenship, provided one accepts the democratic objective and other purposes of democracy as set forth by citizenship theorists. Admittedly, if citizens were not competent in any important sense, we might have to accept inequality in citizenship at least as a temporary expedient. The preceding three chapters demonstrated that citizens do satisfy important though weak forms of the standards of participation, discussion and rational voting; and that they can fulfill stronger forms of these demands in the future. Furthermore, the democratic objective and other objectives toward which the activities of citizenship are aimed cannot be completely satisfied by exclusive rule by experts or any other kind of elite, however competent and benign. That the objectives cannot be met in this way can be shown by examining the functions which equal citizenship is supposed to perform, according to citizenship theorists.

FUNCTIONS OF EQUALITY

The first function of the condition for equal citizenship, implied by the democratic objective, requires that interests of all important social groups be represented in the formation and expression of public opinion and in the electoral processes in proportion to their actual numbers in society. Reflecting a common theme in citizenship theory, Hobhouse writes that in the making of democratic decisions and rules, 'no assignable section [should be] left out'.[6] Although this function does not necessarily require full participation, discussion and voting by everyone but only a proportional distribution of these activities, it does imply that everyone engage in these activities at least to a sufficient degree to be able to form political interests. As we saw in Chapter 3, interests may be created and modified by political participation. In any case, even if this function of equality could be fulfilled by a proportional distribution of citizenship, other functions cannot.

A second function is to increase participation, discussion and rational voting.[7] If more citizenship is distributed more equally, the levels of these activities will increase since the deprivation of citizenship at present is most serious among persons in lower strata.

Equalizing citizenship should also contribute to individual self-realization—what some citizenship theorists consider positive freedom—since we have seen that participation probably enhances political awareness and confidence in one's environment. This effect is the third function of equality. According to Laski, equality is supposed to help make ordinary citizens 'feel significant'.[8]

A fourth function is to promote negative liberty. Here the process is supposed to be that the more that people exercise citizenship, the more likely it is that they will win social, economic and political benefits which will give them more options to live life as they please. This probably has been true for many lower-status groups. However, it seems overly optimistic if applied to the situation of most blacks today, since only part of what blacks need for liberty in this sense can be won by political action.[9]

Equality is also thought to help maintain stability within a polity. This, the fifth function, is stressed by Laski, Smith, Lindsay and Friedrich.[10] Here social and economic equality is perhaps more important than the political equalities of citizenship. The assumptions are that the less sharp are the inequalities in status in society, the less prevalent will be social tensions, the easier will be cooperation among citizens of different strata, and the more widespread will be attitudes that the system is legitimate. Evidence does lend some support to these assumptions. Where absolute and relative inequalities in status (and presumably in political citizenship) are small, the 'potential tension level of a society' is likely to be lower. As people move into higher-status positions in a society, they are more likely to accept the 'orthodox political norms of society'. This change would probably enable them to cooperate more readily with the previously more active citizens in society, as well as make them more likely to feel that the system is legitimate. Further, some studies suggest that higher-status persons are also less likely to develop cynical attitudes toward politics. Finally, we have already seen that the higher levels of participation, which greater equality would bring, are likely to foster a sense of legitimacy.[11]

Despite all this, equality is not on balance very important for preserving stability in developed democracies such as Britain and the United States—first, because much stability is sustained without equality; and second, because increasing equality may cause instability.

The intensity of dissatisfaction felt by lower-status persons in the U.S. and the U.K. is probably much less than is commonly supposed (except for persons who suffer severe deprivation and discrimination). In Lane's study of the ideology of working-class men in New Haven, most of the fifteen subjects felt at least morally equal to upper classes and did not resent the greater material benefits higher-status persons received. British studies report similar findings. Lower-status persons evidently compare their positions now with what they had before, rather than with positions of groups or persons above them. When asked, 'What sort of people do you think are doing noticeably better than you?', very few manual workers in a British survey drew any comparisons with persons in a non-manual class. Disruptive dissatisfactions are also choked off by the belief, widely held in the United States and also to some extent in Britain, that equality of opportunity prevails. Younger men can always hope to rise, and older men can hope that their children will. Where the conflict between this belief and the reality of social life is extreme (as for blacks), greater political activity and some instability are likely to result. But for most citizens the conflict never becomes very acute. They prefer to take their chances with the status quo rather than to engage in disruptive political action. Indeed the threat which inequality in the U.S. and U.K. poses to the stability of these systems is so slight that the greater worry surely is political complacency.[12]

Not only is stability possible without equality but increasing equality can generate dissatisfaction and consequent instability. As inequalities are reduced, people moving up the social ladder may actually feel more dissatisfied because their expectations become greater than before. They begin, often quite justifiably, to compare themselves with other groups higher in the status hierarchy instead of their peers or their own earlier positions. This relative deprivation is particularly striking among blacks. As a group, blacks have expressed more dissatisfaction as they have made some gains in recent years. And among individual blacks, those of higher status are more likely than those of lower status to be militant.[13]

If stability were the only or the primary objective of the standards of citizenship, we should in view of the evidence have to discourage efforts toward greater equality in developed democracies. But it is not. Some stability must be traded to satisfy the other functions of equality and the other standards of citizenship. Where political complacency persists in face of inequalities, the ideals of citizenship enjoin us to disturb it. Where responsible militancy takes hold, the ideals should promote it.

Equal citizenship, insofar as it exists, tends to fulfill four of the five functions assigned to it by citizenship theory. None of these four functions probably could be fulfilled where citizenship is reserved for a political elite. Now we must find out to what extent equality actually prevails in the distribution of citizenship.

THE DISTRIBUTION OF CITIZENSHIP

Earlier chapters revealed that full equality of citizenship is not found in the United States and Britain. Nevertheless, an important though weaker form of the equality condition, still in accord with the formula for equality, would be satisfied by proportional equality. According to the requirements of proportional equality, all significant groups must have proportional shares of citizenship. Although proportional equality would not directly fulfill all of the functions that equality is supposed to perform, it would probably satisfy the democratic objective and would also thus contribute indirectly to the other functions. If the results of the political processes benefited all citizens more equally, circumstances favoring individual self-realization and liberty, as well as circumstances promoting legitimacy and perhaps stability, would be more equally distributed. In addition, incentives to participate would be multiplied. Unfortunately, the demands of even proportional equality are not met at present. This can be illustrated by the unequal distribution of citizenship to lower classes and to American blacks.

Studies consistently show that lower-status persons are less likely to participate in politics than higher-status persons, no matter which of the common measures of status is used. Among the top fifth of the U.S. male labor force with respect to socio-economic status, nearly 80 per cent voted in 1968; only 45 per cent of those in the bottom fifth voted. In a British study, only 29 per cent of the highest of three status groups were not interested in politics; 66 per cent of the lowest group were not interested.[14] Furthermore, each of the common components of lower socio-economic status (lower income, occupation and education) are independently associated with lower levels of participation. For example, among the lowest income group (under $3,000 in 1960 and $4,000 in 1964 and 1968), about one-third were non-voters in each of the last three American presidential elections, compared to only about one-eighth of the higher income group (over $7,500 in 1960, $10,000 in 1964 and 1968).[15] Further inequalities occur in group political activity, since those lower-status persons who do join organizations (except perhaps some unions) find them dominated by higher-status persons and therefore not very likely to pursue programs that would benefit disadvantaged groups and individuals. Groups which might include a larger proportion of lower-status citizens (such as consumer organizations) are not as easily organized as groups dominated by higher-status interests.[16]

Not only do higher-status persons discuss politics more frequently and feel freer to do so than lower-status persons, higher-status persons also benefit from having a disproportionate share of characteristics which have been identified here as encouraging rational discussion. In higher strata, opinion leaders are more numerous, and personal influence is more frequent. The exposure to political information in the media, which is essential for debate, is also more frequent among higher-status persons (with the significant exception of exposure to television). Even in a study in which interest in politics was held constant, 60 per cent of persons of lower socio-economic status were exposed to political material in the media, compared to almost 80 per cent of those of higher status.[17]

Rational voting shows similar patterns of unequal distribution. Only in voting by party images and party identification do lower-status persons match higher-status persons. And one British study casts doubt on this supposedly equal social distribution of party identifiers. The tendency to vote according to status is also greater in higher-status groups. As for the voting *ideal* which requires voters to be informed about their choices, lower-status persons fall far short of higher-status persons' levels of political knowledge, awareness of the impact of government, and ability to see longer-term interests. For example, only 37 per cent of Americans with only grammar school education were able to tell Gallup pollsters what is meant by balancing the federal budget; from 55 to 77 per cent of persons in higher educational groups answered adequately.[18]

The distribution of citizenship between blacks and whites, though improved in recent years, remains strikingly unequal in many ways. In 1960, for example, about 46 per cent of black citizens did not vote, while only 19 per cent of the whites did not. Even in 1964, a high-stimulus election especially for blacks, 35 per cent of the blacks did not vote, compared to 20 per cent of whites. The difference narrowed only slightly in 1968, even though Southern black turnout sharply increased and Northern white turnout declined. The unequal distribution of citizenship is of course most pronounced in the South; one survey showed that 86 per cent of voting-age whites have voted in at least one election; only 41 per cent of the black adults have ever voted. Discussion and media exposure are also distributed unequally, though not quite so sharply.[19]

Much of the unequal distribution of citizenship between blacks and whites can be attributed to the fact that proportionately more blacks than whites fall in lower-status groups. According to one analysis of a 1963 NORC survey, the differences in education completely explain the difference in turnout between black and white registered voters—within as well as outside the South. My analysis of 1968 survey data suggests that education still has a significant impact on the black and white differences in turnout (except among those with only some college education). About 52 per cent of whites with only grade school education voted, while 57 per cent of blacks with that much education voted. College-educated blacks were as likely to vote as college-educated whites.[20] But none of this means that black inequalities in citizenship are simply a class problem exactly like that of other lower-status citizens. Blacks suffer, as the next section emphasizes, from special disadvantages in the opportunities for citizenship.

In several respects, blacks match or surpass whites in citizenship. Blacks are more likely than whites to report taking an active part in organizations, and are more likely than whites to belong to *political* organizations. Proportionately more blacks than whites have strong party attachments, and blacks who vote are more likely than persons of similar status and environment in most other minority groups to vote consistently Democratic. Blacks also more strongly identify with their reference group than do members of most other social groupings. Although politicized blacks thus exhibit certain aspects of participation, discussion and rational voting to greater degrees than do whites, the proportion of politicized blacks is significantly less than for other groups.[21] Obviously, we cannot conclude that blacks enjoy equal citizenship.

In at least some Northern communities blacks as a group vote and participate in other ways more than whites. In Dahl's New Haven study, 44 per cent of the blacks were among the most active in campaigns and elections, compared to 20 per cent of the whites. But this is probably because governmental channels of influence are more open to blacks than are private channels, such as influence by means of business and social connections with community leaders.[22] The fact that Northern blacks may not be so disadvantaged in citizenship merely exposes the inequalities in their social and economic life. It suggests that it is misleading to concentrate exclusively on the distribution of political citizenship. In the next section, we probe beyond these political inequalities.

Thus, in most respects the distribution of citizenship between upper and lower classes and between blacks and whites fails to satisfy the weaker idea of proportional equality. This is true of the activities of citizenship as defined not only in terms of ideals but also in terms of the conditions that were shown probably to be satisfied in previous chapters.

A still weaker form of the condition for equality can be satisfied, however. The absolute number of lower-status persons who participate in politics (and presumably share in most of the other activities of citizenship) is often greater than the absolute number of higher-status persons who do. About three-fifths of the one-quarter of the population classified as high-participators are in lower-income groups.[23] Therefore, the numerical distribution of citizenship often favors those groups which suffer in the proportional distribution. This numerical distribution suggests one form of inequality in which blacks in some communities and lower classes in general are not disadvantaged. Although higher-status persons are at a disadvantage on this standard of numerical equality, an equality condition stated in terms of this standard can still be said to be satisfied. The purpose of the condition is to compensate *partly* for the other forms of inequalities which fall overwhelmingly on lower-status groups. Advantages in numerical inequality of course do not balance the disadvantages in other forms of inequality. Moreover, the advantages do not have any rational justification, based as they are on the fortuitous fact that lower-status persons are more numerous. Nevertheless, the idea of numerical equality should not be discounted in democratic theory. The numerical superiority of the lower strata in suffrage has been a chief cause of the expansion of welfare and other benefits provided by governments in this century.

EQUALITY OF OPPORTUNITY

Faced with patent inequalities in the actual distribution of citizenship, theorists of citizenship turn to the potential distribution—the idea of equality of opportunity. This idea takes two forms: equality of *de jure* opportunity, which stipulates that the enforced laws and other rules dealing with citizenship do not treat persons unequally without a relevant reason; and equality of *de facto* opportunity, which similarly requires equal treatment with respect to circumstances which affect the use of *de jure* opportunities for citizenship.[24] The first is a form of equality which is a condition that probably can be satisfied in the first mode in the schema for citizenship. The second, which reveals the sources of inequalities in the distribution of citizenship, expresses ideals and must be assigned to the second and third modes in the schema.

Explicit legal exclusion from the activities of citizenship has all but ended. Most of the legal provisions and procedures, such as poll taxes and discriminatory registration requirements, which have had the same effect as explicit exclusion are fast disappearing. Undoubtedly, in some areas, notably Southern United States, the enforcement of legal equality is not effective. But on the whole, equality of *de jure* opportunity seems reasonably well met. The best indication that this is so is the declining interest shown in the field by reformers. Now that *de jure* equality in citizenship has been virtually achieved, reformers tend to deny its importance. However, its attainment has had important effects on the distribution of citizenship and of other benefits. As a result of the extension of suffrage, for instance, lower classes have shared more equitably in the benefits of government and have acquired skills and interests which enable them to be more competent citizens. From the evidence cited in Chapter 3 about the impact of registration on turnout, we may infer that the legal barriers to voting (both the formal requirements and the way they are administered) have been significant restraints on black voting in the South, although of course many other factors, especially community social pressure, have affected it too.[25] Moreover, removing these barriers to voting so that blacks become an electoral power does make a difference to what blacks can expect to receive from government. Although giving blacks the vote has not yet had a great impact on the problems of housing and school desegregation, it has had a few significant effects in such areas as the allocation of public goods and the administration of justice.[26]

In Chapter 3, we saw that the second function of participation— the inclusion of all significant interests—could not be satisfied unless some condition for equality of opportunity could also be met. The idea of *de jure* equality will serve this purpose. It is quite compatible with forms of discrimination we encountered in Chapter 3, such as the unfair advantage producers have over consumers, and

higher-income citizens have over lower-income citizens, in organiz-
ing for political action. From the perspective of equality of *de jure*
opportunity, consumers and lower-income citizens have equal
opportunities to organize because like other groups their legal
rights to organize are protected.

Because *de jure* equality is compatible with significant forms of
discrimination, it does not capture very much of the meaning of
the concept of equality. However important *de jure* opportunities
are, no citizenship theorist would deny that a satisfactory ideal of
equality must also recognize *de facto* opportunities. The ideal cannot
be blind to circumstances which discriminate against certain groups
in the actual use of whatever *de jure* opportunities exist. Furthermore, it is mainly through the recognition of *de facto* inequalities
that political systems come to enact the rules to which *de jure*
equality refers. If only *de jure* equality were in question, a system
could become more egalitarian simply by *eliminating* rules which
are enforced in a discriminatory manner.

Theorists such as MacIver and Lindsay who claim that political
equality is possible without social equality do not really deny the
importance of the equality of *de facto* opportunity. These theorists
mean to say no more than that what we call *de jure* equality is
significant enough to deserve the title of 'equality'. They do not
intend to imply that more nearly equal *use* of this sort of political
equality is possible without some equalization of social and economic
conditions. Thus, their alleged dispute with other citizenship
theorists, such as Laski, Cole, Dewey and Simon, who wish to
reserve 'equality' to refer to the idea of *de facto* equality, is mainly
verbal. The first group of theorists use 'equality' to express a
condition which is generally satisfied in existing democracies, *as
well as* to refer to an ideal which is not yet attained. The second
group of theorists restrict the term to the expression of an ideal.[27]

Despite the prominence of some version of the idea of equality of
de facto opportunity in citizenship theories, so seldom is the idea
analyzed that several difficulties in the idea itself are usually overlooked. These conceptual difficulties are: conflicts between equality
and opportunity; conflicts between equality and other values; and
the indeterminacy of opportunity.

The first set of difficulties arises because the idea of opportunity usually implies *in*equality. To speak of opportunities presupposes a hierarchy through which an individual can rise—in short, a society of *un*equals. Since citizenship theorists who advocate equality of opportunity do not wish to abolish all forms of hierarchy entirely, the conflict does not appear as a stark contradiction. It is manifested in two sorts of tensions—first, between specialization and flexibility; and, second, between competitiveness and mutual respect.

The first tension is illustrated by the problem which an educational system faces in balancing the chance to receive specialized training such as college preparation and the chance to switch from one specialized education to another. The British system has favored the former by assigning children (largely on the basis of I.Q. tests) to separate, comparatively specialized educational streams at an early age. The system in effect gives less emphasis to making access to opportunities equal and gives more emphasis to making the accessible opportunities more valuable. In contrast, the American system, at least in theory, preserves longer a child's option of switching to more desirable forms of specialization such as college preparation. Since the system less rigidly segregates children into specialized streams at so early an age, it better allows for the fact that early influences may have disadvantaged a child. In the American system, the equality of the opportunity takes precedence over the value of the opportunity.[28]

A second tension in the ideal occurs because a concern with opportunity engenders in social and political life a competitive spirit which is inimical to what some citizenship theorists, most notably Lindsay, consider an important part of the ideal of equality—the equality of respect for all persons. Although Lindsay sees no serious conflict between equality of respect and equality of opportunity, it is clear that competing for opportunities can discourage according other people genuinely equal respect as persons. Competitive activity engenders continual efforts to prove oneself better than one's rivals; an achievement-oriented society leads to a concern with status, with what others think, with conformity. Persons receive respect mostly insofar as they fill roles into which society places them. The logical outcome of a competitive system, with completely equal opportunities to reach its top positions, is the meritocracy envisioned by Michael Young. In this society, equality of opportunity has been attained, but all traces of equality of respect have vanished. The unmeritorious are disdained by the meritorious. Mutual respect disappears, because it can be sustained only by a belief in the equality of all persons—which in turn partly depends at present on the possibility of blaming one's failures on unequal opportunities. Hence, realization of equality of opportunity without the cultivation of equality of respect would be undesirable. That we may never arrive at a meritocracy does not affect the point that even in present societies the demands of equality of opportunity are not entirely compatible with other standards of equality.[29]

The second set of difficulties concerns conflicts between equality of opportunity and other values or ideals besides equality. The list of conflicts could be extended, but three are most significant for the purposes of this inquiry.

If equality of opportunity is taken (in part) to imply that high rates of upward mobility in a society are desirable, then realization of such equality may unfavorably affect political participation and status and party voting. The more mobile individual is more likely to be subjected to cross pressures than the less mobile person. The mobile individual faces in his new environment experiences and associations which conflict with his old ties and experiences. Persons subjected to cross pressures in this way, many studies have shown, are less likely to participate in politics and are less consistent and firm in their class voting and party attachments.[30]

The presupposition of autonomy may also conflict with efforts to establish more equal opportunities. For if the attitudes of the fifteen 'common men' in Robert Lane's study do not differ greatly from those of the American working class as a whole, many citizens do not desire but fear equality. The representativeness of Lane's group is certainly questionable. All fifteen are white, Eastern seaboard residents in an urban environment, and eleven are Roman Catholics. But since surveys have found some indications that the attitudes Lane describes may be common among white lower-status persons, challenging Lane's methodology is not the best way to deal with this problem. The more straightforward strategy is to recognize, as we have had to do before, that citizens do not always desire what citizenship theory recommends. The theory does not therefore brand these citizens as irrational, but its ideals may urge that their attitudes be changed—especially by the experience of greater political participation. Examining the source of the fear of equality among Lane's men gives some reason to be hopeful about the possibility of undermining the fear of equality. The fear seems to be based on the belief that equality must result in political rule by unqualified leaders, or absolute equality of income, or higher incomes without acceptance by one's social peers. Perhaps if citizens could be shown that equality of opportunity need not have any of these consequences, they would welcome it.[31]

The third potential conflict is between liberty and equality. Some writers have argued that equality requires a common culture in a society—for example, a socialist culture where commercialism and competition are absent, and authentic working-class values are universally respected.[32] In a plurality of cultures, one culture comes to be regarded as superior to another, and acceptance of the superior one is a badge of status. This differentiation would be a serious source of inequality, even if inequalities in education, income and occupation were to disappear. But if a common culture were to prevail, personal liberty would be likely to be limited in two ways. A common culture at least initially would have to be imposed on some persons, and the liberty to draw upon the whole cultural history of civilization would be limited. Therefore, an ideal of equality, if it is to be compatible with liberty, should not be understood to entail a common culture. At the same time, this conclusion suggests a further reason for giving the ideal of equal respect for persons added emphasis. If liberty demands a multiplication of values and cultures, then equality must even more strongly insist upon the respect for persons whatever their values.

The upshot of these first two sets of difficulties with the ideal of equality of *de facto* opportunity is that the ideal, even more than most, must be balanced against other values—including other ideals of equality. We cannot, for example, state constructive or reconstructive ideals of equal opportunity without at the same time stipulating that they be qualified by other ideals such as equality of respect.

A third set of difficulties with the ideal of *de facto* opportunity arises because the notion of opportunity is usually indeterminate in most statements of the ideal, including those in citizenship theory. It is not clear in principle how far the *de facto* ideal demands that we extend the chain of opportunities for citizenship. The point of the ideal is to probe beyond inequalities in the use of citizenship— beyond the first link in the chain—to the conditions which create them. Therefore, the ideal must extend at least to inequalities in those conditions—that is, to the second link, which reveals differences in social and economic status. Probably the ideal should also embrace inequalities at the third link, such as unequal educational opportunities, which affect those at the second link. But does the ideal extend still further to the inequalities which affect the third link in the chain of opportunities? For example, if factors in the family environment such as attitudes toward education increase a child's chances of staying in school or of going to college, does the ideal require that this environment equally provide such stimuli for everyone? Extending the chain to its end, must we equalize the *genetic* opportunities of all children? It might be necessary to do so if children are to have an equivalent chance at every step of the process which determines what sort of education they will receive and finally what sort of citizens they will be.

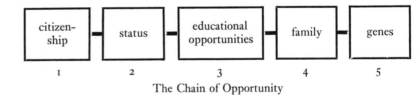

The Chain of Opportunity

At present, the ideal would in practice extend no further on the chain of opportunities than the third link. The application of the ideal is limited in this way for three reasons. First, these inequalities provide sufficient work to keep reformers busy. Second, we cannot yet reliably manipulate the more remote links in the chain. Third, our current ideas of liberty would not tolerate further extensions. With the passage of time all three of these reasons will be undermined. That this is so is obvious in the case of the first and second reasons, but requires some argument in the case of the third. The advance of scientific knowledge of human behavior can be expected to alter our attitudes toward intervention in areas (such as family life) that we now, on grounds of liberty, consider to be largely protected from outside interference. The capacity to discover and to change the conditions in an individual's environment which make him act as he does will probably narrow the area of what we assign mainly to personal responsibility and to enlarge what we attribute to an individual's environment. Intervention to correct what is done to an individual by his environment is not so clearly interference with what *he* does—that is, with his liberty. We shall probably still impute responsibility and freedom to individuals; an individual himself might be able to make use of the new scientific knowledge to alter his environment. But the responsibility will at least be shared by others (including public officials) who have the capacity to change the conditions of action. The absence of intervention, then, will be less and less a measure of liberty even in the most private spheres of action. Indeed, the failure to use scientific knowledge could be considered a violation of liberty. If we possess the knowledge and power to increase individuals' options in life, we should regard intervention as enhancing their liberty, rather than restricting it, provided they agree. Our progeny, therefore, may condone tampering with their family life to equalize opportunities, just as we now largely accept the intervention in our economic life to which most of our progenitors objected in the name of liberty.

Thus, in principle the chain of opportunity implied by the ideal of equality of *de facto* opportunity can be extended almost indefinitely. The ultimate limit to the chain presumably would be set only by our concept of personal identity. If the characteristics of a person which are regarded as essential to making him who he is were altered, we could no longer speak of giving *him* equal opportunity.[33] But apart from this limitation, the chain of opportunity seems logically unlimited and the notion of opportunity in the ideal consequently indeterminate. It follows that the ideal of equal opportunity is not, as some have argued, necessarily a conservative ideal. The ideal need not take inequalities of ability in the present system as given. How much change in present inequalities the ideal requires will depend on which point in the chain of opportunity is at issue. In the next section, it will be seen that we do not have to trace the chain of opportunities very far before we find serious inequalities of opportunity in present British and American society.

UNEQUAL OPPORTUNITIES

If lower-status persons and blacks simply chose to engage less often than others in the activities of citizenship, we could not blame the unequal use of *de jure* opportunities on unequal *de facto* opportunities. However, since lower-status persons are more likely to have the psychological, social and economic traits which would discourage citizenship, the failure to use *de jure* opportunities is not fully a matter of choice for these persons. Examining the distribution of these traits which discourage citizenship will show that the ideal of equality of *de facto* opportunity is not satisfied with respect even to secondary opportunities and will at the same time suggest what factors must be taken into account in any attempt to realize the ideal.

All three of the variables which characterize lower socio-economic status are associated with traits which discourage citizenship. Lower-status occupations give individuals fewer opportunities to develop skills which could carry over into politics. Persons in such occupations protest decisions less often and are consulted on the job less often. They have fewer chances to associate with like-minded people in a way that would create and support rational political opinions. They are less likely to have the leisure to engage in political activities and are more likely to suffer psychological frustrations which would inhibit them in dealing confidently with their political environment.[34] Similarly, persons in lower-income groups have greater financial worry; more financial security would lead to higher levels of self-confidence and self-esteem which are conducive to citizenship. Perhaps lower-income persons also feel that they have less of a stake in government since, as some political theorists have argued, it is psychologically less rewarding to be given something you do not have than it is painful to be deprived of what you already have. It is less pleasant to receive than painful to give. Finally, lack of education, as I pointed out in previous chapters, may inhibit all forms of citizenship. Lower levels of education are associated with lower interest in politics, fewer opinions, less frequent political discussion, greater ignorance of what choices would be in one's own interest, and less confidence to deal with the political environment.[35]

In addition to traits which appear to arise from each of these status variables alone, the cumulative effect of all the variables together seems to affect negatively some of the activities of citizenship. Persons on the bottom of the heap in all respects are very unlikely to have much of a sense of political efficacy or sense of citizen duty, and are quite likely to feel cynical about politics. Repeated failure limits the aspirations of such persons: 'those who have less wish for less'. Thus for the lowest groups, especially many blacks, the obstacles to citizenship are deeper than their deprivations of education, occupation and income; these individuals' hopes for bettering their status have been crushed. And for blacks and other minority racial groups, prejudice raises still another barrier to equal citizenship. The impact of prejudice on efforts of non-whites toward improving their position is obvious in the United States, but it is only less visible in Britain because of the proportionately fewer non-white persons living there. A study of Political and Economic Planning concluded that racial discrimination against non-whites, especially West Indians, in housing, jobs and other areas is 'deep-rooted and widespread in Britain'.[36]

Furthermore, lower-status persons are disproportionately subjected to cross pressures, which discourage participation, discussion, and status and party voting. The 'lower strata', Lipset writes, are

influenced by their life experiences and their class organizations to favor those parties which advocate social and economic reforms, but at the same time they are exposed to strong upper-class and conservative influences through the press, radio, school and churches ... though their social and economic inferiority predisposes them against the status quo, the existing system has many traditional claims to legitimacy which influence them.[37]

That inequalities in status itself are great in the United States and the United Kingdom should not need elaboration. In the case

of income, one of the most familiar indicators of status, the top fifth
of United States income earners in recent years have received more
than two-fifths of the total income, while the bottom fifth got less
than one twentieth of the total. The shape of the distribution of
income (though not wealth) in the United Kingdom is almost
identical to that of the United States except for the very top and
bottom, which are somewhat less extreme. In neither country have
radical changes in the distributions occurred in recent years. Nor
does taxation in either country result in great reductions in the
inequalities, as is often assumed.[38]

At the third link in the chain of opportunities, the chances for
achieving higher status that would promote citizenship are not
equally distributed. In an industrial society, education is the crucial
factor determining whether one attains higher occupations and
incomes. The impact of this on blacks and whites is not equal. For a
given education, a black's chances for better occupations and
incomes at almost every level are significantly inferior to a white's.
Moreover, for both blacks and whites, the opportunity for education is unequally distributed in two respects. First, lower-status
and especially black persons are more likely to attend poorer
schools. In 1965, more than 65 per cent of black first-graders were
still in virtually all black schools with facilities generally inferior to
white schools. Second, in both the United States and Britain, sons
of manual workers are much less likely to go to college than sons of
higher-status fathers. In the United States where this sort of
inequality of educational opportunity is less severe than in Britain,
one study found that two-thirds of the children of professional
fathers were admitted to college but only 16 per cent of children of
manual workers.[39]

From the perspective of the idea of numerical equality, the
distribution of opportunity does not seem so unfavorable. The
absolute number of college-trained persons of lower-class origins
exceed in the United States the number of college-trained persons
of professional-class origins. Half of the college-trained population
consists of children of blue-collar workers and of farmers. In Britain
about one-quarter of those admitted to University come from
working-class background.[40] But plainly it is inequality as it

affects individuals, not categories, that must be the paramount concern of citizenship theory. And many lower-status individuals, we have seen, suffer disadvantages in educational opportunities.

A principal source of these disadvantages is the family and home background, the fourth link in the chain of opportunity. Not merely do lower-status families find it more difficult to afford to send their children to college. More significantly, lower-class families less often foster the values of education and the will to seek more of it. Differences in home environment influence not only whether the child continues his education but also the extent to which he profits from whatever schooling he receives. In 1965 a major U.S. report on *Equality of Educational Opportunity*, based on one of the largest surveys ever undertaken by social scientists, found that a child's achievement on standardized tests depends substantially on his home background (such factors as the kind and amount of reading material in the home, and his parents' attitude toward education). Indeed, even 'schools bring little influence to bear on a child's achievement that is independent of the . . . inequalities imposed on children by home, neighborhood and peers'.[41]

Some critics of this report have argued that the effect of differences in school quality on students' performance is much greater than the report shows. They say that because the quality of the school and the home background are so closely interrelated (good schools are usually in good neighborhoods), the attempt statistically to take out the effects of home background at the same time eliminates the effects of school quality. Moreover, the achievement tests do not measure knowledge of specific subject-matter, such as geography, science and literature, on which schools concentrate their teaching.[42]

The statistical issues which the report raises have not yet been resolved, but it does seem clear that the report establishes that home background has a significant impact on a child's ability to benefit from his education. Whatever the significance of school quality, the disadvantages of an unfavorable home and family background may never be entirely overcome. In any case, the persons most disadvantaged in home background are most likely to go to the poorer schools.

Finally, the combination of home background and school quality, according to data in the report, accounts for not more than 28 per cent of variance in children's achievement.[43] Even if we allow for the unreliability of the tests and other such factors, quite a lot of variance remains unexplained, some of which might be attributable to genetic differences. We arrive, then, at the final point in the chain of opportunity. No matter how far we probe behind the inequalities in the use of *de jure* opportunities for citizenship, we uncover further inequalities in *de facto* opportunities. Plainly, equality of *de facto* opportunity is an ideal, not a reality.

CONSTRUCTIVE IDEALS OF EQUALITY

In the second mode in the schema, the constructive ideal of *de facto* opportunity requires trends and moderate reforms which would diminish inequalities in opportunities for citizenship and hence in the actual distribution of citizenship. Thus, insofar as this ideal is realized, two other constructive ideals, requiring proportional and more nearly equal distribution of citizenship, will tend to be realized also. The same trends and reforms that in earlier chapters were shown to affect the activities of citizenship will be examined in this section for their differential effects on citizenship between strata and between whites and blacks. These trends and reforms are not meant to exhaust the possibilities for constructive change; the ideal of equality of opportunity alone unfolds a wide array of possible reforms.

Since early in this century, trends in differential rates of turnout increases have consistently favored blacks and those of lower education and income. If these trends reflect gains in other forms of citizenship and if they continue, we might expect constructive ideals of equality to come closer to being realized. No doubt some of the causes of this trend in the past, such as the removal of ballot restrictions, will not have any effect in the future. Others, however, can be expected to continue. The 'socialization' of government, giving politics a salience for lower classes more nearly equivalent to that which it has for higher classes, should contribute toward the equalization of opportunities for citizenship.[44]

The increasing tendency for sons to attain higher status than their fathers (insofar as it has occurred) has in the past received some impetus from rapid industrialization which cannot be expected to continue indefinitely. However, the upward trends in mobility may in the future be sustained by increasing urbanization, economic prosperity, and most importantly the expansion of the white-collar sector of the occupational structure. Even now, among sons of unskilled workers, fewer of those in younger age groups than in older age groups hold unskilled jobs. If mobility reduces discrepancies in education, income and occupation, opportunities for some forms of citizenship are likely to become more nearly equal.[45] Finally, as the composition of the labor forces shifts toward a higher proportion of skilled, white-collar technical and managerial positions, the changing character of industrial work will provide more opportunities for the exercise of skill. If these trends persist, lower-status citizens can be expected to become more nearly equal in political competence to higher-status citizens.[46]

Even if the general trends in society were consistently toward more equal status, however, the lowest groups would probably be passed by, caught in that cycle of deprivation which crushes their will to reach for any opportunity. In any case, for blacks a change in the attitude of the white majority toward them is as important as a chance to rise in status. Unfortunately, in the South at present adults in youngest age groups seem to be more segregationist in outlook than some older age groups. This is partly attributable to the fact that the education of the younger generation had sharper anti-black overtones; the younger group acquired their education during the tense and violent period of the 1950s when blacks began to make their first real gains. It might be feared, therefore, that blacks' demands and their gains will continue to have such an unfortunate effect on whites' attitudes, and that the effect will spread northward as blacks push for the equality that they deserve in such areas as housing and job opportunities. However, survey evidence since 1942 shows a steady trend, unshaken in the North or South by civil rights demonstrations and violence of recent years, toward greater white acceptance of racial integration. Now, even in the South a majority of whites say they would not object to a black neighbor and by 1965 55 per cent of Southern whites favored school integration. Whites do not approve of riots, and many do not endorse even orderly demonstrations such as the Poor People's March in 1963. But such events do not seem to increase white resistance to black demands for greater equality. If anything, they seem to weaken that resistance, as whites are made more aware of black grievances.[47]

What non-radical reforms would contribute toward realizing the constructive ideal of equality of *de facto* opportunity? Clearly the familiar social reforms of liberalism, as most citizenship theorists believe, are still vital. From what was shown about the unequal opportunities, we can see that more equal opportunities for better education, for more satisfying jobs and for higher incomes would contribute toward more equal opportunities for citizenship. Of the three sorts of opportunities, higher incomes seem to be the least important for people with at least middle-class incomes. For lower-class persons, including lower-class blacks, large improvements in *any* of these three should have an impact on the other two and, hence on citizenship. As for educational opportunities, school integration probably will help blacks. However, as we have seen, the family background of many lower-class persons, not only blacks, may have to be enriched.[48]

Citizenship theorists also stress the need for reforms which are more clearly political in nature. However, some of these reforms which would increase participation, discussion and rational voting might not reduce the inequalities in their distribution—and could actually intensify such inequalities. For example, 'get-out-the-vote' campaigns based on appeals to civic duty would have their greatest impact on middle-class turnout. Strengthening the activity of existing groups, without a special effort to encourage groups which would support lower-class and black aims, would be likely also to have a negative effect on the equality of opportunity. In Southern counties, attempts to foster competitive two-party systems could actually reduce black participation, if such a system happened to replace a factionalism which offered within one party a candidate relatively favorable to blacks.[49]

In contrast, simplifying registration and voting procedures and making the content of political discussion more concrete are changes which would benefit those most disadvantaged in citizenship. So would efforts toward the dispersion of political power within present structures; persons of lower socio-economic status in some political activities beyond voting are less likely to be outdone by higher-status citizens in local politics than in national politics. Any reforms which would stimulate citizens' interest in campaigns and other political activities could also be expected to contribute toward a more equal distribution of citizenship. If a citizen's interest can be aroused, he is more likely to participate and discuss, whatever his status level. To be sure, sheer excitement is not desirable. The voting ideals, we have seen, stipulate that greater interest include a greater awareness and knowledge of politics. This must be the goal of an educational program which is not confined to the schools and universities. In a proper conception of equality of opportunity, education has a political dimension, as well as a social and economic one.[50]

RECONSTRUCTIVE IDEALS

To each of the constructive ideals of equality corresponds a reconstructive ideal which urges the same kind of equality but to the greater degree which radical change would permit. For example, the reconstructive ideal of equality of *de facto* opportunity might require that any disadvantages in home background of children be eliminated. This would probably entail a radical change in the role of the family in society.

However, one reconstructive ideal of equality has no counterpart in the second mode in the schema. This ideal is not explicitly stated by any citizenship theorist, but some suggestions of it, as we have noticed before, are prominent in the writings of Laski and Cole. Such an ideal pictures a society in which all members equally make political or quasi-political decisions in government or institutions that have authority to allocate social and economic resources. These decision-making powers logically could not be exercised simultaneously by everyone, but could be exercised successively by everyone—for example, by a process of rotation in office in small units.

This reconstructive ideal of equality deals with activities beyond electoral citizenship since it refers to the exercise of direct political

influence, not indirect kinds of influence such as voting and discussion. The ideal, however, is closely related to citizenship construed as a capacity to exercise indirect influence. Were all citizens
to gain greater experience in the making of political and social
decisions in the way that the ideal posits, all would more actively
and more competently engage in all activities of citizenship.

Clearly this reconstructive ideal of equality would not be realized
merely by trends (such as greater equalization of social positions)
which contribute toward realization of constructive ideals of
equality. Some of these trends are in fact more likely to impede
advancement toward the reconstructive ideal since they are in part
a product of the welfare state, which tends to concentrate political
and social authority. The leveling of society, Ralf Dahrehdorf
argues, stops short of the leveling of power and authority—here is
'the structural limit of equality'.[51]

Pluralist theorists of community power claim that power is not
concentrated in the hands of a homogeneous elite; power on different issues is now dispersed among different groups, not cumu-
latively concentrated as it once was in one group which was also
the highest social stratum. It is for this reason that some theorists
are not so disturbed by inequality in political activities beyond
exercise of indirect influence. But many other studies of community
power do not support the pluralist claim without qualification.
There have been (at last count) thirty-one studies covering fifty-five
American communities, and not surprisingly they do not all agree.
Differences in method may account for some of the divergent
findings. The reputational approach (asking who is the most
influential) tends to find pyramidal or concentrated power structures, while the decision-making approach (focusing on who makes
decisions on issues) tends to find pluralist power structures. But
differences in the characteristics of the communities studied is
probably more important. Communities that are smaller and less
industrialized than New Haven, a favorite of the pluralist theorists,
have a much greater degree of concentrated power. Even if a power
elite does not rule in larger, more industrialized communities, the
standards of equality are hardly met. For in a pluralist structure, the
leadership echelon, which is characterized by this dispersed pattern

of power, includes mostly white-collar occupations or higher, heavily biased in favor of professionals, especially lawyers. When power is dispersed, the wage-earner is left out. Furthermore, dispersed power is often not competitive. Although no one group of men dominate on all issues, many small groups dominate and are relatively uncontrolled on the issues within their spheres of influence. Finally, the issues which never arise are often as important as the issues which are decided. Community power studies seldom ask who shapes the climate which provokes issues and who injects them into the political arena. Thus, dispersed power on the pluralist pattern, even where it prevails, is not sufficient to satisfy many of the functions of equality—let alone the reconstructive ideal which demands equal exercise of direct influence.[52]

Although the reconstructive ideal of participation discussed in Chapter 3 probably would, by dispersing power into smaller units, contribute to equality in the exercise of direct political influence, it is not specifically concerned with the distribution of such influence. Even if power were dispersed as this ideal of participation pictures, tendencies toward inequality would be likely to remain. There would be, besides social and economic factors, two important structural impediments to equality. First, the number of positions of authority even in small units obviously would be considerably less than the number of citizens. Second, given specialization of labor, some citizens would still benefit more than others from experience in their work; occupations such as law would help men develop skills for citizenship more readily than, say, work in industrial production. The reconstructive ideal of equality of direct influence is directed against these two structural impediments.

The first impediment perhaps can never be completely overcome, but it is not invulnerable. Leadership positions in private as well as governmental organizations might be made subject to more rapid rotation. Movement into and out of circles of power could be increased by appropriate legal measures. In addition, it should be possible for governments to share authority with some broadly based political movements which are able to sustain organizations with responsible leadership. Finally, developments in communications and information sciences, as was suggested in Chapter 4, may help enlarge the arena of decision-making.

The second impediment may be partially undermined by changes in industrial life. Although the idea of self-government in industry which formed part of the Guild Socialism of Cole and others was never implemented in Britain, substantial traces of the idea survive in various proposals for workers' participation in management. These proposals could have the effect of providing equal opportunities for the actual exercise of power in the work-place, as well as opportunities for rehearsals for political decision-making. Some reformers urge that workers, along with consumers, be at least represented on councils which would oversee larger industries, as well as on councils or committees within divisions and within companies and on boards of directors. At least some European nations appear to be doing a better job than the United States and Britain in providing more opportunities for workers' exercise of power in industry.[53]

Greater industrial democracy could perhaps be achieved without sacrificing the needs of economic efficiency and whatever advantages the British and American economic systems may have. Managers in more progressive industries in the United States and Britain have in recent years shown great interest in applying the recommendations of behavioral scientists who propose greater participation and involvement of people in work-place decisions beyond conventional labor-management negotiations. A major theme in these recommendations is that the needs of production and the needs of people do not inherently conflict. Giving workers and lower-level managers a greater role in industrial decision-making should not only increase production, these writers say, but also contribute toward making employees' work more satisfying and fulfilling. Presumably it would also help make more competent citizens.[54] Although these proposals are sometimes offered and usually taken in the interest of preserving the remnants of a capitalist structure of industry, they could in the future form the basis for more far-reaching, radical reforms.

In the future, educational and leisure activities will be as important as life at work. Citizen involvement in decisions in these activities has been neglected by most citizenship theorists as well as by many reformers. But their significance in the future is bound to increase, as the work-week for most citizens decreases. Greater citizen participation in decisions affecting local schools and recreational activities thus must be an important objective in reform oriented toward enhanced citizenship.

Evidence from social science is not very helpful in determining what the effects of realizing reconstructive ideals of equality might be. The radical changes that the ideals imply, though they might be begun moderately and on a limited scale, fall beyond the reach of most studies conducted under present conditions in the United States and Britain. However, the evidence already examined on the effects of participation does indicate in a general way that realization of the ideal of equality of direct influence would be desirable. Insofar as citizens have a chance to share in the exercise of direct power, their interest and involvement in the exercise of indirect power are likely to be considerably enhanced. Thus, this reconstructive ideal of equality, though greatly emphasized only by British social democrats, must be considered indispensable in any satisfactory democratic theory of citizenship.

CONCLUSION

Citizenship theory, unlike elitist theory, maintains that no acceptable reason can be given to justify unequal distribution of citizenship in violation of the formal idea of equality. The presupposition of autonomy precludes discrimination in the activities of citizenship, and the presupposition of improvability encourages citizenship theorists to see possibilities for distributing citizenship more equally.

The actual distribution of citizenship, however, does not meet most of the versions of the standards which the formal idea of equality underlies. Hence, in the first mode in the schema of citizenship, the two conditions for equality which can be said to be satisfied, or not violated, are very weak conditions. The first, numerical equality, refers to the absolute ratios in the distribution of citizenship between lower- and higher-status groups. Since the distribution favors lower-status groups on this criterion, it does not violate the formal idea of equality in the way that other inequalities do. The second condition deals with the distribution of *de jure* opportunities for citizenship. Since the enforced rules of the British and American political systems no longer discriminate against certain classes and races except in a few areas, this condition for equality of *de jure* opportunity is virtually met.

In the second mode in the schema, two constructive ideals concern the distribution of citizenship; one deals with the distribution of opportunities for citizenship, and another with equality of respect. First, proportional equality requires that major social groups be represented in the activities of citizenship in proportion to their numbers in the population. Second, a stronger form of the ideal stipulates that citizenship be distributed more equally to all citizens. Both of these ideals depend on the realizability of the third constructive ideal, equality of *de facto* opportunity, which requires that opportunities for citizenship be equal (at that point in the chain of opportunities leading to citizenship where radical change would not be necessary). Finally, in order that the value of mutual respect for other citizens is not lost in the scramble for opportunities, the ideal of *de facto* opportunity must be qualified by the ideal of equality of respect.

In the third mode, the belief that structural changes should be undertaken to give citizens more opportunities to exercise direct power in the political and social system is formulated as a re-constructive ideal of equality. In addition, reconstructive ideals corresponding to the constructive ideals of equality also find a place in this mode. The reconstructive ideal of equality of *de facto* opportunity, for example, directs reformers down the chain of opportunities past the point where radical change would not be required.

Conclusion

This book has developed and applied a schema in which a theory of democratic citizenship is related to studies from behavioral social science. Two broad conclusions follow from this analysis: the findings of social science are within certain limits very useful in formulating a theory of democratic citizenship; and citizenship theory can be reconciled with and supported by these findings.

USES AND LIMITATIONS OF SOCIAL SCIENCE

This study has been, in part, an argument in favor of a balanced approach to relating democratic theory and social science. Such an approach falls between prescriptivism and descriptivism; it avoids treating all standards of citizenship as immune to challenge by social science, or treating standards as subject to falsification as descriptive generalizations are. Many citizenship theorists tend toward either prescriptivism or descriptivism; some elitist democratic theorists tend toward descriptivism. Against prescriptivist tendencies, the schema emphasizes the relevance of the findings of social science; against descriptivist tendencies, the limitations of such findings.

Evidence from social science is relevant in three general ways. First, it can be used to evaluate the kinds of citizenship that exist at present—the quality of citizenship in democracies. It can also be used to assess the degree to which certain kinds of citizenship exist, though such an indication cannot be so precise in democratic theory as in strictly empirical inquiry. Both of these uses are demonstrated in the first mode in the schema. The first mode, however, is also relevant to ideals. The picture of weak democracy which is presented in the first mode underscores the need to realize the ideals of citizenship theory. If the first mode does not provoke some deep dissatisfaction with democracy as it exists, the uses of this mode are not fully appreciated.

A second use of social science is to point out the possibilities in present structures for change which would realize these ideals.

Much of the evidence cited here in support of constructive ideals serves this purpose. For example, we saw that although genuine debate does not often occur in political discussion, evidence indicates that such debate can be encouraged under certain conditions which do occasionally occur in present structures.

Finally, evidence from social science can be used to suggest what advantages accrue to citizens if moderate or radical changes take place. Greater participation, for example, may develop more self-confident, politically aware citizens who are more likely to act in accordance with democratic ideals. Such evidence is thus relevant to both constructive and reconstructive ideals.

Three limitations of the use of the findings of social science in framing democratic theory have also been revealed in this study. First, some crucial elements in the ideals, as well as the conditions, can never be completely interpreted in empirical terms. This is chiefly because these standards rest partly on presuppositions which cannot be disproved by empirical evidence. In addition, certain conditions and ideals, such as those referring to the notion of legitimacy, contain an irreducible evaluative element; however legitimate citizens may feel a government or system to be (according to findings of social science), we may still judge that the government or the system does not satisfy our evaluative criteria of legitimacy. This limitation does not imply that empirical evidence cannot be used in making such a judgment; nor does it imply that reasoned argument about the evaluative element is impossible. It means merely that empirical evidence is not decisive on such questions.

A second limitation is that evidence from social science is particularly inconclusive when applied to proposals for radical change. Such change would alter the structure and thus the constants on which the generalizations of social science usually depend. This is why this study has paid less attention to reconstructive ideals than to conditions and constructive ideals. The limitation also explains why those who favor radical change are more inclined to use more sweeping and less quantitative historical and sociological evidence. Nothing said here implies that radical change should not be attempted, nor that arguments in its favor cannot be defended as cogently as those for non-radical change. The implication is merely that we should be cautious in invoking the authority of the social scientific evidence now available in support of reconstructive ideals. That social science does not very well support reconstructive ideals is more to the discredit of social science than the ideals. Thus the use of behavioral social science does not obviate the historical, philosophical and literary styles of discourse in which political theory has traditionally been expressed.

A third limitation of the use of social science in democratic theory arises because strictly empirical inquiry, though affected by values, does not and should not always raise the same questions as the approach to democratic theory adopted here. An empirical explanation of voting behavior, for example, differs from what democratic theory would require, at the very least because such an explanation demands a greater degree of quantitative precision and greater economy of models. Democratic theory as developed here therefore can make use of social science but cannot substitute for it.

CITIZENSHIP AND BEHAVIOR

This study has been an argument not only in favor of a balanced approach to relating democratic theory and social science, but also an argument in partial defense of citizenship theory. That theory is characterized by two presuppositions and four sets of standards of citizenship—which distinguish it from another less satisfactory view of democracy, elitist democratic theory. The presuppositions of citizenship, which incline theorists to respect citizens' present and future capacities for judging their political interests, are not directly affected by empirical evidence but rather influence the kind of evidence which is considered significant. The standards of citizenship—conditions and ideals of participation, discussion, rational voting and equality—are partly based on the presuppositions. However, the standards are also shaped to varying degrees by empirical evidence. To see how these standards are modified and supported by findings of social science, I presented the standards in three modes in a schema. I examined the nature of citizenship which is displayed by two democracies, the citizenship which could be realized, and citizenship which might be realized.

In the first mode, conditions requiring certain kinds or degrees of citizenship to realize various democratic objectives or functions were framed in such a way that they would be likely to be satisfied. The conditions generally express a weaker sense or a lesser degree of the demands made upon citizens by ideals.

Participation functions in three ways which directly contribute toward the democratic objective (i.e., attaining rules and decisions which satisfy the interests of the greatest number of citizens). The first function, to prevent rulers from deliberately violating most citizens' interests, is fulfilled in a minimal sense if a majority does not protest when it has an opportunity to do so. Whether this can be said to be satisfied depends on whether all interests are expressed and considered in the political processes (the second function) and whether citizens develop knowledge of what their political interests are (the third function). The second function is fulfilled if we are prepared to accept symbolic and indirect representation of interests via pressure groups and parties, as well as a form of equality which requires only that *de jure* opportunities to organize be equal. The third function depends on the nature of political discussion, though all forms of participation were shown to contribute toward fulfilling the function.

Two other functions of participation, to some extent independent of the democratic objective, are to promote legitimacy and self-realization. Evidence indicated that these latter two objectives, insofar as they could be interpreted empirically, are furthered by participation in the manner specified by the condition. However, many citizens do not benefit from these results of participation.

The first function of *discussion* is to help people recognize their political interests and thus create rational opinions. This function is furthered by a process in which opinion leaders, the better informed ordinary citizens, shape the opinions of their friends and associates. Three features of the process are likely to generate discussion that is rational in a weak sense: formation of opinions by reference groups; absence of manipulation of citizens by the media; and resistance of opinion leaders to manipulation. A second function of discussion—to establish a sense of community—is fulfilled in the sense that most people show an awareness of interests of people from other social groups. Promotion of stability, the third function, is also encouraged by discussion.

If a rational decision in *voting* is one made in accordance with self-interest, then voters can be said to be rational. Although they do not calculate, most voters behave in such a way that a 'rational explanation' of their action probably can be given. Such explanations provide reasons which a voter could have given, usually in terms of voting by status and by partisan attitude. Even voting for a candidate because of his personal appeal, though this occurs less often than some other voting behavior, can be considered rational. Another sort of rationality—consideration of the general interest—is displayed by voters in a weak sense which refers to the acceptance of the procedures of the political system, especially the electoral verdict, as legitimate. Finally, the collective result of an electoral decision may be interpreted as a broad expression of approval or disapproval of past performance—a more rational result than would be a decision specifically about future issues.

The function of *equality* which is directly connected with the democratic objective is meant to secure equality in citizenship for all significant groups. The conditions which refer to these functions can be satisfied only in weak senses of equality, the most important of which requires only that groups have equal *de jure* opportunities to participate, discuss and vote rationally. Lower-status and black persons do not share even proportionately in the actual distribution of citizenship. Equality in citizenship would also, as citizenship theorists hope, tend to perform three other functions: increase other activities of citizenship, foster individual self-realization and promote negative liberty. Here again we can say only that equality operates in the manner set by the condition, not that these effects of equality are experienced by all citizens, let alone experienced equally. Finally, equality in citizenship turns out on balance not to favor stability in developed democracies.

Taken together these conditions, referring to aspects of citizenship and their functions, reveal a picture of democracy as it exists for ordinary citizens in the United States and Britain. It is a weak but not insignificant form of democracy which the picture presents.

The ideals of citizenship theory which arise in the other two modes in the schema suggest stronger forms.

The second mode in the schema comprises constructive ideals which demand a greater degree of whatever activity the conditions call for, or demand it in a stronger sense. The constructive ideal of *participation* and one of the constructive ideals of *discussion* urge more participation and discussion within existing social and political structures. A second constructive ideal of *discussion* stresses discussion which would foster genuine debate by means of promoting better rational propaganda. The constructive ideal of self-interested *rational voting* demands changes which would make choices more meaningful to voters. A second constructive ideal of *rational voting* prescribes that more voters try to see their own interests in terms of a general interest. Finally, there are four constructive ideals of *equality*—one urging proportional, and one equal distribution of citizenship; another prescribing improvements in equality of *de facto* opportunity; and still another stipulating equality of respect.

Changes which affect the realization of all of these constructive ideals were classified either as trends or reforms, though these sometimes interact. Some trends which appear to affect these ideals favorably are increases in educational opportunities, urbanization, exposure to media, and the continuing extension of governmental activities. One of the important unfavorable trends is the increasing specialization of politics. Moderate reforms which were shown to be likely to contribute to realization of constructive ideals include the simplifying of registration and voting procedures and barriers to other forms of participation, making campaigns and elections more interesting and informative, dispersing some decision-making authority within existing structures, and strengthening group activity (with special efforts to enlist lower-status groups).

In the third mode in the schema, reconstructive ideals picture a state of affairs which, if realizable at all, would require radical change. Evidence from behavioral social science as it now exists is therefore not much help in showing that these ideals are realizable. Such evidence is of some use in indicating in some instances that changes analogous to those implied by a reconstructive ideal would produce desirable consequences. However, in other instances the complete realization of a reconstructive ideal need not be shown to be desirable. A few reconstructive ideals serve as challenges which are not intended as programs of reform.

The reconstructive ideal of *participation* pictures a decentralized political structure which would encourage all citizens to take part much more actively not only in electoral activity but also in more direct kinds of decision-making. This ideal resembles three of the other reconstructive ideals, which at least imply such a structure. The most important reconstructive ideal of *discussion* refers to a media system with a capacity for tailoring programs to small political units and for allowing more than one-way mass communication. A reconstructive ideal of *rational voting* urging that citizens better understand the meaning of their choices would also be promoted in a structure in which power is dispersed. Finally, one reconstructive ideal of *equality* also implies such a structure, but since it pictures citizens sharing equally in influencing decisions it demands further structural reforms such as rotation in office and work-place democracy. Other reconstructive ideals which do not concern the dispersal of power include an ideal in voting which critically challenges the limited range of alternatives which voters have, and one which condemns voting for self-interests rather than the general interest. Also there are additional reconstructive ideals of equality, which correspond to each of the other constructive ideals of equality. Insofar as evidence from social science is relevant to any reconstructive ideals, it gives them some slight support. Furthermore, these ideals are more faithful to the presuppositions of citizenship than are the other standards of citizenship.

Citizenship theory as formulated in these three modes in the schema can thus be reconciled with some findings of social science. While partially supported by these studies, citizenship theory is not acceptable without modification. Among the major revisions or amendments undertaken here were the introduction of the concepts of rational propaganda and rational explanation, and the extension of the idea of equality of opportunity. In addition, certain methodological faults of some citizenship theorists, such as tendency toward prescriptivism, were criticized.

Conclusion

Despite these modifications, most of the essentials of citizenship theory remain intact. Moreover, the modified theory of citizenship should prove more acceptable than theories untainted by social science. Neither the visions of democratic theory nor the findings of social science alone can reveal the full dimensions of citizenship, but together they may. Social science, then, is a worthy if limited ally of a democratic theory which strives to illuminate the present and the future of democratic citizenship.

Notes

Citations are given in full the first time they appear and also in the Bibliography. The notes are longer than otherwise would be necessary so that readers unfamiliar with either social science or democratic theory can more easily find out more about the studies or the theorists with which this work deals. Let those readers uninitiated in social science be warned that the number of citations for any finding is not directly proportional to its degree of certainty.

INTRODUCTION

1 For important pleas for a rapprochement, see David Easton, *The Political System* (New York, 1953), pp. 219–32; and W. G. Runciman, *Social Science and Political Theory* (Cambridge, England, 1963).

2 For a historical analysis of the concept of citizenship, see H. Mark Roelofs, *The Tension of Citizenship* (New York, 1957). To avoid supposing that there is only one Greek idea of democracy, consult Aristotle, *Politics*, 1291 b–1292 a, 1292 b–1293 a.

3 On the meaning of 'democracy', see Richard McKeon (ed.), *Democracy in a World of Tensions* (Chicago, 1951), pp. 453–512; George H. Sabine, 'The Two Democratic Traditions', *Philosophical Review* (Oct. 1952), pp. 451–74; Arne Naess *et al.*, *Democracy, Ideology and Objectivity* (Oslo, Norway, 1956); Richard Wollheim, 'Democracy', *Journal of the History of Ideas* (April 1958), pp. 225–42; S. I. Benn and R. S. Peters, *Social Principles and the Democratic State* (London, 1959), pp. 332–40; Robert A. Dahl, *A Preface to Democratic Theory* (Chicago, 1963), pp. 63–84; Giovanni Sartori, *Democratic Theory* (New York, 1965), esp. pp. 3–30; and Jens A. Christophersen, *The Meaning of 'Democracy'* (Oslo, 1966).

4 On 'behavioralism', see Robert A. Dahl, 'The Behavioral Approach in Political Science: Epitaph for a Monument to a Successful Protest', *American Political Science Review* (Dec. 1961), pp. 763–72; and David Easton, 'The Current Meaning of "Behavioralism" in Political Science', in James C. Charlesworth (ed.), *The Limits of Behavioralism in Political Science* (American Academy of Political and Social Science, Oct. 1962), pp. 1–25. Dahl's essay is reprinted along with other relevant articles in Heinz Eulau (ed.), *Behavioralism in Political Science* (New York, 1969). For critical assaults upon behavioralism, see Eric Voegelin, *The New Science of Politics* (Chicago, 1952); Herbert J. Storing (ed.), *Essays on the Scientific Study of Politics* (New York, 1962); and Dante Germino, *Beyond Ideology* (New York, 1967), pp. 187–214. Cf. John H. Schaar and Sheldon S. Wolin, 'Review Essay: *Essays on the Scientific Study of Politics*: A Critique', *American Political Science Review* (March 1963), pp. 125–50; and reply by Storing *et al.*, pp. 151–60.

5 Bertrand de Jouvenal, 'Political Science and Prevision', *American Political Science Review* (March 1965), pp. 33–4.

6 For examples of attacks on a classical theory where no normative theorists are carefully considered, see Bernard R. Berelson, 'Democratic Theory and Public Opinion', *Public Opinion Quarterly* (Fall 1952), pp. 313–30; Berelson, Paul F. Lazarsfeld and William N. McPhee, *Voting* (Chicago, 1954), pp. 305–23; Gabriel A. Almond and Sidney Verba, *The Civic Culture* (Princeton, 1963), pp. 473–9.

7 Elsewhere I have outlined how John Stuart Mill's democratic theory might be related to twentieth-century empirical studies ['Democratic Theory and Electoral Behavior', paper delivered to the American Political Science Association (Sept. 1966)].

8 See, e.g. Sartori, pp. 43–6, 231–7.

9 John Dewey, *Freedom and Culture* (New York, 1939), pp. 148, 143–54; *Problems of Men* (New York, 1946), pp. 33, 133–40; *Liberalism and Social Action* (New York, 1935), pp. 31–2; *The Public and Its Problems* (Denver, 1927), pp. 198–9, 202–3; *Individualism Old and New* (New York, 1962), pp. 95–100, 154–63; *Theory of Valuation* (Chicago, 1939), pp. 58–60; *Reconstruction in Philosophy* (Boston, 1957), p. 209; *Democracy and Education* (New York, 1961), pp. 83, 86–8; Jerome Nathanson, *John Dewey: The Reconstruction of the Democratic Life* (New York, 1951), p. 114 and Milton R. Konvitz, 'Dewey's Revision of Jefferson', in Sidney Hook (ed.), *John Dewey: Philosopher of Science and Freedom*, (New York, 1950), pp. 72–4.

    Hans Kelsen, 'Absolutism and Relativism in Philosophy and Politics', *American Political Science Review* (Oct. 1948), pp. 913–14; *Ethics* (Oct. 1955), pt II, pp. 4, 14, 27–8, 38–9; and *Vom Wesen und Wert der Demokratie* (Tübingen, 1929), pp. 15–18, 98–104.

    Alf Ross, *Why Democracy?* (Cambridge, Mass., 1952), pp. 119, 153–4.

    T. V. Smith, *The Democratic Tradition in America* (New York, 1941), pp. 14–16, 185–92; *The Democratic Way of Life* (Chicago, 1939), pp. 171, 175, 179–82, 191; *The Legislative Way of Life in America* (Chicago, 1940), pp. 25–31, 98; and *The Promise of American Politics* (Chicago, 1936), pp. 84, 223–56, 284. On compromise, see also, *Legislative*, pp. 25–9, 92; *Discipline for Democracy* (Chapel Hill, 1942), pp. 103–16, 126–32; *The Ethics of Compromise* (Boston, 1956), pp. 40–80; and *Beyond Conscience* (New York, 1934).

10 Charles Merriam, *Political Power* (New York, 1964), pp. 287, 297, 300; *New Aspects of Politics* (Chicago, 1925), p. xi; *Prologue to Politics* (Chicago, 1939), pp. 54–7.

11 Graham Wallas, *Social Judgment* (New York, 1935), pp. 61, 72, 131–44; 156–61; *Our Social Heritage* (New Haven, 1921), pp. 245–57; *The Great Society* (New York, 1923), pp. 15–19, 227–32, *The Art of Thought* (London, 1926), p. 25; and *Human Nature in Politics* (Lincoln, Neb., 1962), pp. 156–82, 185.

12 A. D. Lindsay, *I Believe in Democracy* (London, 1940), pp. 33; *Modern Democratic State* (New York, 1962), pp. 58–63, 77–8, 196, 240–2, 251–9, 278; *The Essentials of Democracy* (London, 1951), pp. 10–11, 19, 45, 61; *The Churches and Democracy* (London, 1934), pp. 14–39; and Lindsay's

comments in Richard McKeon (ed.), *Democracy in a World of Tensions*, p.181.
Yves R. Simon, *Philosophy of Democratic Government* (Chicago, 1951),
pp. 79–83, 296–318; and *Community of the Free* (New York, 1947), pp.
84–101. Also, see *The Traditions of Natural Law* (New York, 1965);
A General Theory of Authority (Notre Dame, 1962); and *Nature and
Functions of Authority* (Milwaukee, 1940).

13 Carl J. Friedrich, *Man and his Government* (New York, 1963), pp. 39–52;
The New Image of the Common Man (Boston, 1950), pp. xxi–xxii and
passim; and *The Philosophy of Law in Historical Perspective* (Chicago, 1963),
p. 197. Friedrich says his doctrine is expressed from an 'ontological
perspective' in *Man and his Government* and from an 'ideological perspective' in *The New Image of the Common Man* [*Man*, p. 47]. For continuation
and modification of the views in the latter book, see *Demokratie als
Herrschafts—und Lebensform* (Heidelberg, 1959), esp. pp. 37–65, 77–81.
Also see *Constitutional Government and Democracy* (Boston, 1950), pp. 237–
56, 259–95, 511–71.

Robert M. MacIver, *Community: A Sociological Study* (London, 1924),
pp. 22–4; *The Modern State* (London, 1964), pp. 6–7, 467–86; *The Web of
Government* (New York, 1947), pp. 51, 192–208; *The Ramparts We Guard*
(New York, 1950), pp. 37–8, 111–12; and *Leviathan and the People*
(Louisiana, 1939), pp. 70–1, 154–5. For MacIver's 'pluralism', see *Modern
State*, pp. 484–5; and *Community*, pp. 45–6. For his definition of democracy,
see *Ramparts*, pp. 50–1, 134–6.

Leonard T. Hobhouse, *Social Evolution and Political Theory* (New York,
1928), pp. 186–7; *The Elements of Social Justice* (London, 1922), pp. 24–5,
199–200, 205; *The Rational Good* (London, 1947), pp. 59–115; 'The
Philosophy of Development', in *Sociology and Philosophy* (Cambridge,
Mass., 1966), pp. 313–19; *Social Development: Its Nature and Conditions*
(New York, 1924), pp. 70–3; and Ernest Barker, *Leonard Trelawny
Hobhouse, 1864–1929*, from the *Proceedings of the British Academy*, vol. xv
(London, n.d.), pp. 4, 11, 14–15. Also see Hobhouse, *Liberalism* (New
York, 1964).

G. D. H. Cole, *Guild Socialism Re-stated* (London, 1920), pp. 30–2;
Social Theory (London, 1930), pp. 81–102; and Cole and Margaret Cole,
A Guide to Modern Politics (New York, 1934), pp. 334–9. Cf. Harold J.
Laski, *A Grammar of Politics* (New Haven, 1930), pp. 138–9. Cf. Hobhouse,
Elements, pp. 195–206.

14 Michel Fourest, *Les Théories du Professeur Harold J. Laski: Le declin de
l'état moniste et l'avènement de l'état pluraliste* (Paris, 1943), p. 166. For
the pluralist ideas, see Harold J. Laski, *Authority in the Modern State* (New
Haven, 1919), p. 65; *The Foundations of Sovereignty* (New Haven, 1921),
pp. 26–9, 169; *A Grammar of Politics* (New Haven, 1930), pp. 44–88. For
general statements of his pluralism, see *Studies in the Problem of Sovereignty*
(New Haven, 1917), pp. 1–25; and *Authority*, pp. 26–32, 42–52, 65–6,
69–89. On changes in his pluralist theory, see Herbert A. Deane, *The
Political Ideas of Harold J. Laski* (New York, 1955), pp. 81, 85–7. Laski
dates his pluralist writings from 1917–25 [Laski, *Introduction to Contemporary Politics* (Seattle, 1939), p. 69], although he was still calling his

theory 'pluralist' as late as 1929 [Deane, p. 78]. For the anarchist tendencies, see Laski, *Grammar*, pp. 39–41. Also, see *Dangers of Obedience* (New York, 1930). For Marxist themes, see Laski, *The Prospects of Democratic Government* (Williamsburg, Va., 1939), pp. 4, 8–9; *Democracy in Crisis* (Chapel Hill, 1933), pp. 144–6; 'The Present Position of Representative Democracy', *American Political Science Review* (August 1932), pp. 629–41; *The State in Theory and Practice* (New York, 1935), pp. 152–3; *Faith, Reason and Civilization* (New York, 1944), p. 67. For a sampling of Laski's views on the incompatibility of capitalism and social democracy, see 'The Present Position', pp. 67–77, 111; *State in Theory*, pp. 111 ff.; *Democracy at the Crossroads* (London, 1937), pp. 20–1; *The Decline of Liberalism* (Oxford, 1940), pp. 16–17. On the move away from Marxism during and after World War Two, see Fourest, p. 162; Deane, pp. 172–8; Laski, *The Rights of Man* (London, 1940), pp. 5–8; *The Strategy of Freedom* (New York, 1941), pp. 106–7; and *Reflections on the Constitution* (Manchester, England, 1951), pp. 92–3. For Laski's account of how he converted to a form of Marxism, see *Introduction to Contemporary Politics*, pp. 69–71. On his Marxist and anti-Marxist attitudes generally, see Deane, pp. 68–74, 131–42, 145 ff., 201–18, 268–85.

15 Other twentieth-century theorists who in at least some important respects could be considered as citizenship theorists include: M. J. Adler and Walter Farrell, 'The Theory of Democracy', *The Thomist* (1941–44); Ernest Barker, *Reflections on Government* (New York, 1942); C. Delisle Burns, *Democracy* (London, 1935); Herbert Croly, *Progressive Democracy* (New York, 1914); *The Promise of American Life* (Cambridge, Mass., 1965); Harold Gosnell, *Democracy—The Threshold of Freedom* (New York, 1948); Sidney Hook, 'The Philosophical Presuppositions of Democracy', *Ethics* (April 1942), pp. 275–96; *Reason, Social Myths and Democracy* (New York, 1966); John H. Hallowell, *The Moral Foundation of Democracy* (Chicago, 1954); Jay William Hudson, *Why Democracy: A Study in the Philosophy of the State* (New York, 1936); Marie Collins Swabey, *Theory of the Democratic State* (Cambridge, Mass., 1937); and Walter E. Weyl, *The New Democracy* (New York, 1918).

CHAPTER I PRESUPPOSITIONS

1 This discussion of presuppositions draws on R. G. Collingwood's metaphysics. See his *An Essay on Metaphysics* (Oxford, 1948), esp. pp. 21–48. My notion of presupposition was suggested mainly by Kant's idea of *regulative Prinzipien* [*Critique of Pure Reason*, Norman Kemp Smith (trans. and ed.) (London, 1952), pp. 246–7, 301–14].

2 Edward Sapir, 'Language', *Encyclopedia of the Social Sciences* (New York, 1933), pp. 156–7. For now classic illustrations of how linguistic-logical categories in a single language affect how we think, see Ludwig Wittgenstein, *Philosophical Investigations*, G. E. M. Anscombe (trans.) (New York, 1953).

3 See John B. Carroll, *Language and Thought* (Englewood Cliffs, N. J., 1964), esp. pp. 109–10; and Roger Brown, *Words and Things* (Glencoe, Ill., 1958),

pp. 229–63, 253–4. For Whorf's views, see his essays, *Language, Thought and Reality*, John B. Carroll (ed.) (Cambridge, Mass., 1956), esp. pp. 145, 147, 151, 153, 216. Also see George A. Miller and David McNeill, 'Psycholinguistics', in Gardner Lindzey and Eliot Aronson (eds.), *Handbook of Social Psychology*, 2nd edition (Reading, Mass., 1969), vol. III, pp. 728–41. For some illustrations of how in natural science cosmological presuppositions affect the way one sees the world, see Norwood Russell Hanson, *Patterns of Discovery* (Cambridge, England, 1965), pp. 4–49, 182; Thomas S. Kuhn, *The Structure of Scientific Revolutions* (Chicago, 1964), esp. pp. 115, 117–24; and Alexandre Koyré, *Newtonian Studies* (Cambridge, Mass., 1965), esp. pp. 3–24.

4 Cf. these recent analyses of the concept of interests: John Plamenatz, 'Interests', *Political Studies* (Feb. 1954), esp. pp. 1–4; Brian Barry, 'The Public Interest'; and W. J. Rees, 'The Public Interest', both in *Proceedings of the Aristotelian Society*, supplementary volume XXXVIII (1964), esp. pp. 1–7, 19–26; S. I. Benn, '"Interests" in Politics', *Proceedings of the Aristotelian Society* (1959–60), pp. 123–40; Brian Barry, *Political Argument* (London, 1965), pp. 173–86; Richard E. Flathman, *The Public Interest* (New York, 1966), pp. 14–31; and Hanna Pitkin, *The Concept of Representation* (Berkeley and Los Angeles, 1967), pp. 156–62. The analyses by Plamenatz, Flathman and Pitkin give some support to the view of interest in the text, while those of Barry, Benn and Rees oppose it more than they support it.

5 Yves Simon, *Philosophy of Democratic Government*, pp. 146–54. Also, see Harold Laski, *The American Presidency* (London, 1940), pp. 35–6.

6 Sidney Hook, *John Dewey: An Intellectual Portrait* (New York, 1939), p. 17; Sidney Ratner (ed.), *The Philosopher of the Common Man: Essays in the Honor of John Dewey to Celebrate his Eightieth Birthday* (New York, 1940); and Jerome Nathanson, *John Dewey*, pp. 83–4 [quote].

7 John Dewey, *Problems of Men*, p. 35; 'Practical Democracy', *The New Republic* (2 Dec. 1925), p. 54; Dewey, *Public and Its Problems*, p. 146 [my italics in second quote]; *Freedom and Culture*, p. 130; and *The Ethics of Democracy* (Ann Arbor, 1888), pp. 21–2.

8 Hans Kelsen, *General Theory of Law and State* (Cambridge, Mass., 1945) pp. 288–9, 291–2, 298–9; and Kelsen, 'Foundations of Democracy', *Ethics* (Oct. 1955), p. 32. Earlier Kelsen did not so scorn representative democracy: see *Vom Wesen und Wert der Demokratie*, p. 27.

9 See Ross's comments in Richard McKeon (ed.), *Democracy in a World of Tensions* (Chicago, 1951), p. 367 and Ross, *Why Democracy?* pp. 202–10.

10 Charles Merriam, *Systematic Politics* (Chicago, 1945), pp. 312, 199; *The New Democracy and the New Despotism* (New York, 1939), pp. 11–49, 179, 244, 246; 'The Education of Charles E. Merriam', in L. White (ed.), *The Future of Government in the United States* (Chicago, 1942), p. 20; *What is Democracy?* (Chicago, 1941), pp. 6, 8; *Political Power*, pp. 53, 125, 136, 157, 303–5; and *Four American Party Leaders* (New York, 1926), pp. vii, 90.

11 T. V. Smith, *The Promise of American Politics*, p. 82; on citizenship, see *The Democratic Way of Life*, pp. xiii–xiv.

12 Graham Wallas, *Human Nature in Politics*, pp. 118, 253–4.

13 A. D. Lindsay, *The Modern Democratic State*, pp. 250, 261, 269–71, 276–9; *The Churches and Democracy*, pp. 48–9; and *I Believe in Democracy*, pp. 15–16, 30–6.

14 Yves Simon, *Philosophy of Democratic Government*, pp. 76, 92, 217, 218–19, 221, 307.

15 Carl Friedrich, *The New Image of the Common Man*, pp. 40, 294–5, 344, 348; *Man and His Government*, pp. 48–52; and *Transcendent Justice* (Durham, N. C., 1964), pp. 95–6, 115.

16 Robert MacIver, *The Ramparts We Guard*, pp. 27–8, 40–7, 52–3, 113–15, 130–3; *Leviathan and the People*, pp. 65–9, 87, 88–9, 150. Other arguments for democracy are in *The Modern State*, pp. 340 ff.

17 Leonard Hobhouse, *The Metaphysical Theory of the State: A Criticism* (London, 1918), pp. 135, 137; 'The Philosophy of Development', in *Sociology and Philosophy*, p. 296; *Liberalism*, pp. 117–18.

18 Harold J. Laski, *Holmes–Laski Letters*, ed. Mark DeWolfe Howe (Cambridge, Mass., 1953), vol. I, pp. 551–2; *The Dangers of Obedience*, pp. 31–58; *The Foundations of Sovereignty*, pp. 29, 247; *A Grammar of Politics*, pp. 42–3, 59–61; *Studies in the Problem of Sovereignty*, pp. 267–85; *Authority in the Modern State*, pp. 74–81; and *Liberty in the Modern State* (London, 1948), pp. 82–8. Also, on his pluralism, see note 14 to the Introduction.

19 For the quasi-anarchist views, see Laski, *Grammar*, p. 68; and *Dangers of Obedience*, pp. 65, 59, 86, 90, 233. For his Marxist perspective, see Laski, *Introduction to Contemporary Politics*, p. 108; and note 14 to the Introduction.

20 G. D. H. Cole and Raymond Postgate, *The Common People, 1746–1946* (London, 1949), p. 687; Cole and Cole, *A Guide to Modern Politics*, pp. vi–vii, 3–4, 28–9, 335, 430; *Social Theory*, p. 208; and *Guild Socialism Re-stated*, pp. 12–13.

21 Charles Merriam, *New Democracy*, p. 96; 'The Education of Charles E. Merriam', p. 19; *Prologue to Politics*, pp. 74–5; *Civic Education in the United States*, pt VI (New York, 1934), p. 44.

22 Simon, *Community of the Free*, p. 136 and generally 122–36; and *Philosophy*, pp. 287–8, 318.

23 Wallas, *Our Social Heritage*, pp. 19–23; *The Great Society*, p. 68; and *Human Nature*, p. 306.

24 Hobhouse, *Morals in Evolution: A Study in Comparative Ethics* (London, 1929), pp. 609–11; *Social Evolution and Political Theory*, pp. 1–16, 127, 149–65; *Liberalism*, p. 73. For Hobhouse's theory of development generally, see 'The Philosophy of Development', *Social Development*, pp. 17–37, 74–129, 246–315, 327–43; and *Morals in Evolution*, pp. 613–37.

25 MacIver, *The Web of Government*, pp. 434–6.

26 Dewey, *Public and Its Problems*, p. 146; 'Public Opinion', *The New Republic* (3 May 1922), pp. 286–8; 'Practical Democracy', p. 54; 'Creative Democracy—The Task Before Us', in Sidney Ratner (ed.), *The Philosopher of the Common Man*, p. 224; *Freedom and Culture*, pp. 124–5; and *The Living Thought of Thomas Jefferson* (New York, 1940), p. 25. On why Dewey was hesitant to call himself a democratic socialist, see Jim Cork, 'John Dewey and Karl Marx', in Sidney Hook (ed.), *John Dewey: Philosopher of Science and Freedom*

(New York, 1950), pp. 348–9. On the motivation for his tendencies toward socialism, see Dewey and James H. Tufts, *Ethics* (New York, 1932), pp. 387, 389.

27 Merriam, *Civic Education in the United States*, pp. x–xiv, 50, 148–52 and generally chs. iv–vi; *New Democracy*, p. 183; Wallas, *Human Nature*, pp. 204–14, 247–8, 253; *The Art of Thought*, pp. 228–308; Dewey, *Democracy and Education*, pp. 1–68, 321–2; *Problems of Men*, pp. 50–1. Cf. MacIver, *Ramparts*, pp. 8–9, 12, 123.

28 Ross, *Why Democracy?* p. 107; Merriam, *New Democracy*, pp. 108–9; Hobhouse, *Liberalism*, pp. 61, 119; *Democracy and Reaction* (New York, 1905), pp. 185–6; and Laski, *Grammar*, pp. 115, 147, 431–2.

29 Other statements or intimations of elitist democratic theory can be found in: Giovanni Sartori, *Democratic Theory*, esp. pp. 72–134; V. O. Key, Jr., *Public Opinion and American Democracy* (New York, 1961), esp. pp. 535–58; 'Public Opinion and the Decay of Democracy', *Virginia Quarterly Review* (Autumn 1961), pp. 481–94; R. T. McKenzie, *British Political Parties* (London, 1964), pp. 645–8; L. S. Amery, *Thoughts on the Constitution* (London, 1947), pp. 15–21; E. Pendleton Herring, *The Politics of Democracy* (New York, 1940), pp. 30–5, 64–7, 309–10; James Q. Wilson, *The Amateur Democrat* (Chicago, 1962), pp. 342–7; Lester W. Milbrath, *Political Participation* (Chicago, 1965), pp. 142–54; Harold D. Lasswell, *The Political Writings* (Glencoe, Ill., 1951), pp. 194–7, 295, 309–10, 443–4, 446, 498–9; Gabriel A. Almond and Sidney Verba, *The Civic Culture*, pp. 473–505; Bernard Berelson, Paul F. Lazarsfeld and William N. McPhee, *Voting*, pp. 305–23; and Morris Janowitz and Dwaine Marvick, *Competitive Pressure and Democratic Consent* (Chicago, 1964), esp. pp. 4–5. The most important precursor of elitist democratic theory is: Gaetano Mosca, *Elementi di scienza politica* (Laterza, 1939), 3rd edition revised.

30 The essentials of Lippman's description of citizens' weaknesses are in *Public Opinion* (New York, 1965), pp. 3–158. On the disappearance of the 'self-governing community', the need for expertise and the role of citizens, see further pp. 167–74, 191, 229–30; *The Phantom Public* (New York, 1930), pp. 61–2, 73–4, 144–5, 150, 199 [quote]. On 'statesmanship' and 'permanent interests', see *A Preface to Morals* (New York, 1929), pp. 282–3 [quotes]; *The Public Philosophy* (New York, 1955), esp. pp. 32 [quote] 35, 41–6, 123–4; *An Inquiry Into the Principles of the Good Society* (Boston, 1938), pp. 260–8; and *The Essential Lippmann*, Clinton Rossiter and James Lare (eds.), (New York, 1965), pp. 3–6, 162–8.

31 Schumpeter's theory and his critique of 'classical doctrine' of democracy are in *Capitalism, Socialism and Democracy* (London, 1954), pp. 235–302. For his distrust of citizens, see especially pp. 256, 263–4; for the definition of the democratic method, pp. 269, 284–5 [my italics]; the undesirability of pressure, pp. 272, 294–5; and the nature of the elite, pp. 288, 291.

32 Schumpeter, pp. 241–3, 256 n., 282; and Lippmann, *Phantom Public*, pp. 146 [quote]–51; *Public Opinion*, pp. 195–97.

33 Lippmann, *Public Philosophy*, esp. pp. 123–7; *Public Opinion*, pp. 197, 239–49, 250–1 [quote]; and Schumpeter, pp. 285, 290–1, 293.

34 Recent critics of elitist democratic theory include: Lane Davis, 'The Cost of Realism: Contemporary Restatements of Democracy', *Western Political Quarterly* (March 1964), pp. 37–46; Graeme Duncan and Steven Lukes, 'The New Democracy', *Political Studies* (June 1963), pp. 156–77; Stephen W. Rousseas and James Farganis, 'American Politics and the End of Ideology', *British Journal of Sociology* (Dec. 1963), pp. 347–62; T. B. Bottomore, *Elites and Society* (London, 1964), pp. 103–21; Jack L. Walker, 'A Critique of the Elitist Theory of Democracy', *American Political Science Review* (June 1966), pp. 285–95; Henry S. Kariel, *The Promise of Politics* (Englewood Cliffs, N.J., 1966); and Peter Bachrach, *The Theory of Democratic Elitism* (Boston, 1967). But see Robert Dahl's critique of Walker ['Further Reflections on "The Elitist Theory of Democracy",' *American Political Science Review* (June 1966), pp. 296–305] and Walker's reply [pp. 391–2].

35 Lippmann, *Phantom Public*, pp. 20–1, 39. Schumpeter similarly attacks some doctrines that citizenship theorists and most other theorists do not hold (pp. 251, 269, 270, 282).

36 Lindsay, *Modern Democratic State*; pp. 233–4; MacIver, *Ramparts*, pp. 22–3; *Modern State*, pp. 204–5, 387–90; Friedrich, *New Image*, pp. 122–4; and Merriam, *New Democracy*, pp. 64, 71, 181; and *Prologue to Politics*, p. 41.

CHAPTER 2 SCHEMA

1 Lane Davis, 'The Cost of Realism: Contemporary Restatements of Democracy', *Western Political Quarterly* (March 1964), p. 39. Cf. Giovanni Sartori, *Democratic Theory*, pp. 63–8, 79–82. Also see Graeme Duncan and Steven Lukes, who tend toward prescriptivism but who do show some concern for the effect of empirical evidence on the validity of ideals ['The New Democracy', *Political Studies* (June 1963), pp. 156–77.]

2 John Dewey, *Democracy and Education*, p. 83; *The Public and Its Problems*, pp. 7–9, 110, 148; *Individualism Old and New*, pp. 72–3, 148, 169–70; *Human Nature and Conduct* (New York, 1922), pp. 259–64, 282–8; and Dewey and James Tufts, *Ethics*, pp. 301, 387–8. Also, Charles Merriam, *Civic Education*, pp. 182–3; and Graham Wallas, *Human Nature in Politics*, pp. 144–5.

3 Yves Simon, *Philosophy of Democratic Government*, p. 116; A. D. Lindsay, *The Essentials of Democracy*, p. 74; M. J. Adler and Walter Farrell, 'The Theory of Democracy', *The Thomist* (July 1941), p. 436.

4 Harold Laski, *The State in Theory and Practice*, pp. 7, 41; and *Introduction to Contemporary Politics*, pp. 35–41. Also, see Leonard Hobhouse, *Liberalism*, p. 30; *The Metaphysical Theory of the State*, pp. 17–18; and Carl Friedrich, *Man and His Government*, pp. 89, 92.

5 Bernard Berelson, 'Democratic Theory and Public Opinion', *Public Opinion Quarterly* (Fall 1952), pp. 327–8. Also, cf. T. V. Smith, *The Democratic Way of Life*, p. 203; C. W. Cassinelli, *The Politics of Freedom* (Seattle, 1961), pp. 13, 82; William Buchanan, 'An Inquiry into Purposive Voting', *Journal of Politics* (May 1956), pp. 284–5; and Gabriel A. Almond and Sidney Verba, *The Civic Culture*, pp. 475–6.

6 Lindsay, *Modern Democratic State*, pp. 37–51; Dewey, *Public*, pp. 143–55; Friedrich, *Man and His Government*, pp. 53–82, 84–8; Robert MacIver, *The Web of Government*, pp. 4–5.

7 See Adler and Farrell, pp. 347–98. For a qualification, see pp. 130–1.

8 Kelsen, *General Theory*, pp. 283–300. In a chapter on 'Das Volk' in *Vom Wesen und Wert der Demokratie*, Kelsen distinguishes ideals and reality but only very briefly mentions the limitations democratic reality places on the ideals (pp. 18–19).

9 Bernard Crick, *The American Science of Politics* (London, 1959), p. 139.

10 The classic discussions of this set of problems are still worth reading: David Hume, *A Treatise of Human Nature*, L. A. Selby-Bigge (ed.), (Oxford, 1960), bk III, pt I, sec. 1; Max Weber, ' "Objectivity" in Social Science and Social Policy", in *The Methodology of the Social Sciences*, E. Shils and H. Finch (tr. and ed.), (Glencoe, Ill., 1949), pp. 50–122; and G. E. Moore, *Principia Ethica* (Cambridge, England, 1959), pp. 1–58. For some modern discussions see Karl Popper, 'What Can Logic Do for Philosophy?' *Proceedings of the Aristotelian Society*, supplementary volume XXII (1948); R. M. Hare, *Language of Morals* (Oxford, 1952), pp. 27–31, 79–93; Patrick Nowell-Smith, *Ethics* (Oxford, 1954), esp. pp. 21–31, 43–54, 157–9; Alan Montefiore, 'Fact, Value and Ideology', in Bernard Williams and Alan Montefiore (eds.), *British Analytical Philosophy* (London, 1966), pp. 179–203; and Phillipa Foot (ed.), *Theories of Ethics* (Oxford, 1967), pp. 16–114. A history of modern arguments about the fact-value distinction is in Arnold Brecht, *Political Theory* (Princeton, 1959), pp. 207–58.

11 Models proposed in recent years by many philosophers of varying meta-ethical views to characterize the justification of value judgments differ significantly from models for the justification of empirical judgments though not necessarily in the way I describe in the text. See, for example, Herbert Feigl, 'Validation and Vindication: An Analysis of the Nature and the Limits of Ethical Arguments', in W. Sellars and J. Hospers, *Readings in Ethical Theory* (New York, 1952), pp. 667–80; Stephen E. Toulmin, *An Examination of the Place of Reason in Ethics* (Cambridge, England, 1953), pp. 121–65; Nowell-Smith, *Ethics*, pp. 43–54, 85–159; Carl G. Hempel, *Aspects of Scientific Explanation* (New York, 1965), pp. 81–96; Paul W. Taylor, *Normative Discourse* (Englewood Cliffs, 1961), pp. 3–188, 255–9; and R. M. Hare, *Freedom and Reason* (Oxford, 1963), esp. pp. 86–111. Philosophers who, without identifying valuational and empirical justification, stress their parallels, include: John Rawls, 'Outline of a Decision Procedure for Ethics', *Philosophical Review* (April 1951), pp. 177–97; Paul Edwards, *The Logic of Moral Discourse* (Glencoe, Ill., 1955), pp. 139–223; and Kurt Baier, *The Moral Point of View: A Rational Basis of Ethics* (Ithaca, N.Y., 1958), pp. 47–84. Also see Orval L. Perry, 'The Logic of Moral Valuation', *Mind* (Jan. 1957), pp. 42–62.

12 Dewey, *Problems of Men*, pp. 220, 227–8, 233; *Reconstruction in Philosophy*, p. 163 and generally 161–86; *Logic* (New York, 1938), pp. 3–4, 17; and *The Quest for Certainty* (New York, 1960), pp. 40 ff., 260–1. Also see Friedrich, *Man*, pp. 8–10, 55.

13 E.g. Leo Strauss, *Natural Right and History* (Chicago, 1953), pp. 49–56. See the criticism by Ernest Nagel, *The Structure of Science* (New York, 1961), pp. 490–5.

14 The best discussion of the issue of objectivity in the social sciences is Nagel, *Structure*, pp. 447–502. Also see, Weber, ' "Objectivity" '; 'The Meaning of "Ethical Neutrality" in Sociology and Economics', in *The Methodology of the Social Sciences*, pp. 1–112; Gunnar Myrdal, *Value in Social Theory*, Paul Streeton (ed.) (London, 1958); Quentin Gibson, *The Logic of Social Enquiry* (London, 1960), pp. 47–87; A. J. Ayer, 'Man as a Subject for Science', in Laslett and Runciman (eds.), *Philosophy, Politics and Society*, 3rd series (Oxford, 1967), pp. 6–24; and Charles Taylor, 'Neutrality in Political Science', *ibid.* pp. 25–57.

15 See Christian Bay, 'Politics and Pseudopolitics: A Critical Evaluation of Some Behavioral Literature', *American Political Science Review* (March 1965), pp. 39–51.

16 Weber, ' "Ethical Neutrality" ' in *Methodology*, pp. 20–2.

17 This and other misrepresentations of the distinction between value judgments and empirical propositions can be found in Leo Strauss, 'An Epilogue', in Herbert J. Storing *Essays on the Scientific Study of Politics*, pp. 307–27; and Eric Voegelin, *The New Science of Politics*, pp. 1–26. For a critical discussion of such misrepresentations, see Brecht, pp. 117–35.

18 E.g. see Seymour Martin Lipset, *Political Man* (New York, 1960), pp. 27–86; and Almond and Verba, pp. 261–2 and literature cited there.

19 Robert Dahl, *A Preface to Democratic Theory* (Chicago, 1963), pp. 63, 73–5, 87. More recently, Dahl begins to recognize some limits of the use of empirical techniques for evaluations: 'The Evaluation of Political Systems', in I. Pool (ed.), *Contemporary Political Science* (New York, 1967), pp. 176–8.

20 Discussions of the democratic objective or ideas that closely approximate it are in: Dewey, *Public*, p. 69; Ross, *Why Democracy?* pp. 14, 312; Merriam, *New Democracy*, p. 39; Lindsay, *Modern Democratic State*, pp. 269–71; *Essentials*, pp. 71–2; *I Believe in Democracy*, pp. 14–16; Simon, *Philosophy*, p. 221; Friedrich, *The New Image of the Common Man*, pp. 207–8; MacIver, *Power Transformed*, pp. 198–200; Laski, *Dangers of Obedience*, pp. 234–5; *Liberty in the Modern State*, pp. 82–3; *Grammar*, pp. 27, 29–35, 60–1; and Cole and Cole, *Guide to Modern Politics*, pp. 406–7.

21 Dewey, *Public*, pp. 207–8; Friedrich, *New Image of the Common Man*, pp. 134–9; *Constitutional Government and Democracy*, pp. 282–3; T.V. Smith, *Democratic Way of Life* (1951), pp. 12, 14, 16, 37, 97; MacIver, *The Modern State*, pp. 201–2; Laski, *The State in Theory and Practice*, pp. 73–4; *Democracy in Crisis*, p. 111, and Lindsay, *Modern Democratic State*, pp. 200, 203.

22 On the theory of majority rule, see Elias Berg, *Democracy and the Majority Principle* (Goteborg, Sweden, 1965), and the bibliography there; and Willmoore Kendall and George W. Carey, 'The "Intensity" Problem and Democratic Theory', *American Political Science Review* (March 1968), pp. 5–24. On the majority principle and its relation to the idea of the public interest, see Brian Barry, *Political Argument*, pp. 58–66, 242–85, 292–5, 312–16. The best brief discussion of the difficulties with the

principle is Dahl, *Preface*, pp. 34–62, 124–31. Also, see Warren E. Miller, 'Majority Rule and the Representative System of Government', i.n E Allardt and Y. Littunen (eds.), *Cleavages, Ideologies and Party Systems* (Helsinki, Proceedings of the Westermarck Society, 1964), pp. 343–76.

23 Kenneth J. Arrow, *Social Choice and Individual Values* (New York, 1963), esp. pp. 46–60, 80. In this new edition of the book, Arrow answers his critics (pp. 92–120).

24 For a lucid survey of the whole problem, see R. Duncan Luce and Howard Raiffa, *Games and Decision* (New York, 1957), pp. 327–70. A history of attempts to deal with the problem, as well as some original contributions, are in: Duncan Black, *The Theory of Committees and Elections* (Cambridge, England, 1958). A bibliographical survey is: W. Riker, 'Voting and Summation of Preferences', *American Political Science Review* (Dec. 1961), pp. 900–11. Also see James M. Buchanan and Gordon Tullock, *The Calculus of Consent* (Ann Arbor, 1965), esp. pp. 131–45.

25 See the different concepts of an ideal developed by Barry, *Political Argument*, pp. 38–41; and Hare, *Freedom and Reason*, pp. 137–56. Also, see Abraham Edel, *Method in Ethical Theory* (London, 1963), pp. 323–53.

26 A. D. Lindsay, *The Modern Democratic State*, pp. 37, 41, 47, 45. Cf. J. C. Rees, 'The Limitations of Political Theory', *Political Studies* (Oct. 1954), pp. 256–7; and John Plamenatz, 'The Uses of Political Theory', *Political Studies* (Feb., 1960), p. 47.

27 MacIver, *The Web of Government*, pp. 4–5, 447–8.

28 Cf. Dewey, *Liberalism and Social Action*, pp. 62, 78.

29 T. V. Smith, *Democratic Way*, p. 11.

30 Robert M. MacIver, *The More Perfect Union* (New York, 1948).

31 G. D. H. Cole, *Guild Socialism Re-stated*, pp. 11, 25.

32 Laski, *Communism* (New York, 1927), p. 78; *State in Theory and Practice*, pp. 163–4.

33 See Hugh D. Forbes and Edward R. Tufte, 'A Note of Caution in Causal Modelling', *American Political Science Review* (Dec. 1968), pp. 1258–64; and Donald E. Farrar and Robert R. Glaubner, 'Multicollinearity in Regression Analysis', *Review of Economics and Statistics* (Feb. 1967), pp. 92–107.

34 Laski, *Parliamentary Government in England*, pp. 163–4; *State in Theory and Practice*, pp. 279–80.

35 See Barrington Moore, Jr., *Social Origins of Dictatorship and Democracy* (Boston, 1966), pp. 509–23.

36 See, e.g. Neal Riemer, *The Revival of Democratic Theory*, p. 62.

37 Cf. Murray B. Levin, *The Alienated Voter* (New York, 1960) pp. 70–4; and Almond and Verba, pp. 179, 482.

38 Sartori, pp. 63–5.

CHAPTER 3 PARTICIPATION

1 U.S. Bureau of the Census, *Statistical Abstract of the United States: 1968* (Washington, 1968), table 531, p. 369; U.K. Central Statistical Office, *Annual Abstract of Statistics, 1967* (London, H.M.S.O., 1967), table 87,

p. 83; Jean Blondel, *Voters, Parties and Leaders* (Baltimore, 1963), pp. 52–3; Walter Dean Burnham, 'The Changing Shape of the American Political Universe', *American Political Science Review* (March 1965), pp. 10–11, 23.

2 William Buchanan, 'An Inquiry into Purposive Voting', *Journal of Politics* (May 1956), pp. 292–4; and Morris Janowitz and Dwaine Marvick, *Competitive Pressure and Democratic Consent*, pp. 5–6.

3 Lester W. Milbrath, *Political Participation* (Chicago, 1965), pp. 19, 21. Also, David Butler and Donald Stokes, *Political Change in Britain* (London, 1969), p. 25; Robert E. Lane, *Political Life* (New York, 1965), pp. 53–4, 67–8; Blondel, p. 94; and Julian L. Woodward and Elmo Roper, 'Political Activity of American Citizens', *American Political Science Review* (Dec. 1950), pp. 872–85.

4 Robert Dahl, *Who Governs?* (New Haven, 1961), pp. 276–9.

5 Robert MacIver, *Power Transformed*, pp. 198–200; Yves R. Simon, *Philosophy of Democratic Government*, p. 221; John Dewey, *The Public and Its Problems*, p. 69; Charles Merriam, *The New Democracy and the New Despotism*, p. 39; Carl J. Friedrich, *The New Image of the Common Man*, pp. 63–5; and Harold J. Laski; *A Grammar of Politics*, pp. 27, 115–16; *The Foundations of Sovereignty*, pp. 227–8; *The Dangers of Obedience*, pp. 234–35; *Liberty in the Modern State*, pp. 80–1. For a nineteenth-century use of 'sinister interests' argument, see James Mill, *An Essay on Government* in Edwin Burtt (ed.), *The English Philosophers from Bacon to Mill* (New York, 1939), esp. pp. 872–5. A discussion of the whole problem (emphasizing non-governmental abuses of power as well) is David Spitz, *Democracy and the Challenge of Power* (New York, 1958).

6 A. D. Lindsay, *The Modern Democratic State*, pp. 269–71; *The Essentials of Democracy*, pp. 71–2; and *I Believe in Democracy*, pp. 14–16. Other citizenship theorists who use some form of the 'shoes-pinching' argument include: Dewey, *Public*, p. 207; Leonard Hobhouse, *Liberalism*, p. 119; *The Elements of Social Justice*, p. 186; Friedrich, *New Image*, pp. 211, 265; and Laski, *Liberty*, pp. 81–2.

7 Lindsay, *Modern Democratic State*, pp. 271, 276.

8 Friedrich, *New Image*, p. 233; *Man and His Government*, p. 149; Laski, *Grammar*, pp. 323–7; *Politics* (Philadelphia, 1931), pp. 89–90; and MacIver, *The Pursuit of Happiness*, p. 76.

9 Samuel J. Eldersveld, 'American Interest Groups: A survey of Research and Some Implications for Theory and Method', in Henry W. Ehrmann (ed.), *Interest Groups on Four Continents* (Pittsburgh, 1958), p. 186. For other discussions of this whole general area, see David B. Truman, *The Governmental Process* (New York, 1951), pp. 501–35 and bibliography, pp. 537–44; Raymond A. Bauer, Ithiel de Sola Pool, and Lewis Anthony Dexter, *American Business and Public Policy* (New York, 1963); V. O. Key, Jr., *Politics, Parties and Pressure Groups* (New York, 1964), pp. 20–161; and *Public Opinion and American Democracy*, pp. 500–31; Harry Eckstein, *Pressure Group Politics* (Stanford, 1960); and Samuel H. Beer, *British Politics in the Collectivist Age* (New York, 1965), esp. pp. 318–51.

10 See Charles R. Wright and Herbert H. Hyman, 'Voluntary Association Membership of American Adults: Evidence From National Sample

Surveys', *American Sociological Review* (June 1958), pp. 284–94; Key, *Public Opinion*, pp. 502–4, 511, 530; Lane, *Political Life*, p. 75; Blondel, pp. 172, 176–84. For the objection that groups do not significantly influence political decisions, see Robert Presthus, *Men at the Top* (New York, 1964), pp. 264–81.

11 For very similar concepts, see C. J. Friedrich, *Constitutional Government and Democracy*, p. 267; *Man and His Government*, pp. 304, 365; Harold F. Gosnell, *Democracy* (New York, 1948), esp. p. 130; and Alfred de Grazia, *Public and Republic* (New York, 1951), esp. pp. 3–4. The best analysis of the concept and further references are in Hanna Pitkin, *The Concept of Representation*, pp. 92–111. Also, cf. Susanne Langer, *Philosophy in a New Key* (New York, 1942), esp. pp. 32–3.

12 Pitkin, pp. 107–8.

13 See Murray Edelman, *The Symbolic Uses of Politics* (Urbana, 1964), esp. pp. 22–72.

14 Key, *Public Opinion*, pp. 518–24.

15 Dewey, *Democracy and Education*, pp. 275–76, 336–9; Laski, *Liberty*, pp. 71–7; *Grammar*, pp. 42–3; and Hobhouse, *Democracy and Reaction*, pp. 185–6; *Liberalism*, pp. 61, 119.

16 Samuel J. Eldersveld, 'Experimental Techniques and Voting Behavior', *American Political Science Review* (March 1956), p. 163; Milbrath, *Political Participation*, pp. 64–5; Key, *Public Opinion*, pp. 185–6; Angus Campbell and Robert L. Kahn, *The People Elect a President* (Ann Arbor, 1952), p. 59; and Bernard R. Berelson, Paul F. Lazarsfeld and William N. McPhee, *Voting*, pp. 337–8.

17 Gordon M. Connelly and Harry H. Field, 'The Non-Voter: Who He Is, What He Thinks', *Public Opinion Quarterly* (Summer 1944), pp. 184–5; Angus Campbell, Gerald Gurin, and Warren E. Miller, *The Voter Decides* (Evanston, Ill., 1954), p. 126; and Frank Bealey, J. Blondel and W. P. McCann, *Constituency Politics* (London, 1965), p. 237; L. J. Sharpe, *A Metropolis Votes* (London, 1962), pp. 71–4; Ian Budge and Derek W. Urwin, *Scottish Political Behavior* (London, 1966), pp. 81–2; and Eric A. Nordlinger, *The Working-Class Tories* (Berkeley, 1967), p. 119.

18 E.g. Milbrath, *Political Participation*, pp. 64–5.

19 Charles Merriam, *The Making of Citizens* (Chicago, 1931), p. 238 and generally ch. 1; and Simon, *Philosophy*, pp. 193–4; Laski, *Liberty*, pp. 71–2; and Dewey, *Individualism Old and New*, pp. 59–60.

20 Gabriel Almond and Sidney Verba, *The Civic Culture*, pp. 243, 231, 236, 238–9.

21 Cf. Edgar Litt, 'Political Cynicism and Political Futility', *Journal of Politics* (May 1963), pp. 314–20; Angus Campbell, 'The Passive Citizen', *Acta Sociologica* (1962), vol. VI, p. 14; and Donald H. Stokes, 'Popular Evaluations of Government: An Empirical Assessment', in Harlan Cleveland and Harold Lasswell (eds.), *Ethics and Bigness* (New York, 1962), pp. 61–72.

22 See Connelly and Field, pp. 181–3; Paul F. Lazarsfeld, Bernard Berelson and Hazel Gaudet, *The People's Choice* (New York, 1948), pp. 46–7; S. M. Lipset, *Political Man* (New York, 1960), p. 227; Murray B. Levin, *The Alienated Voter* (New York, 1960), p. 62.

23 Campbell, 'The Passive Citizen', pp. 15–16. For the community studies, see Robert E. Agger and Vincent Ostrom, 'Political Participation in a Small Community', in Heinz Eulau *et al.* (eds.), *Political Behavior* (Glencoe, Ill., 1956), pp. 139–40, 144; Alice S. Kitt and David B. Gleicher, 'Determinants of Voting Behaviour', *Public Opinion Quarterly* (Fall 1950), p. 409; and Morris Rosenberg, 'Some Determinants of Political Apathy', *Public Opinion Quarterly* (Winter 1954–5), pp. 349–66; and W. Buchanan, pp. 290–1. A cross-national survey which reaches a similar conclusion on this point is Almond and Verba, pp. 241–63.

24 Almond and Verba, p. 102.

25 T. V. Smith, *The Promise of American Politics*, p. 84; and *The Democratic Way of Life*, p. 191. Also Carl J. Friedrich, *Transcendent Justice*, pp. 95–6, 115; Hobhouse, *Liberalism*, p. 117; Laski, *Dangers of Obedience*, p. 233; and Hans Kelsen, *General Theory of Law and State*, pp. 284–5; *Vom Wesen und Wert der Demokratie*, pp. 14–15.

26 Christian Bay, *The Structure of Freedom* (New York, 1965), pp. 83–5, 155–239.

27 Lane, *Political Life*, pp. 128–31, 162; and Rosenberg, pp. 350–4. On the effect of participation on unconscious needs and intra-psychic tensions, and on the effect on conscious needs (such as the need to understand), see Lane, pp. 115–24, 111–14 (respectively).

28 Campbell *et al.*, *The American Voter*, pp. 515–19; Campbell, 'The Passive Citizen', pp. 11–12; and Lane, p. 154. The sense of efficacy is related to but not identical to Almond and Verba's 'satisfaction with the role of participant' discussed above.

29 Campbell *et al.*, *The Voter Decides*, pp. 187, 192–4; Key, p. 193; Berelson *et al.*, *Voting*, pp. 25–6; Arthur Kornhauser, Harold L. Sheppard, and Albert J. Mayer, *When Labor Votes* (New York, 1956), pp. 158–9, 156 (n. 4); and Dahl, *Who Governs?*, pp. 287–8.

30 Merriam, *The New Democracy*, p. 42; and Friedrich, *New Image*, pp. 293, 295; *The Philosophy of Law in Historical Perspective*, p. 198.

31 Almond and Verba, pp. 261–99.

32 See Robert C. Angell, 'The Moral Integration of American Cities', *American Journal of Sociology* (July 1951), pt. 2; and Lane, *Political Life*, pp. 108–11, 271.

33 Some form of this argument is used by E. Pendleton Herring, *The Politics of Democracy* (New York, 1940), pp. 32–3; Bernard Berelson, 'Democratic Theory and Public Opinion', p. 317; Berelson *et al.*, *Voting*, pp. 314–16; Talcott Parsons, ' "Voting" and the Equilibrium of the American Party System', in Eugene Burdick and Arthur J. Brodbeck (eds.), *American Voting Behavior* (Glencoe, Ill., 1957), pp. 80–120; Herbert Tingsten, *The Problem of Democracy*, pp. 113–16; Almond and Verba, pp. 473–6, 480–1. At least one citizenship theorist is tempted to use this argument at least once: Laski, *Democracy in Crisis*, p. 72.

34 Almond and Verba, pp. 473–505.

35 Herbert Tingsten, *Political Behavior* (Totowa, N.J., 1963), pp. 225–6.

36 For a more fruitful approach to explaining stability and governmental performance (in terms of the relations between authority patterns in society

and those in government), see Harry Eckstein, *A Theory of Stable De-mocracy* (Princeton, 1961); and *Authority Relations and Governmental Performance* (Princeton, 1968, mimeo).

37 See William N. McPhee and Jack Ferguson, 'Political Immunization', in William McPhee and William Glaser (eds.), *Public Opinion and Con-gressional Elections* (New York, 1962), pp. 155–78; and Burnham, pp. 27–8. For a general discussion of the conditions which encourage or discourage disruptive mass movements in democracies, see William Kornhauser, *The Politics of Mass Society* (Glencoe, Ill., 1959), and the literature cited there.

38 For the characteristics of non-participants, see Campbell *et al.*, *The American Voter*, pp. 110–15; Janowitz and Marvick, pp. 33–4; Philip K. Hastings, 'The Voter and the Non-Voter', *American Journal of Sociology* (Nov. 1956), p. 307; Berelson *et al.*, *Voting*, pp. 31–2; Lane, *Political Life*, pp. 340–2, and Key, *Public Opinion*, pp. 187–8. Also, cf. Chapter 5, note 52 below.

39 Campbell *et al.*, *American Voter*, pp. 510–15. On the link between authori-tarianism and non-participation, see Bernard Hennessy, 'Politicals and Apoliticals: Some Measurements of Personality Traits', *Midwest Journal of Political Science* (Nov. 1959), pp. 351–3; Robert Lane, 'Political Per-sonality and Electoral Choice', *American Political Science Review* (March 1955), pp. 177–9, and Arthur Kornhauser *et al.*, pp. 167–76. The *locus classicus* on authoritarianism is: Theodore W. Adorno, Else Frenkel-Brunswik, Daniel J. Levinsen, and R. N. Sanford, *The Authoritarian Personality* (New York, 1950). The methods of this study are criticized and further work in the field is discussed in: Richard Christie and Marie Jahoda (eds.), *Studies in the Scope and Method of the Authoritarian Personality* (Glencoe, Ill., 1954); and Christie and Peggy Cook, 'A Guide to the Published Literature Relating to the Authoritarian Personality Through 1956', *Journal of Psychology* (April 1958), pp. 171–99. Also see Dean Peabody, 'Authoritarianism Scales and Response Bias', *Psychological Bulletin* (Jan. 1966), pp. 11–23. For a survey which focuses on the political aspects of authoritarianism, see Fred I. Greenstein, 'Personality and Political Socialization', *Annals of the American Academy of Political and Social Science* (Sept. 1965), pp. 81–95.

40 Cf. Blondel, pp. 55–6; and Lane, *Political Life*, p. 344.

41 Christopher Martin, *The Bored Electors* (London, 1961), pp. 93, 97–8; W. H. Morris Jones, 'In Defense of Apathy', *Political Studies* (Feb. 1954), p. 25; and Milbrath, *Political Participation*, pp. 147–9.

42 Cf. H. L. A. Hart, 'Legal and Moral Obligation', in Abraham I. Melden (ed.), *Essays in Moral Philosophy* (Seattle, 1958), pp. 82–107; and Friedrich, *Man*, pp. 163–70.

43 MacIver, *Leviathan and the People*, p. 143.

44 This argument is seldom supported so baldly in serious writing but sugges-tions of it can be found in: Walter Lippmann, *Public Opinion*, p. 195; Nelson Polsby, *Community Power and Political Theory* (New Haven, 1963), pp. 116–17; Almond and Verba, pp. 480–1; Nordlinger, p. 100; and Leslie Lipson, *The Democratic Civilization* (New York, 1964), pp. 293, 586–7. Also see criticisms and citations in Charles Merriam and Harold F.

Gosnell, *The American Party System* (New York, 1949), pp. 456–7; and Jack L. Walker, 'A Critique of the Elitist Theory of Democracy', *American Political Science Review* (June 1966), pp. 289–91.

45 Anthony Downs, *An Economic Theory of Democracy* (New York, 1957), pp. 36–50, 260–76. Cf. Brian Barry, *Political Argument*, pp. 281, 328–30; Mancur Olson, Jr., *The Logic of Collective Action* (Cambridge, Mass., 1965), *passim*; and William H. Riker and Peter C. Ordeshook, 'A Theory of the Calculus of Voting', *American Political Science Review* (March 1968), pp. 25–42.

46 Graham Wallas, *Human Nature in Politics*, p. 247.

47 Campbell, 'The Passive Citizen', p. 20. See Campbell *et al.*, *The American Voter*, pp. 476–7; *The Voter Decides*, p. 72; Lipset, *Political Man*, p. 187; Key, *Public Opinion*, pp. 325–6, 331, 342; Buchanan, p. 289; Campbell and Kahn, p. 37; Mark P. Benney, A. P. Gray and R. H. Pear, *How People Vote* (London, 1956), p. 127; Agger and Ostrom, pp. 138–9; Almond and Verba, pp. 86–8; 204–9, 380–81; Lazarsfeld *et al.*, *The People's Choice*, pp. 42–3. But at least one study (NORC, 1944) found no independent effect where economic status was controlled: see Berelson *et al.*, p. 336.

48 *U.S. Bureau of Census, Statistical Abstract, 1968*, table 149 (includes projections), p. 107; and U.K. Central Statistical Office, *Annual Abstract, 1967*, table 88, p. 85.

49 Janowitz and Marvick, p. 98; and Burnham, p. 22.

50 On residential mobility and participation, see Robert R. Alford and Eugene C. Lee, 'Voting Turnout in American Cities', *American Political Science Review* (Sept. 1968), p. 803; Alford and Harry M. Scoble, 'Sources of Local Political Involvement', *American Political Science Review* (Dec. 1968), pp. 1197–9; Sharpe, pp. 62, 74; Milbrath, *Political Participation*, pp. 93, 133; and Harry Sharp, 'Migration and Voting Behavior in a Metropolitan Community', *Public Opinion Quarterly* (Summer 1955), p. 209. On urban residence and participation, see Connelly and Field, pp. 180–1; Campbell *et al.*, *American Voter*, pp. 405–8, 464; Campbell and Kahn, p. 21; and and Milbrath, *Political Participation*, pp. 128–30. On turnout and state-rankings by urban characteristics, see Milbrath, 'Political Participation in the States', in Herbert Jacob and Kenneth Vines (eds.), *Comparative State Politics* (Boston, 1965), pp. 51–2. Three studies seem difficult to treat any way but as counter-instances to the generalization that urban residents are more likely to participate than non-urban residents: Agger and Ostrom, pp. 138, 148 (n. 4); and James A. Robinson and William H. Standing, 'Some Correlates of Voter Participation', *The Journal of Politics* (Feb. 1960), pp. 99–106; and Bealey *et al.*, p. 247.

51 Campbell, 'The Passive Citizen', p. 20. Cf. Lane, *Political Life*, pp. 265–7.

52 Berelson *et al.*, *Voting*, pp. 248–9, 337; Lazarsfeld *et al.*, *The People's Choice*, pp. 40–2; and William A. Glaser, 'Television and Voting Turnout', *Public Opinion Quarterly* (Spring 1965), pp. 71–86. Also see Chapter 4, note 59 below.

53 G. D. H. Cole and Margaret Cole, *A Guide to Modern Politics*, p. 425.

54 Lipset, *Political Man*, pp. 191–2, 194; Campbell and Kahn, p. 58; Louis Harris, *Is There a Republican Majority?* (New York, 1954), pp. 16–17; and

E. Wight Bakke, *Citizens Without Work* (New Haven, 1940), p. 46. Also see Lipson, pp. 285–6.

55   Almond and Verba, p. 263; and Lipset, *Political Man*, p. 207.

56   Alford and Lee, pp. 803, 808; and Lane, *Political Life*, pp. 262–3.

57   E.g. Lane, *Political Life*, pp. 356–7.

58   Campbell and Kahn, p. 21.

59   Stanley Kelley, Jr., Richard E. Ayres and William G. Bowen, 'Registration and Voting: Putting First Things First', *American Political Science Review* (June 1967), pp. 362–3, 367 and literature cited *passim*.

60   Samuel J. Eldersveld and Richard W. Dodge, 'Personal Contact or Mail Propaganda? An Experiment in Voting Turnout and Attitude Change', in Daniel Katz *et al.*, (eds.), *Public Opinion and Propaganda* (New York, 1954), pp. 538, 541; and Eldersveld, 'Experimental Techniques and Voting Behavior', pp. 160, 162–3.

61   For evidence of the relationship between citizen duty and participation, see Campbell *et al.*, *The American Voter*, pp. 105–6. On the disproportionate concentration of feeling of citizen duty among the higher status groups, see Campbell *et al.*, *American Voter*, p. 480; Heinz Eulau, *Class and Party in the Eisenhower Years* (New York, 1962), pp. 82–3; and Lipset, p. 208.

62   See Berelson, *et al.*, pp. 174–6, 337; Eldersveld, *Political Parties* (Chicago, 1964), pp. 448–56, 459–60, 463–7, 495–6, 499–500; Janowitz and Marvick, p. 79; Raymond E. Wolfinger, 'The Influence of Precinct Work on Voting Behavior', *Public Opinion Quarterly* (Fall 1963), p. 398; Kitt and Gleicher, pp. 395–6; R. S. Milne and H. C. Mackenzie, *Straight Fight* (London, 1954), pp. 71–2, 143; and Campbell and Kahn, p. 39; Campbell *et al.* (*The American Voter*) challenge the generalization that non-voters tend to be Democratic (pp. 110–15).

63   Simon, *Philosophy*, pp. 296–9, 305; Hobhouse, *Liberalism*, p. 118; Laski, *Foundations*, p. 247; Lindsay, *Essentials*, pp. 72–4; and Dewey, *Public*, pp. 143, 147–9.

64   On the diagnosis, see Key, *Public Opinion*, p. 196; and Lipset, *Political Man*, pp. 197–8. The shipyard workers study is by Robert K. Merton (cited by Lipset, p. 200).

65   Rosenberg, pp. 358–9.

66   For the effect of group membership on political participation, see Campbell, 'The Passive Citizen', p. 13; Lipset, *Political Man*, p. 187; Key, pp. 504–6; Buchanan, pp. 290–1; Campbell and Kahn, pp. 25–6; Almond and Verba, pp. 307–9; Butler and Stokes, pp. 163–4; Benney *et al.*, p. 127; Bealey *et al.*, p, 200; and Nordlinger, pp. 122–3, 153, 149–50. On the 'cumulative effect' of group membership, see Almond and Verba, pp. 320–1. On 'shared behavior', see Campbell *et al.*, *The Voter Decides*, p. 202. On organizations' potential to affect the least interested citizen, see Key, *Public Opinion*, p. 506.

67   For the factors affecting organization membership and its varying effects on persons of different status, see Lipset, *Political Man*, 318; Presthus, pp. 246–7; Lazarsfeld *et al.*, *The People's Choice*, p. 146; Campbell and Kahn, pp. 24–8; Lipset, Martin A. Trow and James S. Coleman, *Union Democracy* (Glencoe, Ill., 1956), pp. 97–105. On membership and group

conflict, see Sidney Verba, 'Organizational Membership and Democratic Consensus', *Journal of Politics* (August 1965), pp. 467–97. On cross-pressures, see Chapter 6, note 30 below.

68 See, e.g. Dewey, *Public*, pp. 132–7.

69 Angus Campbell and Henry Valen, 'Party Identification in Norway and the United States', *Public Opinion Quarterly* (Winter 1961), p. 512; and Berelson *et al.*, *Voting*, pp. 25–8, 30; Budge and Urwin, pp. 82–4; Sharpe, pp. 70–1; and Campbell *et al.*, *The American Voter*, pp. 96–101.

70 Campbell *et al.*, *The Voter Decides*, pp. 107–8, 124–35, 139.

71 Milbrath, *Political Participation*, p. 96; 'Political Participation in the States', p. 50; Burham, pp. 22–8; Peter Fletcher, 'The Results Analyzed', in L. J. Sharpe (ed.), *Voting in Cities* (London, 1967), pp. 298–303 [only in local elections]; Kelley *et al.*, pp. 365–6 and Alford and Lee, p. 804. No evidence that competitiveness by itself increases voting is found by: Warren E. Miller, 'One-Party Politics and the Voter', *American Political Science Review* (Sept. 1956), p. 711; Robinson and Standing, pp. 96–9; Key, *Southern Politics* (New York, 1949), p. 523; David Butler's appendix in H. G. Nicholas, *The British General Election of 1950*, pp. 319–20; Blondel, pp. 53–4; and Bealey *et al.*, pp. 224–6.

72 Angus Campbell, 'Surge and Decline: A Study of Electoral Change', *Public Opinion Quarterly* (Fall 1960), p. 398; Campbell, 'The Passive Citizen', pp. 16–19; and Bealey *et al.*, pp. 246–7. On the effect of concurrent elections, see Alford and Lee, p. 802. On 'psychological involvement', see Campbell *et al.*, *American Voter*, pp. 101–10.

73 Lane, *Political Life*, pp. 54–5, 61.

74 Lindsay, *Modern Democratic State*, p. 210; Friedrich, *Man*, p. 281; and Laski, *Liberty in the Modern State*, pp. 73–4; *Authority in the Modern State*, pp. 53–4; *Dangers*, pp. 1–30.

75 See especially Frederic Solomon and Jacob R. Fishman, 'Youth and Peace: A Psychosocial Study of Student Peace Demonstrators', *Journal of Social Issues* (Oct. 1964), pp. 54–73; and Edward R. Tufte, *The Civil Rights Movement and Its Opposition*, unpublished doctoral dissertation (Yale, 1968), pp. 31–48. This paragraph is based largely from Tufte's discussion. For a general survey, see Jerome H. Skolnick, *The Politics of Protest* (New York, 1969). For evidence on youth and activism, see Jeanne H. Block, Norma Hann and M. Brewster Smith, 'Activism and Apathy in Contemporary Adolescents', in J. F. Adams (ed.), *Contributions to the Understanding of Adolescence* (Boston, 1967); Jacob R. Fishman and Frederic Solomon, 'Youth and Social Action: An Introduction', *Journal of Social Issues* (Oct. 1964), pp. 1–27; Joseph Katz, 'The Student Activists: Rights, Needs and Powers of Undergraduates', report prepared for the U.S. Office of Education (Stanford, 1967); and Seymour Martin Lipset, 'Student Opposition in the United States', *Government and Opposition* (April 1966), pp. 351–74. More specifically on civil rights activism are: James H. Lave, 'The Changing Character of the Negro Protest', *The Annals* (Jan. 1965), pp. 119–26; John M. Orbell, 'Protest Participation Among Southern College Students', *American Political Science Review* (June 1967), pp. 446–56; Ruth Searles and J. Allen Williams, 'Negro College Students' Participa-

tion in Sit-ins', *Social Forces* (March 1963), pp. 215–20; Samuel J. Surface and Melvin Seeman, 'Some Correlates of Civil Rights Activism', *Social Forces* (Dec. 1967), pp. 197–207; and Jack L. Walker, *Sit-Ins in Atlanta* (New York, 1967).

76 Cole and Cole, *Guide*, pp. 436, 443–8; Cole, *Social Theory*, pp. 161, 158–71; *The Future of Local Government* (London, 1929), pp. 23–5, 27–8, 33–4; Laski, *Dangers of Obedience*, pp. 69–74; *Studies in the Problem of Sovereignty*, pp. 83–8; *Foundations of Sovereignty*, pp. 29, 86–7, 241–4; *Grammar*, pp. 59–61. Also Hobhouse, *Liberalism*, pp. 118–19; and Kelsen, *General Theory*, p. 312.

77 See James W. Fesler, 'Approaches to the Understanding of Decentralization', *Journal of Politics* (August 1965), pp. 536–66.

78 For the evidence favorable to local politics, see Almond and Verba, pp. 80–2, 185; Robert E. Agger, Daniel Goldrich, and Bert E. Swanson, *The Rulers and the Ruled* (New York, 1964), pp. 624–5; and Robert A. Dahl, *Pluralist Democracy in the United States* (Chicago, 1967), pp. 198–202. On the difference in turnout rates between local and national elections, see Edward C. Banfield and James Q. Wilson, *City Politics* (Cambridge, 1963), p. 225; Fletcher, p. 298; and Budge and Urwin, p. 73. The relationship between size and turnout is most fully explored in Robert A. Dahl and Edward R. Tufte, *Size and Democracy* (Stanford, forthcoming). This whole section draws heavily from the work of Dahl and Tufte.

79 Robert A. Dahl, 'The City in the Future of Democracy', *American Political Science Review* (Dec. 1967), p. 967; and Dahl and Tufte.

80 This objection is urged by Henry Kariel, *The Decline of American Pluralism* (Stanford, 1961), esp. pp. 179–87. Cf. Grant McConnell, *Private Power and American Democracy* (New York, 1966), pp. 91–118.

CHAPTER 4 DISCUSSION

1 A. D. Lindsay, *The Essentials of Democracy*, pp. 1, 32–46; John Dewey, in Richard McKeon (ed.), *Democracy in A World of Tensions* (Chicago, 1951), pp. 62–8; and Alf Ross, *Why Democracy?* p. 111. Also see Hans Kelsen 'Absolutism and Relativism in Philosophy and Politics', *American Political Science Review* (Oct. 1948), pp. 913–14.

2 Leonard T. Hobhouse, *Democracy and Reaction*, p. 151; Robert M. MacIver, *The Web of Government*, p. 199; Ross, pp. 122–3; and Charles E. Merriam, *Prologue to Politics*, p. 36.

3 Sidney Verba, *Small Groups and Political Behavior* (Princeton, 1961), pp. 206–43. For other surveys of the studies, see Elihu Katz and Paul F. Lazarsfeld, *Personal Influence* (Glencoe, Ill., 1955), pp. 66–81; Joseph T. Klapper, *The Effects of Mass Communication* (Glencoe, Ill., 1960), pp. 80–4; and Harold H. Kelley and John W. Thibaut, 'Group Problem Solving', in Gardiner Lindzey and Elliott Aronson (eds.), *The Handbook of Social Psychology*, 2nd edition (Reading, Mass., 1969), vol. IV, pp. 1–101.

4 Verba, pp. 233–5; and D. G. Marquis, H. Guetzkow and R. W. Heyns, 'A Social-Psychological Study of the Decision-Making Conference', in H. Guetzkow (ed.), *Groups, Leadership and Men* (Pittsburgh, 1951), pp. 55–67.

5 Robert E. Lane, *Political Life*, p. 86; Gabriel A. Almond and Sidney Verba, *The Civic Culture*, pp. 115–16; Angus Campbell, Gerald Gurin and Warren E. Miller, *The Voter Decides*, p. 31; David Butler and Donald Stokes, *Political Change in Britain*, pp. 217–19; Joseph Trenaman and Denis McQuail, *Television and the Political Image* (London, 1961), pp. 81–2; and Bernard Berelson, Paul F. Lazarsfeld, and William N. McPhee, *Voting*, p. 240.

6 For numbers and characteristics of opinion leaders, see Angus Campbell, Philip E. Converse, Warren E. Miller and Donald E. Stokes, *The American Voter*, p. 271; Campbell *et al.*, *The Voter Decides*, p. 30; Mark P. Benney, A. P. Gray and R. H. Pear, *How People Vote*, pp. 132–4; Robert E. Agger and Vincent Ostrom, 'Political Participation in a Small Community', in Heinz Eulau *et al.* (eds.), *Political Behavior*, pp. 141–5; Key, *Public Opinion*, p. 361; Paul F. Lazarsfeld, Bernard Berelson, and Helen Gaudet, *The People's Choice*, pp. 50–1; Katz and Lazarsfeld, pp. 309–20; Morris Janowitz and Dwaine Marvick, *Competitive Pressure and Democratic Consent*, pp. 72–6; and Berelson *et al.*, *Voting*, pp. 110–12, 114 [quote, my italics]. For evidence that personal influence is an important source of political information and opinions, see note 15 below. For general summaries of the literature on personal influence, see Katz and Lazarsfeld, pt 1; and Elihu Katz, 'The Two-Step Flow of Communication: An Up-To-Date Report on An Hypothesis', *Public Opinion Quarterly* (Spring 1957), pp. 61–78.

7 See especially, Philip E. Converse, 'The Nature of Belief Systems in Mass Publics', in David R. Apter (ed.), *Ideology and Discontent* (New York, 1964), pp. 231–3 and generally 206–61. Also, Key, *Public Opinion*, pp. 362, 363; and Lane, *Political Life*, pp. 87–8.

8 For the impact of reference groups on opinions and attitudes, see Harold H. Kelley, 'Salience of Membership and Resistance to Change of Group-Anchored Attitudes', *Human Relations* (August 1955), pp. 275–89; Katz and Lazarsfeld, pp. 48–65; and Alberta E. Siegel and Sidney Siegel, 'Reference Groups, Membership Groups and Attitude Change', *Journal of Abnormal and Social Psychology* (Nov. 1957), pp. 360–4; and more generally, Robert K. Merton, *Social Theory and Social Structure* (New York, 1968), pp. 279–440; and Herbert H. Hyman, 'Reference Groups', in David L. Sills (ed.), *International Encyclopedia of the Social Sciences* (New York, 1968), pp. 353–61. For the specifically political effect and the bias in survey data, see Campbell *et al.*, *American Voter*, pp. 76–7, 307 and more generally 295–332; Robert D. Putnam, 'Political Attitudes and the Local Communities', *American Political Science Review* (Sept. 1966) pp. 646–52; and Lazarsfeld *et al.*, *The People's Choice*, pp. 137 [quote] 138–49.

9 Dewey, *The Public and Its Problems*, pp. 214, 218; and *Freedom and Culture*, pp. 160–1 [where Dewey modifies his earlier view to include secondary groups]; Carl J. Friedrich, *The New Image of the Common Man* pp. 344, 347; Graham Wallas, *The Great Society*, pp. 285–6, 281–3; and Lindsay, *The Modern Democratic State*, pp. 279–81; *I Believe in Democracy* p. 23.

10 Dewey, *Public*, pp. 26–7, 95–102, 186–9; *Liberalism and Social Action*, pp. 38–41; MacIver, *The Ramparts We Guard*, pp. 18–20; Lindsay, *Modern Democratic State*, p. 83; and Harold J. Laski, *The Dangers of Obedience*, pp. 59–60.

11 The quote about India is from Lloyd and Susanne H. Rudolph, 'Opinion Surveys in India', *Public Opinion Quarterly* (Fall 1958), p. 237. For citizenship theorists' views see, Dewey, *Liberalism*, p. 54; *Democracy and Education*, p. 305; *Individualism Old and New*, pp. 85–8; *I Believe*, ed. C. Fadiman (New York, 1939), pp. 347–8 [where Dewey avers a conversion to an even more individualist view]; Dewey and James Tufts, *Ethics*, pp. 354–76; MacIver, *The Modern State*, pp. 455–67; Merriam, *Political Power*, pp. 67–72; and Laski, *Dangers*, p. 59, 233; *A Grammar of Politics*, pp. 66–7; *Faith, Reason and Civilization*, p. 33; *Authority in the Modern State*, p. 120. On the individualist character of Laski's pluralism and the shift away from individualism in his Marxist writings, see also Herbert A. Deane, *The Political Ideas of Harold J. Laski*, pp. 23–4, 39, 172. Dewey's quasi-idealist theory is in *The Ethics of Democracy* (Ann Arbor, 1888), esp. pp. 13–14.

12 Katz and Lazarsfeld, p. 65; Berelson *et al.*, *Voting*, pp. 120–2; and Harmon Zeigler, *Interest Groups in American Society*, p. 40.

13 Lindsay, *Modern Democratic State*, p. 259.

14 Lazarsfeld *et al.*, *The People's Choice*, p. 151.

15 Berelson *et al.*, *Voting*, p. 115; Lazarsfeld *et al.*, *The People's Choice*, pp. 50–1, 150–7; Milbrath, p. 23; R. S. Milne and H. C. Mackenzie, *Straight Fight* (London, 1954), pp. 124–5; Elihu Katz, 'Communication Research and the Image of Society: Convergence of Two Traditions', *American Journal of Sociology* (March 1960), p. 436; Katz and Lazarsfeld, pp. 15–133; May Brodbeck, 'The Role of Small Groups in Mediating the Effects of Propaganda', *Journal of Abnormal and Social Psychology* (March 1956), pp. 166–70; and Key, *Public Opinion*, pp. 362–3, 363 n. Some findings that are contrary to the 'two-step flow' hypothesis are reported in Katz and Lazarsfeld, p. 142; Benney *et al.*, p. 137; and Dahl, *Who Governs?*, pp. 262–3.

16 See Frederick T. C. Yü, *Mass Persuasion in Communist China* (New York, 1964), pp. 78–89.

17 Klapper, pp. 72, 109–10. Summaries of research on mass communication include: Klapper; Key, *Public Opinion*, pp. 344–405; and Walter Weiss, 'Effects of the Mass Media of Communication', in Gardner Lindzey and Elliot Aronson (eds.), *The Handbook of Social Psychology*, 2nd edition (Reading, Mass. 1969), vol. v.

18 Quoted by Richard Rose, *Influencing Voters* (New York, 1967), p. 205. See pp. 195–219, 240–7 on institutional and other constraints on U.S. and U.K. propagandists.

19 MacIver, *Web of Government*, pp. 221–3; *Ramparts*, p. 33; G. D. H. Cole and Margaret Cole, *A Guide to Modern Politics*, pp. 322–3, 394–8; Simon, *Philosophy of Democratic Government*, pp. 126–7; and Merriam, *The New Democracy*, p. 183.

20 On patterns of newspaper competition and bias in the U.S., see Key, *Public Opinion*, pp. 372–3, 391; Berelson *et al.*, *Voting*, p. 239; Lazarsfeld *et al.*, *People's Choice*, pp. 111, 113; Raymond B. Nixon and Jean Ward, 'Trends in Newspaper Ownership and Inter-Media Competition', *Journalism Quarterly* (Winter 1961), pp. 3–14; and Ole R. Holsti, 'Content Analysis', in Gardner Lindzey and Elliot Aronson (eds.), *Handbook of Social Psychology*, 2nd edition (Reading, Mass., 1968), vol. II, pp. 614–15. On the problems of British newspapers, see Francis Williams, *Dangerous Estate: The Anatomy of Newspapers* (London, 1957); and *Report of the Royal Commission on the Press, 1961–2*, H.M.S.O., Cmnd. 1811 (London, 1962).

21 Trenaman and McQuail, p. 78. Also, Janowitz and Marvick, p. 70; and Lazarsfeld *et al.*, *The People's Choice*, p. 111.

22 Janowitz and Marvick, p. 88.

23 Key, *Public Opinion*, p. 349; Berelson *et al.*, *Voting*, pp. 248–50; Janowitz and Marvick, pp. 62–6; Bernard Berelson, 'Communication and Public Opinion', in Wilbur Schramm (ed.), *Mass Communications* (Urbana, Ill., 1960), p. 537; and Carl I. Hovland, Irving L. Janis and Harold H. Kelley, *Communication and Persuasion* (New Haven, 1953), pp. 188, 198.

24 Wallas, *Human Nature in Politics*, pp. 66–8, 115; Laski, *Democracy in Crisis*, p. 75; *The American Democracy* (New York, 1948), p. 713; MacIver, *Ramparts*, p. 129; and Friedrich, *New Image*, pp. 119–20.

25 Trenaman and McQuail, pp. 192, 194–5, 203–4, 233–4. See also Milne and Mackenzie *Straight Fight*, p. 121. For some examples of the negligible impact of media propaganda campaigns, see Key, *Public Opinion*, pp. 514–18, 352–3; and Herbert H. Hyman and Paul B. Sheatsley, 'Some Reasons Why Information Campaigns Fail', *Public Opinion Quarterly* (Fall 1947), pp. 412–23. Also see Gerhard D. Wiebe's discussion of why the media cannot sell political ideas as easily as commodities ['Merchandising Commodities and Citizenship on Television', *Public Opinion Quarterly* (Winter 1951–2), pp. 679–91].

26 Berelson *et al.*, *Voting*, pp. 246–8; Klapper, pp. 15, 38–43; Wilbur Schramm and Richard F. Carter, 'Effectiveness of a Political Telethon', *Public Opinion Quarterly* (Spring 1959), pp. 121–7; Katz and Lazarsfeld, pp. 21–2; and Key, *Public Opinion*, pp. 395–6.

27 Kurt Lang and Gladys Engel Lang, 'The Mass Media and Voting', in Eugene Burdick and Arthur J. Brodbeck (eds.), *American Voting Behavior*, pp. 221, 227–8; and Klapper, p. 63. On numbers of undecided voters before campaign, see Lazarsfeld *et al.*, *The People's Choice*, p. 53; Campbell *et al.*, *American Voter*, p. 78; D. E. Butler, *The British General Election of 1951* (London, 1952), p. 239; R. S. Milne and H. C. Mackenzie, *Marginal Seat* (London, 1958), pp. 36–7; Jay G. Blumler and Denis McQuail, *Television in Politics* (Chicago, 1969), pp. 52 n., 184; and Butler and Stokes, pp. 428–9.

28 Lang and Lang give this example among others ('The Mass Media and Voting', pp. 230–1).

29 Key, *Public Opinion*, p. 397.

30 Carl I. Hovland, 'Reconciling Conflicting Results Derived from Experimental and Survey Studies of Attitude Change', *American Psychologist* (Jan. 1959), pp. 8–17 [quote, p. 15].

31 Dewey, *Public*, p. 208; and *Experience and Education* (New York, 1938), pp. 25–6. Also, Simon, *Philosophy*, pp. 118–19; Merriam, *The New Democracy*, p. 44; *Prologue*, p. 13; and Ross, *Why Democracy?*, pp. 111–13, 122–3.

32 See Berelson *et al.*, *Voting*, pp. 235–8; Lazarsfeld *et al.*, *The People's Choice*, pp. 115–16, 118; Stanley Kelley, Jr., *Political Campaigning* (Washington, 1960), pp. 51–61; David B. Butler and Anthony King, *The British General Election of 1964* (London, 1965), pp. 153–5; Butler and Richard Rose, *The British General Election of 1959* (London, 1960), pp. 71–4; Lane, *Political Life*, pp. 280–1; and Rose, pp. 180–1.

33 David O. Sears and Jonathan L. Freedman, 'Selective Exposure to Information: A Critical Review', *Public Opinion Quarterly* (Summer 1967), pp. 194–213; Milne and Mackenzie, *Marginal Seat*, p. 99; Benney *et al.*, pp. 162–4; Klapper, pp. 19–25; Berelson *et al.*, *Voting*, p. 339 [reporting NORC survey, 1944]. But see note 64 below.

34 Dewey, *Public*, p. 207; *Liberalism*, pp. 79–80; Lindsay, *Modern Democratic State*, p. 241; *Essentials*, pp. 1, 33–40, *The Churches and Democracy*, pp. 48–9; Friedrich, *Man and His Government*, p. 151; and Simon, *Philosophy*, pp. 33, 39–48, 70–1.

35 Michael Argyle, *The Scientific Study of Social Behavior* (London, 1957), p. 119. The significance of this conclusion is questioned by Robert F. Bales, A. Paul Hare, and Edgar F. Borgatta, 'Structure and Dynamics of Small Groups: A Review of Four Variables', in Joseph Gittler (ed.), *Review of Sociology: Analysis of a Decade* (New York, 1957), p. 398.

36 Dewey, *Democracy and Education*, pp. 120–1; also, see *Public*, pp. 142, 152–6, 167–9; John Herman Randall, Jr., 'The Religion of Shared Experience', in Sidney Ratner (ed.), *The Philosopher of the Common Man*, pp. 109–10.

37 Berelson *et al.*, *Voting*, pp. 105–9; Benney, *et al.*, pp. 132–3; Arthur Kornhauser, Harold L. Sheppard and Albert J. Mayer, *When Labor Votes*, pp. 77, 125; Frank Bealey, J. Blondel and W. P. McCann, *Constituency Politics*, p. 189.

38 Berelson, *et al.*, pp. 105, 119, 107 n.; Lane, *Political Life*, p. 90; and Trenaman and McQuail, pp. 179–80 [quote]. But see Blumler and McQuail, p. 175.

39 Merriam, *On the Agenda of Democracy* (Cambridge, Mass., 1941), p. 23; *The New Democracy*, pp. 169–70; Dewey, *Experience and Education*, pp. 25–6; MacIver, *Web of Government*, pp. 200–1; Ross, p. 117; Kelsen, *General Theory of Law and State*, p. 288; 'Absolutism', pp. 906–14; and Laski, *Democracy in Crisis*, pp. 156–60, 189–220.

40 Simon, *Philosophy*, p. 109; and Merriam, *The New Democracy*, p. 44. Cf. T. V. Smith, *The Ethics of Compromise*, p. 43. Also see Ernest Barker, *Reflections on Government*, pp. 63 ff.

41 See James S. Coleman, *Community Conflict* (Glencoe, Ill., 1957); 'Community Disorganization', in Robert Merton and Robert Nisbet (eds.), *Contemporary Social Problems* (New York, 1961), pp. 569, 604; David Riesman, *The Lonely Crowd* (New Haven, 1950), pp. 217–23; and Berelson *et al.*, *Voting*, pp. 119, 138–42.

42 See Dewey, *Public*, pp. 182–3, 208–9; *Liberalism*, pp. 72–3.

43 The proposal is made, for example, by Ross, *Why Democracy?*, p. 175; and Kelley, *Political Campaigning*, pp. 127–45. Ross explicitly says, however, that education is more important. For the empirical studies see Carl Hovland and Walter Weiss, 'The Influence of Source Credibility on Communication Effectiveness', *Public Opinion Quarterly* (Winter 1951–2), pp. 635–50; Herbert C. Kelman and Carl I. Hovland, ' "Reinstatement" of the Communicator in Delayed Measurement of Attitude Change', *Journal of Abnormal and Social Psychology* (July 1953), pp. 327–35; Klapper, pp. 99–103; and more generally William J. McGuire, 'The Nature of Attitudes and Attitude Change', in Gardner Lindzey and Elliot Aronson (eds.), *Handbook of Social Psychology*, 2nd edition (Reading, Mass., 1969), vol. III, pp. 177–200, 254–6.

44 Laski, *Democracy in Crisis*, pp. 69–71; and *The Dangers of Obedience*, p. 41.

45 For the debate survey, see Samuel Lubell, 'Personalities v. Issues', in Sidney Kraus (ed.), *The Great Debates* (Bloomington, Ind., 1962), p.153. Also, on concrete discussion see Trenaman and McQuail, p. 110; Klapper, pp. 116–17; W. Phillips Davidson, 'On the Effects of Communication', *Public Opinion Quarterly* (Fall 1959), p. 359; Blumler and McQuail, pp. 84, 171; and Butler and Stokes, p. 344.

46 See e.g. Kelley, *Political Campaigning*, pp. 9–10, who defines rationality in communication in a way which omits emotional elements.

47 For the approaches to the study of propaganda, see Dennis F. Thompson, 'Rational Propaganda', in John D. Montgomery and Arthur Smithies (eds.), *Public Policy* (Cambridge, Mass., 1966), pp. 86–92. An example of a model of campaign strategy which assumes the necessity of irrational propaganda is: Lewis A. Froman, Jr., 'A Realistic Approach to Campaign Strategies and Tactics', in M. Kent Jennings and L. Harmon Zeigler (eds.), *The Electoral Process* (Englewood Cliffs, N. J., 1966), pp. 16–17.

48 Alf Ross, *On Law and Justice* (Berkeley, 1959), pp. 305–13, 325–6; and Aristotle, *Rhetoric* [*The Basic Works of Aristotle*, Richard McKeon (ed.) (New York, 1941)], esp. 1354 a: 12–31, 1356 a: 1–21, and more generally Bks 1–2. A good modern treatment of the same subject in a very Aristotelian manner is Chaim Perelman and L. Olbrechts–Tyteca, *Traité de l'argumentation* (Brussels, 1959). See also *Logique et Analyse* (Dec. 1963) and the literature cited there.

49 See Robert A. Lane and David O. Sears, *Public Opinion* (Englewood Cliffs, N.J., 1964), p. 74.

50 For a survey of the meanings of this family of terms and theories associated with the various meanings, see William K. Frankena, 'Some Aspects of Language', and ' "Cognitive" and "Noncognitive" ', in Paul Henle (ed.), *Language, Thought and Culture* (Ann Arbor, 1958), pp. 121–72. Also, see McGuire, pp. 155–7.

51 The Coles emphasize the importance of an affective element in democratic discussion. See *A Guide to Modern Politics*, pp. 433–4. Also, see Dewey, *Public*, pp. 183–4.

52 See Kelley, *Political Campaigning*, p. 13; and E. Pendleton Herring, *The Politics of Democracy* (New York, 1940), p. 289.

53 See note 23 above.

54 Walter Lippmann, *The Phantom Public*, pp. 114, 144. MacIver expresses a similar view in *The Modern State*, pp. 200–1.

55 Raymond A. Bauer and D. F. Cox, 'Rational Versus Emotional Communications: A New Approach', in Leon Arons and Mark A. May (eds.), *Television and Human Behavior* (New York, 1963), p. 144. Also, Klapper, pp. 117–19; and Hovland *et al.*, *Communication and Persuasion*, p. 271. However, the limits on the effectiveness of fear appeals are less than earlier studies suggested (see McGuire, pp. 203–5).

56 See note 45 above.

57 For a summary of the relevant experimental research, see Hovland *et al.*, *Communication and Persuasion*, p. 110; and Klapper, pp. 113–16 [for qualifications]. An attempt to confirm one generalization in a political context is reported by Trenaman and McQuail, pp. 202, 224–5. On the British public's attitude toward debates, see Blumler and McQuail, pp. 101–3.

58 Dewey, *Reconstruction in Philosophy*, p. 31.

59 Klapper, pp. 234–48; Angus Campbell, 'Has Television Reshaped Politics?' *Columbia Journalism Review* (Fall 1962), pp. 10–13; Trenaman and McQuail, p. 82; and Ithiel de Sola Pool, 'TV: A New Dimension in Politics', in Eugene Burdick and Arthur J. Brodbeck (eds.), *American Voting Behavior* (Glencoe, Ill., 1959), pp. 239–40, 243. In a small sample of college students, Pool found some favorable effect of television on political interest (pp. 257–8).

60 Trenaman and McQuail, pp. 87–8, 91; and Janowitz and Marvick, p. 60.

61 On the 'authenticity' of TV, see Arthur Kornhauser *et al.*, pp. 89–90; Lang and Lang, 'Mass Media and Voting', p. 232. For the examples which are alleged to prove that television distorts the reality of an event, see Kurt Lang and Gladys Engel Lang, 'The Unique Perspective of Television and Its Effect: A Pilot Study', *American Sociological Review* (Feb. 1953), pp. 9–12; and 'The Inferential Structure of Political Communications', *Public Opinion Quarterly* (Summer 1955), pp. 168–83 [both reprinted with slight changes in Lang and Lang, *Politics and Television* (Chicago, 1968), pp. 36–103; also see pp. 289–310]. On the lack of bias in television, see note 21 above.

62 For evidence that TV is the most informative of media for the most people, see Elmo Roper, *The Public's View of Television and Other Media, 1959–1964* (New York, 1965); Trenaman and McQuail, pp. 187–90, 233; Blumler and McQuail, pp. 43, 162, 205, 255; Angus Campbell, 'Civil Rights and the Vote for the President', *Psychology Today* (Feb. 1968), p. 30; Key, *Public Opinion*, p. 346; Butler and Stokes, pp. 219–20; and Bealey *et al.*, pp. 189–90, 193. On retention of material, see Klapper, pp. 110–12. For the criticism that TV has no 'tradition of political enlightenment', see Key, pp. 389–90.

63 On the St Louis campaign, see Henry J. Schmandt, Paul G. Steinbicker and George D. Hendel, *Metropolitan Reform in St. Louis* (New York, 1961), pp. 46–7. For the general findings, see note 3 above.

64 Trenaman and McQuail, pp. 200–1; Blumler and McQuail, pp. 51–64; Benney *et al.*, pp. 155–6; Berelson *et al.*, *Voting*, p. 245; and Klapper, p. 25.

65 On 'new ideas', see Klapper, pp. 53–61. On 'personalities', see Key, *Public Opinion*, p. 400. On impact generally, Blumler and McQuail, pp. 157–258. On communicating facts without intended opinions, see Klapper, pp. 84–90; Hovland and Weiss, pp. 635–50; and Raymond A. Bauer and Alice H. Bauer, 'America, Mass Society and Mass Media', *The Journal of Social Issues* (1960), p. 29. On the need for a mechanism, see Robert K. Merton, Marjorie Fiske and Alberta Curtis, *Mass Persuasion: The Social Psychology of a War Bond Drive* (New York, 1946).

66 Elihu Katz and Jacob J. Feldman, 'The Debates in Light of Research: A Survey of Surveys', in Sidney Kraus (ed.), *The Great Debates* (Bloomington, Ind., 1962), p. 191. But cf. Blumler and McQuail, p. 53.

67 The debate texts and many of the texts of single appearances are in: U.S. Congress, Communications Subcommittee of the Senate Committee on Interstate and Foreign Commerce, *Freedom of Communications* (87th Cong., 1st and 2nd Sess., 1961–2), pts. I–III. My comparison in part draws on Stanley Kelley, Jr., 'Campaign Debates: Some Facts and Issues', *Public Opinion Quarterly* (Fall 1962), pp. 351–66. Kelley also briefly compares the debates with interviews and panel programs (pp. 363–65). Kelley's conclusions about the debates are supported by John W. Ellsworth, 'Rationality and Campaigning: A Content Analysis of the 1960 Presidential Debates', *Western Political Quarterly* (Dec. 1965), pp. 794–802.

68 See, e.g. Nixon's Chicago speech on 29 October and Kennedy's Canton, Ohio, speech on 27 September. Compare *Freedom of Communications*, pt. III, pp. 214–18; pt. II, pp. 863–8; with pt. I, pp. 1057–9.

69 *Freedom of Communications*, pt. III, pp. 75–6, 78, 89, 90–1; and Kelley, 'Campaign Debates', pp. 359–60.

70 *Freedom of Communications*, pt. III, pp. 83–4, 215–16; pt. I, pp. 91, 447; and pt. III, pp. 86–8.

71 *Freedom of Communications*, pt. II, pp. 1282–3 [index]; pt. II, pp. 78–80, 84–5. Also compare the solo and debate discussions on Quemoy-Matsu (pt. III, pp. 205–10; pt. II, p. 574; pt. I, pp. 881–8).

72 Kelley, 'Campaign Debates', pp. 361–2; and J. Jeffrey Auer, 'The Counterfeit Debates', in Sidney Kraus (ed.), *The Great Debates*, p. 149.

73 Katz and Feldman, pp. 195–205, 218. Also see Kurt Lang and Gladys Engel Lang, 'Ordeal by Debate: Viewer Reaction', *Public Opinion Quarterly* (Summer 1961), pp. 277–88 [reprinted with slight changes in *Politics and Television*, pp. 212–49]. On British leaders' images, see Blumler and McQuail, pp. 224–58.

74 Critics who object to this result of the debates include: Charles A. Siepmann, 'Were They "Great"?' in Sidney Kraus (ed.), *The Great Debates*, pp. 134–5; Sidney Hyman, 'What Trendex for Lincoln?' *New York Times Magazine* (17 Jan. 1960), p. 26; and Auer, p. 148.

75 Pool, 'TV', pp. 254, 261; and Philip E. Converse, 'Religion and Politics: The 1960 Election', in Angus Campbell *et al.*, *Elections and the Political Order* (New York, 1966), p. 124; Trenaman and McQuail, pp. 118–21, 223; Butler and Stokes, pp. 227–8, 377–81; and Blumler and McQuail,

pp. 114–21, 239–47. For a more sceptical view of the ability of television to project authentic images of political figures, see also Lang and Lang, 'The Television Personality in Politics: Some Considerations', *Public Opinion Quarterly* (Spring 1956), pp. 103–12, [revised and expanded in *Politics and Television*, pp. 186–211].

76   See Theodore H. White, *The Making of the President 1960* (New York, 1961), p. 293; and Harold D. Lasswell, 'Introduction', in Sidney Kraus (ed.), *The Great Debates*, p. 20.

77   Auer, p. 148.

78   American Political Science Association, *Report of the Commission on Presidential Campaign Debates* (Washington, 1964), pp. 6–8. On the disadvantage of complex and remote issues, see note 45 above. For some practical objections and proposed solutions concerning debates in Britain, see Blumler and McQuail, pp. 296–300.

79   For surveys of the problem and some recommendations, see Kelley, *Political Campaigning*, pp. 40, 45–58; and Herbert E. Alexander, 'Broadcasting and Politics', in M. Kent Jennings and L. Harmon Zeigler (eds.), *The Electoral Process* (Englewood Cliffs, N.J., 1966), pp. 82–97; and Rose, pp. 248–77. Also see U.S. Congress, Senate Special Committee to Investigate Political Activities, Lobbying and Campaign Contributions, *Campaign Contributions, Political Activities and Lobbying* (84th Cong., 2nd Sess.).

80   On these legal restrictions and reforms, see John E. Coons (ed.), *Freedom and Responsibility in Broadcasting* (Evanston, Ill., 1961); and U.S. Congress, Communications Subcommittee of the Senate Committee on Interstate and Foreign Commerce, *Review of Section 314* (87th Cong., 1st Sess., 1961); Trenaman and McQuail, pp. 66–74; and *Conference on Electoral Law*, H.M.S.O., Cmnd. 3275 (London, 1967), pt. III.

81   White, pp. 292–3.

82   On press conferences, see Thompson, 'Rational Propaganda', pp. 107–13. On the Granada marathon, see Trenaman and McQuail, pp. 71–4, 90–3. On the New York campaign debates and on voters' pamphlets, see Kelley, *Political Campaigning*, pp. 41–2, 67–9.

83   On the Press Council, see H. P. Levy, *The Press Council: History, Procedure and Cases* (New York, 1967).

84   See note 27 above.

85   Laski, *Democracy at the Crossroads*, pp. 10–11; *Parliamentary Government in England*, pp. 3–52; *The State in Theory and Practice*, pp. 148–50; *Politics*, pp. 125–7; *Democracy in Crisis*, pp. 73–5; *Liberty in the Modern State*, pp. 162–70, 188–91; and Dewey, *Public*, pp. 181–2. The best contemporary British statements of this general view (as much concerned with the quality of culture as political offerings) are: Raymond Williams, *The Existing Alternatives in Communications* (London, 1962); *Britain in the Sixties— Communications* (London, 1962), esp. pp. 88–130; and *The Long Revolution* (London, 1961). The more usual view in America—that the government should enter the communications field only when the media fail and then not on a permanent basis—is expressed by Wilbur Schramm, *Responsibility in Mass Communication* (New York, 1957).

86   See the Carnegie Commission on Educational Television, *Public Television*:
      A Program for Action (New York, 1967); [Pilkington] *Report of the Com-*
      mittee on Broadcasting, 1960 (London, 1962), pp. 44–6, 63, 68, 65; and
      J. T. Suchy, 'How Does Commercial TV Affect British Viewing?' *Journal-*
      ism Quarterly (Winter 1958), pp. 65–71.
87   See J. C. R. Licklider, 'Televistas: Looking Ahead through Side Windows',
      in Carnegie Commission on Educational Television, *Public Television*,
      pp. 201–25.

CHAPTER 5   VOTING

1   See Richard Rose and Harve Mossawir, 'Voting and Elections: A Functional
     Analysis', *Political Studies* (June 1967), pp. 173–201.
2   For a sampling of some other approaches to rationality, as well as further
     discussion of those which could be included within the dichotomy here,
     see Paul Diesing, *Reason in Society* (Urbana, Ill., 1962); Carl G. Hempel,
     Aspects of Scientific Explanation (New York, 1965), pp. 463–87; Carl
     J. Friedrich (ed.), *Rational Decision* (New York, 1964); Robert E. Lane and
     David O. Sears, *Public Opinion*, pp. 72–82; and Bernard Berelson, 'Demo-
     cratic Theory and Public Opinion', *Public Opinion Quarterly* (Fall 1952),
     pp. 325–7; Quentin Gibson, *The Logic of Social Enquiry*, pp. 156–78;
     Jonathan Bennett, *Rationality: An Essay toward Analysis* (London, 1964);
     Anthony Downs, *An Economic Theory of Democracy*; and note 3 below.
3   The most useful applications of the calculation model are found (in a more
     refined form) in modern welfare economics, especially cost-benefit analysis,
     and in game and utility theory. See R. Duncan Luce and Howard Raiffa,
     Games and Decisions, chs. 1–4; William J. Baumol, *Economic Theory and*
     Operations Analysis (Englewood Cliffs, N.J., 1961), chs. 17–18; and C. West
     Churchman, *Prediction and Optimal Decision* (Englewood Cliffs, N.J.,
     1961), pp. 219–49.
        On the usefulness and limitations of this general approach in explaining
     social and political phenomena, see Hempel, pp. 466–8. Also, David
     Braybrooke and Charles E. Lindblom, *Strategy of Decision* (New York, 1963).
4   Leonard T. Hobhouse, *Liberalism*, pp. 41–2; Alf Ross, *Why Democracy?*,
     pp. 49–53; Graham Wallas, *Human Nature in Politics*, pp. 45, 47, 118;
     The Art of Thought, p. 119; Friedrich, *New Image of the Common Man*;
     and John Dewey, *The Public and Its Problems*, pp. 103–4. Dewey objects
     to the model also because he believes the ends-means distinction which it
     assumes is mistaken (*Reconstruction in Philosophy*, pp. 170–2, 175–6; and
     Theory of Valuation, pp. 40–50, 52).
5   Joseph Schumpeter, *Capitalism, Socialism, and Democracy*, p. 262; and
     Harold D. Lasswell, *Psychopathology and Politics*, in *The Political Writings*
     of Harold D. Lasswell, p. 194.
6   Philip E. Converse, Review of *The Responsible Electorate*, by V. O. Key,
     Jr., *Political Science Quarterly* (Dec. 1966), pp. 630–1.
7   Angus Campbell, Philip E. Converse, Warren E. Miller, and Donald E.
     Stokes, *The American Voter*, pp. 505–10; and V. O. Key, Jr., *The Responsible*
     Electorate (Cambridge, Mass., 1966), pp. 89–90.

8 Walter Berns, 'Voting Studies', in Herbert J. Storing (ed.), *Essays on the Scientific Study of Politics*, pp. 40–1.

9 I have shortened and paraphrased respondents' replies given in Campbell *et al.*, *The American Voter*, pp. 242, 245.

10 See Patrick Nowell-Smith, *Ethics*, pp. 100–6; and A. I. Melden, *Free Action* (London, 1961), pp. 148–9, 162. For a survey and further development of the literature on this problem, see Raziel Abelson, ' "Because I Want To" ', *Mind* (Oct. 1965), pp. 547–53.

11 Campbell *et al.*, *The American Voter*, pp. 542–3; David Butler and Donald Stokes, *Political Change in Britain*, pp. 174–82, 355–8; Mark P. Benney, A. P. Gray and R. H. Pear, *How People Vote*, p. 140; Bernard Berelson, Paul F. Lazarsfeld and William N. McPhee, *Voting*, p. 227; Angus Campbell and Robert L. Kahn, *The People Elect a President*, p. 59; and Hazel Gaudet Erskine, 'The Polls: The Informed Public', *Public Opinion Quarterly* (Winter 1962), pp. 669–77. But for evidence more favorable to citizens' knowledgeability of issues, see Campbell and Kahn, p. 55; Morris Janowitz and Dwaine Marvick, *Competitive Pressure and Democratic Consent*, p. 46; Joseph Trenaman and Denis McQuail, *Television and the Political Image*, p. 166; and Lane and Sears, *Public Opinion*, p. 59.

12 Berelson *et al.*, *Voting*, pp. 220–3, 344; Campbell *et al.*, *The American Voter*, pp. 180–1; and Philip E. Converse, Aage R. Clausen and Warren E. Miller, 'Electoral Myth and Reality: The 1964 Election', *American Political Science Review* (June 1965), p. 329.

13 V. O. Key, *Public Opinion and Democracy*, pp. 154–63, 168, 172 n.; Campbell *et al.*, *The American Voter*, pp. 194–6, 209–11, 349; Herbert McCloskey, 'Conservatism and Personality', *American Political Science Review* (March 1958), pp. 44–5; Butler and Stokes, pp. 193–208, 211; Converse *et al.*, 'Electoral Myth and Reality', p. 335 n.; Philip E. Converse, 'The Nature of Belief Systems in Mass Publics', in Apter (ed.), *Ideology and Discontent*, pp. 206–61; and Lane and Sears, p. 69.

14 See Gilbert Ryle, *The Concept of Mind* (London, 1949), esp. pp. 27–32. But see W. B. Gallie, 'The Idea of Practice', *Proceedings of the Aristotelean Society* (1967–8), esp. pp. 76–8.

15 Dewey, *Human Nature and Conduct*, pp. 14–18, 177–8, 193–8; *Public*, pp. 158–60; *How We Think* (New York, 1933), pp. 96–116; *Democracy and Education*, pp. 131–2; Lindsay, *The Good and the Clever* (Cambridge, England, 1945), pp. 5–8, 13–18; *Kant* (London, 1934), pp. 164–5; Friedrich, *New Image*, pp. 295, 345; Wallas, *Human Nature*, pp. 122–5; *The Great Society*, pp. 36–8, 43; Yves Simon, *A General Theory of Authority* pp. 33–41, esp. pp. 34–35 n.; and Laski, *Grammar of Politics*, pp. 22–3; *The Dangers of Obedience*, pp. 59–61. For MacIver's notion of explanation, see his *Social Causation* (New York, 1964), esp. pp. 371–93; and *Society* (New York, 1931), esp. p. 530.

16 For the most able contemporary exposition of this concept, see William Dray, *Laws and Explanation in History* (Oxford, 1957), esp. pp. 122–6; and 'The Historical Explanation of Actions Reconsidered', in Sidney Hook (ed.), *Philosophy and History* (New York,) pp. 105–35. Dray's precursors include R. G. Collingwood, *The Idea of History* (Oxford, 1946); Wilhelm

Dilthey, *Pattern and Meaning in History* (New York, 1962); Charles H. Cooley, *Sociological Theory and Social Research* (New York, 1930), pp. 290–308; and Max Weber, *Wirtschaft und Gesellschaft* (Tübingen, 1925), pt. I, esp. pp. 12–13. Weber's concept of *verstehen* (roughly, understanding from the subject's point of view) is applied by him also to actions which are not strictly rational (*zweckrational* or *wertrational*), such as emotional and habitual ones. Also see John Plamenatz, 'Electoral Studies and Democratic Theory', *Political Studies* (Feb. 1958), pp. 1–9.

17 Dray presents his notion of 'rational explanation', if not in opposition, then in contrast to the widely accepted 'covering law' model of scientific explanation. The classic formulation of that model is by Carl G. Hempel, 'The Function of General Laws in History', *Journal of Philosophy* (15 Jan. 1942), pp. 35–48 (reprinted with modifications in *Aspects of Scientific Explanation*, pp. 231–43). Dray does not claim that rational explanation is the only relevant kind of explanation even in historical writings. Hempel and his followers, however, insist that any rational explanation, if it is to explain must at least implicitly contain a general law (such as 'A rational agent when in a situation of kind C will usually do X') [Hempel, *Aspects*, p. 471; and John Passmore, 'Review Article: Law and Explanation in History', *Australian Journal of Politics and History* (Nov. 1958), p. 275]. Dray replies that (1) such a a 'law' is not an empirical generalization but an explication of what we mean by calling an agent rational; and (2) it is not necessary, in order to understand an action, to know that the agent usually does what reason requires [Dray, *Philosophy of History* (Englewood Cliffs, N.J., 1964), p. 15].

18 Even though some social scientists do not claim the status of causal laws for most of their generalization, other social scientists are already urging that causal language is appropriate in many cases. See, e.g. Hubert M. Blalock Jr., *Causal Inference in Non-Experimental Research* (Chapel Hill, 1961); Hayward R. Alker, Jr., *Mathematics and Politics* (New York, 1965), pp. 112–29; and Arthur S. Goldberg, 'Discerning a Causal Pattern Among Data on Voting Behavior', *American Political Science Review* (Dec. 1966), pp. 913–22.

19 Versions of this doctrine, influenced by Ryle and Wittgenstein, include: Melden, *Free Action*; and Peter Winch, *The Idea of a Social Science* (London, 1958).

20 Alasdair MacIntyre, 'The Idea of a Social Science', *Proceedings of the Aristotelian Society*, supplementary vol. XLI (1967), pp. 95–114; 'The Antecedents of Action', in Bernard Williams and Alan Montefiore (eds.), *British Analytical Philosophy* (London, 1966), pp. 205–25; Donald Davidson, 'Actions, Reasons and Causes', *Journal of Philosophy* (7 Nov. 1963), pp. 685–700; and Stuart Hampshire, *Thought and Action* (London, 1960), esp. pp. 169–222. An argument that supports compatibility of rational explanation and social science is in Arthur L. Kalleberg, 'Concept Formation in Normative and Empirical Studies: Toward Reconciliation in Political Theory', *American Political Science Review* (March 1969), pp. 26–39.

21 Seymour Martin Lipset, *Political Man*, p. 234.

22 For Britain, see Jean Blondel, *Voters, Parties and Leaders*, p. 68; Benney
et al., pp. 103, 115; R. S. Milne and H. C. Mackenzie, *Straight Fight*,
pp. 41, 42; Trenaman and McQuail, pp. 140–1; L. J. Sharpe, *A Metropolis
Votes*, pp. 85–6; Frank Bealey, J. Blondel and W. P. McCann, *Constituency Politics*, pp. 168–9; Henry Durant, 'Voting Behavior in Britain,
1945–1964', in Richard Rose (ed.), *Studies in British Politics* (New York,
1966), pp. 122–8; David E. Butler and Anthony King, *The British
General Election of 1964*, p. 296; Butler and King, *The British General
Election of 1966* (London, 1966), p. 260; and Butler and Stokes
pp. 65–94. For the United States, see Lipset, *Political Man*, pp. 303–18;
Robert R. Alford, *Party and Society*, p. 233; Janowitz and Marvick, p. 26;
Key, *Public Opinion*, p. 125; Campbell and Kahn, pp. 24, 29, 32; Berelson
et al., *Voting*, p. 55; Paul F. Lazarsfeld, Bernard Berelson and Hazel
Gaudet, *The People's Choice*, pp. 19, 21, 26; Campbell et al., *The American
Voter*, p. 159; Survey Research Center, *Who Votes and For Whom* (Uni-
versity of Michigan, 1965, mimeo), pp. 3, 4, 8; Dewey Anderson and Percy
E. Davidson, *Ballots and the Democratic Class Struggle*, pp. 1–163; and
Robert Presthus, *Men at the Top* (New York, 1965), p. 285. On the differ-
ences and similarities between the U.S. and Britain, see Alford, pp. 101–21;
and Morris Janowitz and David R. Segal, 'Social Change and Party
Affiliation: Germany, Great Britain and the United States', *American
Journal of Sociology* (May 1967), pp. 601–18.

23 On correlates of subjective status, see Lazarsfeld et al., pp. 20–1; Berelson
et al., *Voting*, p. 56; Heinz Eulau, *Class and Party in the Eisenhower Years*,
pp. 57–86; Benney et al., p. 115; and Milne and Mackenzie, *Straight Fight*,
pp. 41, 42.

24 See esp. Butler and Stokes, pp. 67–8, 80–94, 115–22. On the absence of
class consciousness, Berelson et al., *Voting*, pp. 57–9, 79–80; Benney et al.,
p. 123; Key, *Public Opinion*, pp. 143–4; Alford, p. 337; and Ferdynand
Zweig, *The Worker in An Affluent Society* (New York, 1961), p. 135. For
some positive findings, see Bealey et al., pp. 176–7, 413; and Eric
Nordlinger, *The Working-Class Tories*, pp. 175–9. On the early development
of class consciousness, see Richard Hoggart, *The Uses of Literacy* (Harmondsworth, 1958), pp. 72–101; and Herbert H. Hyman, *Political Socialization* (Glencoe, Ill., 1959), pp. 35–9.

25 Campbell et al., *The American Voter*, pp. 382–401; and Butler and Stokes,
pp. 389–418.

26 Blondel, pp. 58, 67; Bonham, *The Middle Class Vote*, pp. 167–74; Benney
et al., p. 112; Nordlinger, p. 198; Milne and Mackenzie, *Straight Fight*,
pp. 62–4; Benney et al., p. 112; and Lipset, *Political Man*, p. 262. But see
Robert McKenzie and Allan Silver, *Angels in Marble: Working Class
Conservatives in Urban England* (Chicago, 1968), pp. 98–9; W. G. Runciman,
Relative Deprivation and Social Justice (London, 1966), pp. 142–7,
170–87; and Butler and Stokes, pp. 104–15, 127–9, 145–6, 156.
For the U.S., see Campbell and Kahn, p. 24; Berelson et al., pp. 47,
49–52; Campbell et al., *The Voter Decides*, p. 75. For other factors in lower-
class rightward voting, see Mark Abrams, 'Press, Polls and Votes in Britain
Since the 1955 General Elections', *Public Opinion Quarterly* (Winter 1957–

8), pp. 543–7; Fred I. Greenstein and Raymond E. Wolfinger, 'The Suburbs and Shifting Party Loyalties', *Public Opinion Quarterly* (Winter 1958–9), pp. 473–82; and Lipset, pp. 241–9, 267–78.

27 Nordlinger, p. 171; and McKenzie and Silver, pp. 106–13, 248–9.

28 Campbell *et al.*, *The American Voter*, pp. 153–60; and Lipset, *Political Man*, pp. 281–2. For similar effects in Britain, see Butler and Stokes, pp. 53–5, 58–60; and Trenaman and McQuail, p. 138. Hyman points out that the 'generational' concept must be used cautiously because it is difficult empirically to distinguish the effects of chronological age (simply getting older) from the effects of generational age (the impact of a historical event) [pp. 123–51].

29 See, e.g. V. O. Key, Jr., and Frank Munger, 'Social Determinism and Electoral Decision: The Case of Indiana', in Eugene Burdick and Arthur J. Brodbeck (eds.), *American Voting Behavior*, p. 287. Also see Bealey *et al.*, p. 185.

30 Lipset, *Political Man*, p. 296. For the factors which prevent the parental transmission of political attitudes indefinitely through generations, see Hyman, pp. 93–111.

31 On the inadequacy of status and shifts across status lines, see Converse, 'The Nature of Belief Systems in Mass Publics', pp. 247–8; Angus Campbell and Homer C. Cooper, *Group Differences in Attitudes and Votes* (Ann Arbor, 1956), p. 36; Campbell *et al.*, *The Voter Decides*, pp. 74, 85; Butler and Stokes, pp. 79, 123–50; and Bonham, p. 179. On the permanence of the status basis of voting, see Oscar Glantz, 'Unitary Political Behavior and Differential Political Motivation', *Western Political Quarterly* (Dec. 1957), pp. 833–46; and Key, *The Responsible Electorate*, pp. 116–17. On the independent effects of attitudes toward issues, candidates and parties, see Campbell *et al.*, *The Voter Decides*, ch. 10. For another attitudinal approach to rationality and voting, see Samuel Eldersveld, *Political Parties* (Chicago, 1964), pp. 483–9.

32 Milne and Mackenzie, *Straight Fight*, p. 139; Alfred de Grazia, 'The Limits of External Leadership over a Minority Electorate', *Public Opinion Quarterly* (Spring 1956), p. 121; Benney *et al.*, p. 192; and Lazarsfeld *et al.*, p. 37. But see Ian Budge and Derek Urwin, *Scottish Political Behavior*, pp. 89–100.

33 Campbell *et al.*, *The American Voter*, pp. 168–87; *The Voter Decides*, pp. 112–35; Key, *Public Opinion*, pp. 461–2; *The Responsible Electorate*, p. 150; Janowitz and Marvick, p. 49; Berelson *et al.*, *Voting*, pp. 194–6; Campbell and Kahn, pp. 55, 56; Benney *et al.*, pp. 141–2, 146, 150; Blondel, pp. 75–9. For the significant impact of issues on voters who split their tickets, see Milton C. Cummings, Jr., *Congressmen and the Electorate* (New York, 1966), esp. p. 89.

34 Angus Campbell, Review of *The Responsible Electorate*, *American Political Science Review* (Dec. 1966), p. 1007. On the idea of critical elections, see V. O. Key, Jr., 'A Theory of Critical Elections', *Journal of Politics* (Feb. 1955), pp. 3–18; and 'Secular Realignment and the Party System', *Journal of Politics* (May 1959), pp. 198–210. See Angus Campbell *et al.*, *Elections and the Political Order* (New York, 1966), pt I.

35 Campbell *et al.*, *The American Voter*, p. 187.
36 Campbell *et al.*, *The Voter Decides*, pp. 140, 173–4; Herbert Hyman and Paul B. Sheatsley, 'The Political Appeal of President Eisenhower', *Public Opinion Quarterly* (Winter 1953–4), pp. 443–60; Janowitz and Marvick, pp. 55–6; Campbell and Kahn, p. 53; Donald E. Stokes, 'Some Dynamic Elements of Contests for the Presidency', *American Political Science Review* (March 1966), pp. 19–28; and Butler and Stokes, pp. 384–8. R. S. Milne's remarks on candidate orientation in Britain are in 'Second Thoughts on "Straight Fight" ', in Eugene Burdick and Arthur J. Brodbeck *American Voting Behavior*, pp. 210–11.
37 Hobhouse, *Democracy and Reaction*, p. 150; C. J. Friedrich, *Constitutional Government and Democracy* (Boston, 1950), pp. 238, 267; and Lindsay, *The Essentials of Democracy*, p. 44.
38 See Robert E. Lane, *Political Life*, p. 240. Cf. Nathan Glazer and Daniel Patrick Moynihan, *Beyond the Melting Pot* (Cambridge, Mass., 1965), pp. 17, 301–2; and Raymond E. Wolfinger, 'Some Consequences of Ethnic Politics', in M. Kent Jennings and L. Harmon Zeigler (eds.), *The Electoral Process* (Englewood Cliffs, N.J., 1966), pp. 51–2.
39 See Campbell and Kahn, pp. 43, 49, 51; Lazarsfeld *et al.*, *The People's Choice*, p. 29; Lane, *Political Life*, pp. 24–5; and Campbell *et al.*, *The American Voter*, p. 56.
40 Campbell *et al.*, *The American Voter*, pp. 120–45 [percentages calculated from table G-5, p. 139]; Survey Research Center, *Who Votes and For Whom*, p. 6; Campbell *et al.*, *The Voter Decides*, pp. 88–111; Campbell *et al.*, *Elections and the Political Order*, pp. 9–157; Campbell and Cooper, pp. 37, 57, 93, 101–2; Key, *Public Opinion*, pp. 449–52; *The Responsible Electorate*, p. 150; Lazarsfeld *et al.*, pp. 147–8; David Wallace, *First Tuesday: A Study of Rationality in Voting* (Garden City, 1964), pp. 130–52; Mark Abrams, 'Social Trends and Electoral Behavior', *British Journal of Sociology* (Sept. 1962), pp. 230, 238–40; Milne and Mackenzie, *Straight Fight*, pp. 136–38, 140–1; David Butler, *The Electoral System in Britain 1918–1951* (Oxford, 1953), p. 201; Blondel, pp. 80–1; and Butler and Stokes, pp. 37–43, 45–55. But cf. Trenaman and McQuail, p. 147.
41 Bonham, p. 181 [1st quote]; Arthur S. Goldberg, 'Social Determinism and Rationality as Bases of Party Identification', *American Political Science Review* (March 1969), pp. 5–25; Butler and Stokes, pp. 360–72; Trenaman and McQuail, pp. 40–1, 223; Bealey *et al.*, pp. 210, 214–15, 217–18; Milne and Mackenzie, *Straight Fight*, pp. 144, 100–12; Benney *et al.*, pp. 120–3, 151; Blondel, pp. 81–4; and Key, *Public Opinion*, pp. 433, 443, 445, 453–4.
42 Blondel, pp. 97–108, 131–53; and Key, *Public Opinion*, pp. 439–42, and Herbert McCloskey, Paul J. Hoffman, and Rosemary O'Hara. 'Issue Conflict and Consesus Among Party Leaders and Followers', *American Political Science Review* (June 1960), pp. 406–27.
43 See J. Roland Pennock (*Liberal Democracy*, pp. 224–7) for an example of an analysis of an election to determine whether voters got what they voted for. On parties' contribution to rationality, see Robert Dahl, *Pluralist Democracy in the United States*, pp. 250–7. For some views of citizenship theorists, see Wallas, *Human Nature in Politics*, pp. 103–4, 111; MacIver,

The Web of Government, pp. 208–19; Yves Simon, *Philosophy of Democratic Government*, p. 104. Also, cf. A. Lawrence Lowell, *Public Opinion and Popular Government* (New York, 1913), pp. 75–6.

44 Ross, *Why Democracy?*, pp. 156–7, 161; MacIver, *Leviathan and the People*, pp. 148–50; *The Ramparts We Guard*, p. 28; *The Modern State*, pp. 202, 205; Friedrich, *New Image*, p. 36; and Laski, *A Grammar of Politics*, p. 78. (But see Laski, *Democracy in Crisis*, p. 69.)

45 See Campbell *et al.*, *The American Voter*, pp. 64–88.

46 See Campbell *et al.*, *The American Voter*, pp. 16–17. W. G. Runciman argues persuasively that even a scientific explanation of voting is incomplete without using historical, sociological and psychological approaches [*Social Science and Political Theory*, pp. 189–90].

47 Lindsay, *The Modern Democratic State*, p. 203. Cf. Lindsay, *The Two Moralities* (London, 1940), pp. 92–3, and *Kant*, p. 208 (where the ethical foundations of his views of the common good are discussed). Other discussions in citizenship theory are: MacIver, *Community*, pp. 98–127; *Ramparts*, p. 75; Friedrich, *Man and His Government*, p. 264; Simon, *Philosophy*, pp. 39–48, 70–1; *General Theory*, pp. 23–79, 143–56; Dewey, *Public*, pp. 15–16, 75–6; Hobhouse, *Liberalism*, p. 69; Laski, *Foundations of Sovereignty*, pp. 225–30; and G. D. H. Cole, *Guild Socialism Restated*, p. 34.

48 The following contemporary literature on the concept is useful: Wayne A. R. Leys and Charner Marquis Perry, *Philosophy and the Public Interest* (Chicago, 1959); Brian Barry, *Political Argument*, pp. 190–236; Carl J. Friedrich (ed.), *The Public Interest* (New York, 1962); and Richard E. Flathman, *The Public Interest* (New York, 1966). None of these writers defines 'public interest' exactly as I do, but Barry's definition is closest to mine.

49 James Q. Wilson and Edward Banfield, 'Public-Regardingness as a Value Premise in Voting Behavior', *American Political Science Review* (Dec. 1964), pp. 876–87. Cf. Campbell *et al.*, *The American Voter*, pp. 195–6.

50 Procedural forms of the general interest are mentioned in: MacIver, *Ramparts*, pp. 79–80; *The Modern State*, pp. 11–12; *Web of Government*, pp. 217, 220; Simon, *Philosophy*, p. 30; *General Theory*, p. 41; Merriam, *Political Power*, pp. 130, 101; and Friedrich, *Man*, p. 146; *New Image*, pp. 153, 157, 160–71, 178–81.

51 Key, *Public Opinion*, pp. 45–8, 445, 447–8, 479; Kornhauser *et al.*, *When Labor Votes*, pp. 135, 161; Berelson *et al.*, *Voting*, pp. 186–92; Campbell *et al.*, *The American Voter*, p. 184; Dahl, *Pluralist Democracy*, pp. 325–70; Almond and Verba, *The Civic Culture*, pp. 131–45; Butler and Stokes, pp. 431–7; Trenaman and McQuail, pp. 52–4; Blondel, pp. 77–9; Bealey *et al.*, pp. 206–15, 413; McKenzie and Silver, pp. 109–11, 134–7, 246; Nordlinger, pp. 143, 183–8; and Budge and Urwin, pp. 107–11.

52 The major studies are: Samuel A. Stouffer, *Communism, Conformity and Civil Liberties* (New York, 1966), pp. 37, 40, 44–5; James W. Prothro and Charles M. Grigg, 'Fundamental Principles of Democracy: Bases of Agreement and Disagreement', *Journal of Politics* (May 1960), pp. 276–94; and most important Herbert McClosky, 'Consensus and Ideology in

American Politics', *American Political Science Review* (June 1964), pp. 361–82. But on racial discrimination, see the much more favorable findings reported by Paul Sheatsley, 'White Attitudes toward the Negro', *Daedalus* (Winter 1966), p. 224.

53 See note 50 above.

54 But for rejections of the substantive sense, see Ross, *Why Democracy?*, p. 117; Kelsen, 'Foundations of Democracy', *Ethics* (Oct. 1955), p. 2; and T. V. Smith, *Discipline for Democracy*, pp. 123–5; *The Democratic Way of Life*, p. 204. For contemporary rejections, see Frank J. Sorauf, 'The Public Interest Reconsidered', *Journal of Politics* (Nov. 1957), pp. 616–39; Glendon Schubert, *The Public Interest* (Glencoe, Ill., 1961); and J. D. B. Miller, *The Nature of Politics* (London, 1962), ch. IV.

55 E.g. John Stuart Mill, *Considerations on Representative Government* (Everyman), ch. 6, pp. 255–6; and Ferdinand Lundberg, *The Treason of the People* (New York, 1964), pp. 11–12.

56 For the studies which suggest that voters who change between elections are less likely to be competent than those who do not, see Philip E. Converse, 'Information Flow and the Stability of Partisan Attitudes', *Public Opinion Quarterly* (Winter 1962), esp. pp. 581–2; Butler and Stokes, pp. 221–7 [but cf. 437]; Milne and Mackenzie, *Marginal Seat* (London, 1958), p. 192; Blondel, pp. 69–73; and Campbell *et al.*, *The American Voter*, pp. 256–65, 546–7. Janowitz and Marvick support this general finding only in upper-status groups (p. 37). They find that lower-status switchers may have been more competent than regular voters in 1952. Key finds no difference between 'switchers' and 'stand-patters' in education or information (except in 1960) but some indication that 'switchers' may be less interested (*The Responsible Electorate*, pp. 94 ff., 147). Also see Milne and Mackenzie, *Straight Fight*, pp. 48–9; and Blumler and McQuail, pp. 271–4. For similar findings about voters who change *during* a campaign, see Lazarsfeld *et al.*, *The People's Choice*, pp. 66, 69; Berelson *et al.*, *Voting*, p. 347; and Benney *et al.*, pp. 175–87. Cf. Trenaman and McQuail, pp. 207–21. For the objection that changers have not been shown to form a constant bloc (and other criticisms), see Harry Daudt, *Floating Voters and the Floating Vote* (Leiden, 1959); Milne and Mackenzie, *Straight Fight*, p. 34; and Trenaman and McQuail, pp. 221–2. On the related but less common activity of independent voting, see Robert E. Agger, 'Independents and Party Identifiers: Characteristics and Behavior in 1952', in Eugene Burdick and Arthur J. Brodbeck (eds.), *American Voting Behavior*, pp. 308–29; Alan S. Meyer, 'The Independent Voter', in William N. McPhee and William A. Glaser, *Public Opinion and Congressional Elections* (New York, 1962), pp. 65–77; and Samuel J. Eldersveld, 'The Independent Voter: Measurement, Characteristics, and Implications for Party Strategy', *American Political Science Review* (Sept. 1952), pp. 732–53; Campbell *et al.*, *American Voter*, pp. 143–5; and Key, *The Responsible Electorate*, pp. 91 ff.

57 Lindsay, *Modern Democratic State*, p. 272. Also, Friedrich, *New Image*, pp. 191–2; Hobhouse, *Democracy and Reaction*, p. 150; Laski, *Grammar*, p. 78; MacIver, *Leviathan*, pp. 149–50; and Ross, *Why Democracy?*, p. 161.

58 Key, *Public Opinion*, pp. 473–6; Campbell *et al.*, *The American Voter*, pp. 525–7; Converse, Review of *The Responsible Electorate*, p. 633; and Campbell *et al.*, *The Voter Decides*, p. 165.

59 Key, *The Responsible Electorate*, pp. 53–6, 71–7, 81–9, 125, 132–7; and *Public Opinion*, pp. 465, 466; and Campbell *et al.*, *The American Voter*, pp. 545–7.

60 See Laski, *Liberty in the Modern State*, pp. 48–65; Dewey, *Reconstruction in Philosophy*, pp. 207–8; and *Quest for Certainty*, p. 250.

61 See note 49 above and Budge and Urwin, pp. 87–8.

62 Campbell *et al.*, evidently believe that party voting is a 'restraint' (*The Voter Decides*, p. 96 n.).

63 E.g. Merriam, *What is Democracy?*, p. 58; *Systematic Politics*, p. 209; *New Aspects of Politics*, pp. 203–10; Wallas, *Human Nature*, pp. 206, 209. Also see Chapter 1, notes 27–8.

64 Campbell *et al.*, *The American Voter*, pp. 250–1; *The Voter Decides*, p. 96 n; Hyman, pp. 144–5; Goldberg, esp. p. 19; Lane and Sears, p. 70 [quote]; and Prothro and Grigg, pp. 289–91.

65 Campbell *et al.*, *The American Voter*, pp. 360, 377; Berelson *et al.*, *Voting*, pp. 229, 330; Alford, p. 112; and Eldersveld, *Political Parties*, pp. 517–18.

66 Alford, p. 248. Against the findings of Campbell *et al.* (*The American Voter*, pp. 347–59) which show a decline in status polarization from 1948 through 1956, Alford argues that this is a short-term fluctuation (pp. 225–31). Also see Lipset, p. 325; and Bonham, pp. 194–5.

67 Such a reform is proposed by the Committee on Political Parties of the American Political Science Association, *Toward a More Responsible Two-Party System* (New York, 1950), and E. E. Schattschneider, *Party Government* (New York, 1942). For criticisms, see Austin Ranney and Willmoore Kendall, *Democracy and the American Party System*, pp. 525–33; and Edward C. Banfield, 'In Defense of the American Party System', in Robert A. Goldwin (ed.), *Political Parties, U.S.A.* (Chicago, 1961), pp. 32–7.

68 Cf. Philip E. Converse and Georges Dupeux, 'Politicization of the Electorate in France and the United States', *Public Opinion Quarterly* (Spring 1962), pp. 1–23.

CHAPTER 6 EQUALITY

1 See S. I. Benn and R. S. Peters, *Social Principles and the Democratic State* (London, 1961), p. 111; Isaiah Berlin, 'Equality', *Proceedings of the Aristotelian Society* (1955–6), p. 311; R. H. Tawney, *Equality* (London, 1931), esp. pp. 50–3; John Wilson, *Equality* (New York, 1966), pp. 109–34; Bernard Williams, 'The Idea of Equality', in Peter Laslett and W. G. Runciman (eds.), *Philosophy, Politics and Society*, 2nd series (Oxford, 1962), p. 123; J. Roland Pennock and John W. Chapman (eds.), *Equality*, *Nomos* IX (New York, 1967), *passim*; and G. W. Mortimore, 'An Ideal of Equality', *Mind* (April 1968), pp. 222–42. My interpretation of the equality formula in terms of purposes or functions is not explicitly suggested by these writers, though I do not think it is incompatible with the views of most of them.

2 Charles E. Merriam, *The New Democracy and the New Despotism*, p. 41; Harold J. Laski, *The Limitations of the Expert* (London, 1931), pp. 12–13; and Robert M. MacIver, *The Ramparts We Guard*, pp. 45–6.

3 Laski, *Democracy in Crisis*, pp. 169–79; *A Grammar of Politics*, pp. 115–16; MacIver, *Ramparts*, p. 29; and Carl J. Friedrich, *Man and His Government*, pp. 50–2, 320; *The New Image of the Common Man*, pp. 31–5, 114, 119. For a more sceptical argument which comes to similar conclusions, see Thomas L. Thorson, *The Logic of Democracy* (New York, 1962).

4 A. D. Lindsay, *The Modern Democratic State*, p. 277; John Dewey, *The Public and Its Problems*, pp. 206–7; Laski, *Limitations*, pp. 4, 9–10; *The Dangers of Obedience*, p. 18; and G. D. H. Cole and Margaret Cole, *A Guide to Modern Politics*, pp. 434–7.

5 Laski, *Limitations*, p. 9.

6 Leonard T. Hobhouse, *The Elements of Social Justice*, p. 192. Also, Lindsay, *Modern Democratic State*, p. 270.

7 Friedrich, *Man*, pp. 295–6.

8 Laski, *Grammar*, p. 170. Also Dewey, *The Ethics of Democracy*, p. 25.

9 See James Q. Wilson, 'The Negro in Politics', *Daedalus, The Negro American* (Fall 1965), pp. 949–73; and Donald B. Matthews and James W. Prothro, *Negroes and the New Southern Politics* (New York, 1966), pp. 478–80. See also the U.S. Commission on Civil Rights, *1961 Report*, 'Voting' (Washington, D.C., 1961), vol. I, pt. III, pp. 143–99 (esp. pp. 191–3); Allan P. Sindler, 'Protest Against the Political Status of the Negro', *The Annals of the American Academy of Political and Social Science* (Jan. 1965), pp. 48–54; and William R. Keech, *The Impact of Negro Voting* (Chicago, 1968), pp. 40–92.

10 Laski, *Liberty in the Modern State*, pp. 183–6; *The Prospects of Democratic Government*, pp. 5–7; T. V. Smith, *The Democratic Tradition in America*, p. 283; *The American Philosophy of Equality* (Chicago, 1927), pp. ix–x, 276–99; Lindsay, *Modern Democratic State*, pp. 246–8; and Friedrich, *Man*, p. 296.

11 On the 'potential tension level', see Seymour Martin Lipset, *Political Man*, pp. 444–5. For the effects of higher status on acceptance of prevailing norms and likelihood of cynicism, see Key, *Public Opinion and American Democracy*, pp. 340–1; Lester W. Milbrath, *Political Participation*, p. 80; and William Erbe 'Social Involvement and Political Activity', *American Sociological Review* (April 1964) pp. 198–215. Edgar Litt finds no relationship between socio-economic status and his measure of cynicism ['Political Cynicism and Political Futility', *Journal of Politics* (May 1963), pp. 312–23]. For the effect of participation on legitimacy, see ch. 3, notes 20–4.

12 Robert E. Lane, *Political Ideology* (New York, 1962), esp. pp. 67–8; W. G. Runciman, *Relative Deprivation and Social Justice*, pp. 192–208; Ferdynand Zweig, *The Worker in an Affluent Society*, pp. 134, 195–9; Eric Nordlinger, *The Working-Class Tories*, p. 166; and Seymour Martin Lipset and Reinhard Bendix, *Social Mobility in Industrial Society* (Berkeley, 1959), pp. 76–113.

13 Jerome H. Skolnick, *The Politics of Protest* (New York, 1969), pp. 202–5, 207; Gary T. Marx, *Protest and Prejudice* (New York, 1967), pp. 58, 62, 63, 66–70; and Thomas F. Pettigrew, *A Profile of the Negro American* (Princeton, 1964), pp. 178–92.

14 The American figures based on my analysis of 1968 SRC election data:

	Percent voting in each fifth of male population with work experience, according to Duncan socio-economic index				
	Bottom fifth	Second fifth	Third fifth	Fourth fifth	Top fifth
Voting	45	67	59	73	79
Not voting	38	25	29	18	11
No answer/ don't know	17	8	12	9	10

The Duncan index is an occupational ranking based on income and education for occupations [See Otis Dudley Duncan, 'A Socio-economic Index for all Occupations', in Albert J. Reiss, Jr., *Occupations and Social Status* (New York, 1961), esp. pp. 128–9]. For the British findings, see Mark P. Benney, A. P. Gray and R. H. Pear, *How People Vote*, pp. 127, 185–6; and Frank Bealey, J. Blondel and W. P. McCann, *Constituency Politics*, pp. 403–4. For other (mainly) U.S. findings, see Milbrath, *Political Participation*, pp. 114–28; Julian L. Woodward and Elmo Roper, 'Political Activity of American Citizens', *American Political Science Review* (Dec. 1950), p. 877; Genevieve Knupfer, 'Portrait of the Underdog', *Public Opinion Quarterly* (Spring 1947), pp. 112–13; Lane, *Political Life*, pp. 67, 73; Bernard R. Berelson, Paul F. Lazarsfeld and William N. McPhee, *Voting*, p. 25; Angus Campbell, Gerald Gurin and Warren E. Miller, *The Voter Decides*, pp. 70–3; Morris Janowitz and Dwaine Marvick, *Competitive Pressure and Democratic Consent*, pp. 97–8; Paul F. Lazarsfeld, Bernard Berelson and Hazel Gaudet, *The People's Choice*, pp. 43, 145; and Robert Dahl, *Who Governs?* pp. 283, 285, 292–3.

15 The 1968 findings for voting by annual family income are based on my analysis of unpublished SRC data:

	Under $4,000	$4,000–$9,999	$10,000 and over
Voting	53%	68%	78%
Not voting	35	22	11
No answer, don't know	12	10	11

For data on all three status variables, see Survey Research Center, *Who Votes and For Whom*, pp. 3, 4, 8; and Angus Campbell and Homer C. Cooper, *Group Differences in Attitudes and Votes* (Ann Arbor, 1956), pp. 27, 30, 34. For education, see Berelson *et al.*, *Voting*, p. 336; and Key, *Public Opinion*, pp. 329–31. For occupation, see Angus Campbell and

Robert L. Kahn, *The People Elect a President*, pp. 24, 29, 31, 38; Joseph Trenaman and Denis McQuail, *Television and the Political Image*, p. 209; and Jean Blondel, *Voters, Parties and Leaders*, p. 55. For evidence that there is *no* significant difference in turnout between occupational classes in some *local* British elections, see Ian Budge and Derek Urwin, *Scottish Political Behavior*, p. 80; and L. J. Sharpe, *A Metropolis Votes*, pp. 67–9.

16 Anthony M. Orum, 'A Reappraisal of the Social and Political Participation of Negroes', *American Journal of Sociology* (July 1966), pp. 35–6 [findings for whites also]; Lazarsfeld *et al.*, *People's Choice*, pp. 146–7; Lipset, *Political Man*, p. 203; Campbell and Kahn, pp. 24–8; and Seymour Martin Lipset, M. Trow and J. S. Coleman, *Union Democracy*, pp. 97–105.

17 Generally see Lane, *Political Life*, p. 85; Gabriel Almond and Sydney Verba, *The Civic Culture*, pp. 121–2; and Knupfer, pp. 109–10. On the social distribution of opinion leaders and personal influence, see Lipset, *Political Man*, p. 203; and Knupfer, pp. 105–6, 108–9. On a group reference, see Berelson *et al.*, *Voting*, pp. 75, 243; Benney *et al.*, pp. 126–7; Campbell and Cooper, p. 125; Janowitz and Marvick, *Competitive Pressure*, p. 60; Lane, *Political Life*, p. 91; Trenaman and McQuail, p. 99; R. S. Milne and H. C. Mackenzie, *Straight Fight*, p. 94; and Wilbur Schramm and David M. White, 'Age, Education and Economic Status as Factors in Newspaper Reading: Conclusions', in Wilbur Schramm (ed.), *The Process and Effects of Mass Communications* (Urbana, Ill., 1954), pp. 72–3. On the relative equality of television exposure, see ch. 4, notes 60, 62.

18 For the social distribution of party images and party identification, see Milne and Mackenzie, p. 132; Campbell *et al.*, *The Voter Decides*, pp. 152–3, 154; and Benney *et al.*, pp. 130–1, 134. On the distribution of political information and related properties, see Key, *Public Opinion*, pp. 150, 199–200, 332–3, 338–9; Knupfer, pp. 108–9, 112; Almond and Verba, pp. 86, 87; and ch. 3, notes 16, 17.

19 The 1960 and 1964 figures on non-voting are based on *Who Votes*, p. 2. The Southern data (partly SRC) are reported in Matthew and Prothro, pp. 39–41, 44–5, 261–63. The 1968 unpublished SRC data for the U.S. electorate shows:

	White	Black
Voting	69%	58%
Not voting	21	29
No answer, don't know	10	13

20 Orum, pp. 42, 44. The 1968 figures are based on unpublished SRC data for the U.S. electorate:

| | Per cent voting in each category | | | |
	Grade school	High school	Some college	College
Black	57	65	50	84
White	52	74	76	83

21 On organızations, see Orum, pp. 37–9. On Democratic distinctiveness of the black vote and group identification, see Angus Campbell, Philip E. Converse, Warren E. Miller, and Donald E. Stokes, *The American Voter*, pp. 306, 310. According to my analysis of 1968 unpublished SRC data, 27% of whites in the U.S. electorate have 'strong' identifications with one of the two major parties, while 57% of the blacks have 'strong' identifications (almost entirely Democratic).

22 Robert Dahl, *Who Governs?* pp. 294–5; Dahl, 'Equality and Power in American Society', in William V. D'Antonio and Howard J. Ehrlich, *Power and Democracy in America* (Notre Dame, 1961), pp. 80–1; Milbrath, *Political Participation*, p. 138; and Lane, *Political Life*, p. 83.

23 V. O. Key, *Politics, Parties and Pressure Groups*, p. 595; *Public Opinion*, pp. 198–9; and Dahl, *Who Governs?*, p. 284.

24 Citizenship theorists who specifically discuss some version of what I call equality of *de jure* opportunity include: Yves R. Simon, *Philosophy of Democratic Government*, pp. 202–3; Cole and Cole, p. 407; Friedrich, *The Philosophy of Law in Historical Perspective*, p. 193; Hobhouse, *Liberalism*, p. 70; *Elements*, pp. 94–120; MacIver, *Leviathan and the People*, pp. 80–1; *Ramparts*, pp. 13–18, 125–7; Smith, *Democratic Tradition*, pp. 23–7; *American Philosophy*, pp. 142, 308; Merriam, *What is Democracy?*, pp. 44–5; Hans Kelsen, *General Theory of Law and State*, p. 287; and Ross, *Why Democracy?*, p. 131. For broader ideas of equality of opportunity (including what I call the *de facto* form), see in addition to the previous citations: Dewey, *Public*, p. 150; 'Creative Democracy—The Task Before Us', in Sidney Ratner (ed.), *The Philosopher of the Common Man*, pp. 223–4; Laski, *Liberty*, pp. 250–4; *Grammar*, pp. 154–6; and Friedrich, *Man*, pp. 292–3, 299.

25 See Chapter 3, note 59. On community pressure, see Campbell *et al.*, *American Voter*, pp. 278–9, 281.

26 See note 9 above.

27 The view that some significant form of equality is possible without social and economic equality can be found in MacIver, *Leviathan*, pp. 161–3; Laski, *Studies in the Problem of Sovereignty*, pp. 134–7; and Lindsay, *Modern Democratic State*, p. 258. For the opposite view, see Lindsay, *ibid.*, pp. 247–8; *I Believe in Democracy*, pp. 45–52; Cole and Cole, pp. 406–7; Laski, *Grammar*, pp. 154–6; *Foundations of Sovereignty*, p. 77; *Dangers*, pp. 162, 211–12; 'Democracy', *Encyclopedia of Social Sciences* (New York, 1930), p. 83; Dewey, *Democracy and Education*, pp. 88, 99; and Simon, *Philosophy*, pp. 229, 253–9; *Community of the Free*, pp. 153–72. It is MacIver who, most notably, tries to represent these differences as cause for a genuine dispute (*Leviathan*, pp. 80–1, 161–3).

28 Cf. Ralph H. Turner, 'Modes of Social Ascent Through Education: Sponsored and Contest Mobility', in A. H. Halsey *et al.* (eds.), *Education, Economy and Society* (New York, 1961), pp. 121–39. For evidence showing that the British system succeeds in separating children according to I.Q., see Jean Floud (ed.), A. H. Halsey and F. M. Martin, *Social Class and Education Opportunity* (London, 1956), pp. 42–61.

29 For the citizenship theorists, see Lindsay, *Modern Democratic State*, p. 258; *The Churches and Democracy*, pp. 15–23; and Smith, *Democratic Tradition*, pp. 33–4. For a social scientist's view on this tension, see Lipset, *Political Man*, p. 449. Cf. Williams, 'The Idea of Equality', pp. 129–31. The reference to Michael Young is *The Rise of the Meritocracy* (New York, 1959), pp. 85, 92–3 and *passim*. For an argument that distinctions (e.g. inequalities in praise) are possible without inequality of respect, see Runciman, *Relative Deprivation*, pp. 274–84.

30 Lipset and Bendix, pp. 68–9; Robert R. Alford, *Party and Society*, pp. 118–19, 150, 170; Lipset, *Political Man*, pp. 211–26; Lazarsfeld *et al.*, *People's Choice*, pp. 56–64; Campbell *et al.*, *The Voter Decides*, pp. 157–61, 183; *The American Voter*, pp. 80–1, 83, 85; Berelson *et al.*, *Voting*, p. 27; Janowitz and Marvick, *Competitive Pressure*, p. 94; and Campbell and Kahn, p. 24. Notice that these studies do not all refer to the same kinds of cross pressures. Also notice that the findings do not apply to *inter*generational mobility [See Eleanor E. Maccoby, Richard E. Matthews, and Anton S. Morton, 'Youth and Political Change', *Public Opinion Quarterly* (Spring 1954), pp. 34–6].

31 See Lane, *Political Ideology*, esp. pp. 60, 73–5 and note 12 above.

32 On this issue, see Richard Wollheim, *Socialism and Culture* (London, 1961), esp. pp. 44–8. For a brilliant description of the inequality that is generated by the division of society into working-class and non-working-class cultures, see George Orwell, *The Road to Wigan Pier* (New York, 1958), pp. 186–201.

33 Cf. Williams, 'The Idea of Equality', p. 127 and *passim*.

34 Lane, *Political Life*, p. 334; Lipset, *Political Man*, pp. 205–6; Almond and Verba, p. 344; Arthur Kornhauser, 'Toward an Assessment of the Mental Health of Factory Workers: A Detroit Study', *Human Organization* (Spring 1962), p. 45; Lewis Lipsitz, 'Work Life and Political Attitudes: A Study of Manual Workers', *American Political Science Review* (Dec. 1964), pp. 951, 957; and ch. 3, note 64. Notice, however, that Lipsitz finds no difference between assembly line workers and others in voting, discussion and interest in politics (p. 958). Generally on equality of opportunity in the U.S., see Seymour Martin Lipset, *The First New Nation* (New York, 1963), pp. 366–402.

35 On income, see Lane, *Political Life*, pp. 224–5. On education, see ch. 3, notes 47–9 and ch. 5, note 64. The argument that it is less pleasant to receive than painful to give is in David Hume, *A Treatise of Human Nature*, ed. Selby-Bigge, bk. III, pt. II, sec. 1, p. 482; and Jeremy Bentham, *Theory of Legislation* (Boston, 1840), vol. I, pp. 133–4.

36 Arthur Kornhauser, Harold L. Sheppard and Albert J. Mayer, *When Labor Votes*, p. 156; Dahl, *Who Governs?*, pp. 288–93; Almond and Verba, pp. 176–8; Campbell *et al.*, *The Voter Decides*, pp. 191–4, 198; and Knupfer, pp. 113–14. More specifically on American blacks, see Rashi Fein, 'An Economic and Social Profile of the Negro American', *Daedalus*, *The Negro American* (Fall 1965), p. 841 and *passim*; and Pettigrew, pp. 3–26. The substance of the British Political and Economic Planning study is in W. W. Daniel, *Racial Discrimination in England* (Harmondsworth, Middlesex, 1968) (quote is on p. 211). Also, see Nicholas Deakin (ed.),

Colour and the British Electorate, 1964 (London, 1965); and Butler and Stokes, *Political Change in Britain*, p. 350.

37 Lipset, *Political Man*, p. 213. See also Blumler and McQuail, *Television in Politics*, p. 194; Campbell and Kahn, p. 24; and note 30 above.

38 For continuing data on income distribution, consult Department of Commerce, Bureau of Census, *Current Population Reports* (Series P–60); Survey Research Center, *Survey of Consumer Finances*; and U.K. Central Statistical Office, *Annual Abstract of Statistics* (H.M.S.O.). Also, see Harold Lydall and John B. Lansing, 'A Comparison of the Distribution of Personal Income and Wealth in the United States and Great Britain, *American Economic Review* (March 1959), pp. 43–67; Simon Kuznets 'Income Distribution and Changes in Consumption', in Hoke S. Simpson (ed.), *The Changing American Population* (New York, 1962), esp. p. 30; Richard M. Titmuss, *Income Distribution and Social Change* (London 1962); and Bruce M. Russett, Hayward R. Alker, Karl W. Deutsch, and Harold D. Lasswell, *World Handbook of Economic and Social Indicators* (New Haven, 1964), pp. 245, 247. On the negligible impact of taxation on inequality, see esp. Hayward Alker, *Mathematics and Politics*, pp. 45–50.

39 On the importance of educational background for occupational achievement, see Peter M. Blau and Otis Dudley Duncan, *The American Occupational Structure* (New York, 1967), pp. 402–3, 425; and Lipset and Bendix, pp. 99, 227. On the blacks compared to whites, see Blau and Duncan, pp. 207–41; and James S. Coleman *et al.*, *Equality of Educational Opportunity* (U.S. Department of Health, Education and Welfare, 1966), pp. 3, 5, 8–20, 120, 122. On difference between classes in educational opportunity, see Lipset and Bendix, pp. 94–6.

40 Key, *Public Opinion*, p. 319; and R. K. Kelsall, *Report on an Inquiry Into Applications for Admission to Universities* (London, 1957), p. 9.

41 Coleman *et al.*, *Equality of Educational Opportunity*, pp. 290–325. Also, Floud *et al.*, pp. 93–5, 107–8. For the significance of family background on blacks, see also Lee Rainwater and William L. Yancey (eds.), *The Moynihan Report and the Politics of Controversy* (Cambridge, Mass., 1967).

42 See Samuel Bowles and Henry M. Levin, 'The Determinants of Scholastic Achievement—An Appraisal of Some Recent Evidence', *Journal of Human Resources* (Winter 1968), esp. pp. 7–17; James S. Coleman, 'Equality of Educational Opportunity: Reply to Bowles and Levin', *Journal of Human Resources* (Spring 1968), pp. 237–46; Bowles and Levin, 'More on Multicollinearity and the Effectiveness of Schools', *Journal of Human Resources* (Summer 1968), pp. 393–400. Also see the special issue of the *Harvard Educational Review* (Winter 1968), which is devoted to the Coleman Report and other aspects of educational opportunity.

43 Coleman *et al.*, p. 299.

44 On differential turnout rates, see Orum, pp. 39–40; Lane, *Political Life*, pp. 50–1. On impact of 'socialization', see Chapter 3, note 54.

45 Blau and Duncan, pp. 103, 105, 424, 429; James N. Morgan, Martin H. David, Wilbur J. Cohen and Harvey E. Brazer, *Income and Welfare in the United States*, (New York, 1962), p. 337; Lipset and Bendix, pp. 13–28, 83–91, 108–9; Butler and Stokes, pp. 96–7; and Rose Knight, 'Changes in

the Occupational Structure of the Working Population', *Journal of the Royal Statistical Society*, pt. III (1967), pp. 408–22. On reduction of status discrepancies, see Lane, *Political Ideology*, p. 59; and Blondel, p. 43.

46 Arthur Kornhauser, *Mental Health of the Industrial Worker* (New York, 1965), pp. 260–2, 263, 267; Georges Friedmann, *The Anatomy of Work* (London, 1962); Robert Blauner, 'Work Satisfaction and Industrial Trends in Modern Society', in Walter Galenson and Seymour Martin Lipset (eds.), *Labor and Trade Unionism* (New York, 1960), pp. 339–60; and Almond and Verba, p. 345.

47 On differences in segregationist attitudes by age groups, see Paul B. Sheatsley, 'White Attitudes Toward the Negro', *Daedalus, The Negro American-2* (Winter 1966), pp. 226, 228; and Matthews and Prothro, pp. 349–50. On the trend toward acceptance of integration, see Sheatsley, pp. 219, 222, 233–7; Skolnick, pp. 181–201; and Herbert Hyman and Paul B. Sheatsley, 'Attitudes Toward Desegregation', *Scientific American* (July 1964) [more detail here on 1963 NORC survey discussed in Sheatsley]. For attitudes toward riots and demonstrations, see Skolnick, pp. 205–7.

48 Orum, pp. 38, 44; Janowitz and Marvick, *Competitive Pressure*, pp. 98–9; Lane, *Political Life*, p. 326; Milbrath, *Political Participation*, p. 121; John M. Foskett, 'Social Structure and Social Participation', *American Sociological Review* (August 1955), p. 434; and Matthews and Prothro, pp. 84, 87. But cf. Campbell *et al.*, *The Voter Decides*, p. 72. On integration, see Coleman *et al.*, pp. 302–12, 330–1; and Bowles and Levin, 'Determinants . . .', pp. 21–3.

49 On citizen duty, see Chapter 3, note 61. For group activity, see note 16 above.

50 On the effects of concrete discussion, see Chapter 4, note 45. For the differences between lower- and higher-status persons in contacting local and national politicians, see Lane, *Political Life*, p. 67. On the effects of interest, see Lazarsfeld *et al.*, pp. 47–8, 125.

51 Ralf Dahrendorf, *Class and Class Conflict in Industrial Society* (Stanford, 1959), pp. 64, 107, 241 ff.

52 For the pluralist theories, see Nelson Polsby, *Community Power and Political Theory*, pp. 122–32; Dahl, *Who Governs?*, esp. pp. 85, 230–3; 'Equality and Power', pp. 81–2. For supporting evidence from a study of Newcastle-under-Lyme, see Bealey *et al.*, pp. 386–400. A survey of 31 studies is in John Walton, 'Substance and Artifact: The Current Status of Research on Community Power Structure', *American Journal of Sociology* (Jan. 1966), esp. pp. 434–7. For other findings different from the pluralists', see Presthus, *Men at the Top*, esp. pp. 420–1, 430. On dispersed, *non-competitive* elites, see Wallace S. Sayre and Herbert Kaufman, *Governing New York City* (New York, 1960), pp. 719–20. Also, see Peter Bachrach and Morton S. Baratz, 'Decisions and Non-Decisions: An Analytical Framework', *American Political Science Review* (Sept. 1963), pp. 632–42.

53 Adolf Sturmthal, *Workers Councils* (Cambridge, Mass., 1964), pp. 82–3, 86–139, 168–79; Paul Blumberg, *Industrial Democracy* (London, 1968), esp. pp. 188–234; and Robert W. Cox *et al.*, 'Workers' Participation in Management', *International Institute for Labour Studies Bulletin* (Feb. 1967), pp. 64–125.

54 See Paul Blumberg, *Industrial Democracy*, pp. 70–138. Also, Rensis Likert, *New Patterns of Management* (New York, 1961); and Robert S. Blake, Jane S. Mouton, Louis Barnes and Larry Greiner, 'Breakthrough in Organizational Development', *Harvard Business Review* (Nov.–Dec. 1964), pp. 133–55. Cf. Peter F. Drucker, *The New Society: The Anatomy of the Industrial Order* (New York, 1949), esp. pp. 281–8.

Bibliography

Only works cited in the notes are listed here. Brackets which contain only a date of publication refer to the first edition of the later edition used in this study. Brackets following most of the social science studies contain the following information (where appropriate): location, or types of people, studied; date of study; organization that collected the data, and the principal type of data.

Abelson, Raziel. ' "Because I Want To" ', *Mind* (Oct. 1965), pp. 540–53.

Abrams, Mark. 'Press, Polls and Votes in Britain Since the 1955 General Elections', *Public Opinion Quarterly* (Winter 1957–8), pp. 543–7.

——'Social Trends and Electoral Behavior', *British Journal of Sociology* (Sept. 1962), pp. 228–42 [U.K.; 1959, 1960; surveys].

Adorno, Theodore N., Else Frenkel-Brunswik, Daniel J. Levinson and R. N. Sanford. *The Authoritarian Personality*, New York, 1950 [Calif., mostly middle-class sample; 1945–6].

Agger, Robert E. 'Independents and Party Identifiers: Characteristics and Behavior in 1952', in Eugene Burdick and Arthur J. Brodbeck (eds.), *American Voting Behavior*, Glencoe, Ill., 1959, pp. 308–29 [U.S.; 1952; SRC].

Agger, Robert E. and Vincent Ostrom. 'Political Participation in a Small Community', in Heinz Eulau *et al.* (eds.), *Political Behavior*, Glencoe, Ill., 1956, pp. 138–48 [Rural town of 3,000; survey].

Alexander, Herbert E. 'Broadcasting and Politics', in M. Kent Jennings and L. Harmon Zeigler (eds.), *The Electoral Process*, Englewood Cliffs. N.J., 1966, pp. 81–104.

Alford, Robert R. *Party and Society: The Anglo-American Democracies*, New York, 1963.

Alford, Robert R. and Eugene C. Lee. 'Voting Turnout in American Cities', *American Political Science Review* (Sept. 1968), pp. 796–813 [80% of U.S. cities over 25,000 as of 1962; agg.]

Alford, Robert R. and Harry M. Scoble. 'Sources of Local Political Involvement', *American Political Science Review* (Dec. 1968), pp. 1192–1206 [Four middle-sized Wisconsin cities; 1962; survey].

Alker, Hayward R., Jr. *Mathematics and Politics*, New York, 1965.

Almond, Gabriel A. and Sidney Verba. *The Civic Culture*, Princeton, 1963 [National samples in U.S., U.K., Italy, Germany, Mexico; sometime 1958–62; private polling organizations in each country].

Bibliography

American Political Science Association. *Report of the Commission on Presidential Campaign Debates*, Washington, 1964.

Amery, L. S. *Thoughts on the Constitution*, London, 1947.

Anderson, Dewey and Percey E. Davidson. *Ballots and the Democratic Class Struggle*, Stanford, 1943 [Santa Clara Co., Calif.; 1932, 1934; agg.].

Angell, Robert C. 'The Moral Integration of American Cities', *American Journal of Sociology* (July 1951), pt. 2 [Four medium-large Northern or border cities; 1940, 1946–7; surveys and agg.].

Argyle, Michael. *The Scientific Study of Social Behavior*, London, 1957.

Aristotle. *Rhetoric*, in *The Basic Works of Aristotle*, Richard McKeon (ed.), New York, 1941.

Arrow, Kenneth J. *Social Choice and Individual Values*, New York, 1963 [1951].

Auer, J. Jeffrey. 'The Counterfeit Debates', in Sidney Kraus (ed.), *The Great Debates*, Bloomington, Indiana, 1962, pp. 142–50.

Ayer, A. J. 'Man as a Subject for Science', in Peter Laslett and W. G. Runciman (eds.), *Philosophy, Politics and Society*, 3rd series, Oxford, 1967, pp. 6–24.

Bachrach, Peter and Morton S. Baratz. 'Decisions and Non-Decisions: An Analytical Framework', *American Political Science Review* (Sept. 1963), pp. 632–42.

Baier, Kurt. *The Moral Point of View: A Rational Basis of Ethics*, Ithaca, N.Y., 1958.

Bakke, E. Wight. *Citizens Without Work*, New Haven, 1940 [Unemployed families in New Haven; 1932–9; detailed interviews and survey].

Bales, Robert F., A. Paul Hare and Edgar F. Borgatta. 'Structure and Dynamics of Small Groups: A Review of Four Variables', in Joseph Gittler (ed.), *Review of Sociology: Analysis of a Decade*, New York, 1957, pp. 391–422.

Banfield, Edward C. 'In Defense of the American Party System', in Robert A. Goldwin (ed.), *Political Parties, U.S.A.*, Chicago, 1961, pp. 21–39.

Banfield, Edward C. and James Q. Wilson. *City Politics*, Cambridge, Mass., 1963.

Barker, Ernest. *Leonard Trelawny Hobhouse, 1864–1929*. From *Proceedings of the British Academy*, vol. xv, London, n.d. [Harvard College Library date: 1931].

——*Reflections on Government*, New York, 1942.

Barry, Brian. *Political Argument*, London, 1965.

——'The Public Interest', *Proceedings of the Aristotelian Society*, supplementary vol. xxxviii (1964), pp. 1–18.

Bauer, Raymond A. and Alice H. Bauer, 'America, Mass Society, and Mass Media', *Journal of Social Issues* (1960), pp. 3–66.

234

Bibliography

Bauer, Raymond A. and D. F. Cox. 'Rational Versus Emotional Communications: A New Approach', in Leon Arons and Mark A. May (eds.), *Television and Human Behavior*, New York, 1963, pp. 140–54.

Bauer, Raymond A., Ithiel de Sola Pool and Lewis Anthony Dexter. *American Business and Public Policy: The Politics of Foreign Trade*, New York, 1963.

Baumol, William J. *Economic Theory and Operations Analysis*, Englewood Cliffs, N.J., 1961.

Bay, Christian. 'Politics and Pseudopolitics: A Critical Evaluation of Some Behavioral Literature', *American Political Science Review* (March 1965), pp. 39–51.

——*The Structure of Freedom*, New York, 1965 [1958].

Bealey, Frank, J. Blondel and W. P. McCann. *Constituency Politics: A Study of Newcastle-under-Lyme*, London, 1965 [1959 General Election; post-election survey].

Beer, Samuel H. *British Politics in the Collectivist Age*, New York, 1965.

Benn, S. I. ' "Interests" in Politics', *Proceedings of the Aristotelian Society* (1959–60), pp. 123–40.

Benn, S. I. and R. S. Peters. *Social Principles and the Democratic State*, London, 1959.

Bennett, Jonathan. *Rationality: An Essay Toward Analysis*, London, 1964.

Benney, Mark P., A. P. Gray and R. H. Pear. *How People Vote: A Study of Electoral Behavior in Greenwich*, London, 1956 [1950 General Election; survey, three waves].

Bentham, Jeremy. *Theory of Legislation*, trans. from the French of E. Dumont by R. Hildreth, Boston, 1840.

Berelson, Bernard. 'Communications and Public Opinion', in Wilbur Schramm (ed.), *Mass Communications*, Urbana, Ill., 1960, pp. 527–43 [1949].

——'Democratic Theory and Public Opinion', *Public Opinion Quarterly* (Fall 1952), pp. 313–30.

Berelson, Bernard, Paul F. Lazarsfeld and William N. McPhee. *Voting: A Study of Opinion Formation in a Presidential Campaign*, Chicago 1954 [Elmira, N.Y.; 1948; four waves of panel interviews; includes, appendix summarizing other panel studies].

Berg, Elias. *Democracy and the Majority Principle*, Göteborg, Sweden, 1965.

Berlin, Isaiah. 'Equality', *Proceedings of the Aristotelian Society* (1955–6), pp. 301–26.

Berns, Walter. 'Voting Studies', in Herbert J. Storing (ed.), *Essays on the Scientific Study of Politics*, New York, 1962, pp. 3–62.

Black, Duncan. *The Theory of Committees and Elections*, Cambridge, Mass., 1958.

Bibliography

Blake, Robert S., Jane S. Mouton, Louis Barnes and Larry E. Greiner. 'Breakthrough in Organizational Development', *Harvard Business Review* (Nov.–Dec. 1964), pp. 133–55.

Blalock, Hubert, Jr. *Causal Inferences in Non-Experimental Research*, Chapel Hill, 1961.

Blau, Peter M. and Otis Dudley Duncan. *The American Occupational Structure*, New York, 1967 [U.S.; 1962; census survey].

Blauner, Robert. 'Work Satisfaction and Industrial Trends in Modern Society', in Walter Galenson and Seymour Martin Lipset (eds.), *Labor and Trade Unionism: An Interdisciplinary Reader*, New York, 1960, pp. 339–60.

Bloc, Jeanne H., Norma Hann and M. Brewster Smith. 'Activism and Apathy in Contemporary Adolescents', in J. F. Adams (ed.), *Contributions to the Understanding of Adolescence*, Boston, 1967.

Blondel, Jean. *Voters, Parties, and Leaders: The Social Fabric of British Politics*, Baltimore, 1963.

Blumberg, Paul. *Industrial Democracy: The Sociology of Participation*, London, 1968.

Blumler, Jay G. and Denis McQuail. *Television in Politics: Its Uses and Influence*, Chicago, 1969 [Leeds West and Pudsey; June, September, October 1964; panel.].

Bogart, Leo. *The Age of Television*, New York, 1956.

Bowles, Samuel S. and Henry M. Levin. 'The Determinants of Scholastic Achievement—An Appraisal of Some Recent Evidence', *Journal of Human Resources* (Winter 1968), pp. 3–24.

——'More on Multicollinearity and the Effectiveness of Schools', *Journal of Human Resources* (Summer 1968), pp. 393–400.

Braybrooke, David and Charles E. Lindblom. *Strategy of Decision: Policy Evaluation as a Social Process*, New York, 1963.

Brecht, Arnold. *Political Theory*, Princeton, 1959.

Brodbeck, May. 'The Role of Small Groups in Mediating the Effects of Propaganda', *Journal of Abnormal and Social Psychology* (March 1956), pp. 166–70.

Brown, Roger. *Words and Things*, Glencoe, Ill., 1958.

Buchanan, James M. and Gordon Tullock. *The Calculus of Consent: Logical Foundations of Constitutional Democracy*, Ann Arbor, 1965[1962].

Buchanan, William. 'An Inquiry Into Purposive Voting', *Journal of Politics* (May 1956), pp. 281–96 [278 persons in Southern county seat; non-election year; survey].

Budge, Ian and Derek W. Urwin. *Scottish Political Behavior: A Case Study in British Homogeneity*, London, 1966 [Four Glasgow parliamentary constituencies; 1964–5; survey; also U.K., Almond and Verba data, 1959, survey].

Bibliography

Burns, C. Delisle. *Democracy*, London, 1935.

Butler, David E. *The Electoral System in Britain, 1918–1951*, Oxford, 1953 [agg.].

Butler, David E. and Anthony King. *The British General Election of 1964*, London, 1965 [agg. and private polls].

——*The British General Election of 1966*, London, 1966 [agg. and polls].

Butler, David E. and Richard Rose. *The British General Election of 1959*, London, 1960 [agg. and polls].

Butler, David E. and Donald Stokes. *Political Change in Britain: Forces Shaping Electoral Choice*, London, 1969 [U.K.; summer 1963, fall 1964, spring 1966; panel].

Campbell, Angus. 'Civil Rights and the Vote for the President', *Psychology Today* (Feb. 1968), pp. 26–31 ff. [U.S.; 1952–64; SRC].

——'Has Television Reshaped Politics?' *Columbia Journalism Review* (Fall 1962), pp. 10–13 [U.S.; 1952, 1956, 1960; SRC panels and agg.].

——'The Passive Citizen', *Acta Sociologica* (1962), vol. VI, pp. 9–21.

——Review of *The Responsible Electorate*, by V. O. Key, Jr., *American Political Science Review* (Dec. 1966), pp. 1007–8.

——'Surge and Decline: A Study of Electoral Change', *Public Opinion Quarterly* (Fall 1960), pp. 397–418 [U.S.; 1952, 1956, 1958; SRC].

Campbell, Angus, Philip E. Converse, Warren E. Miller and Donald E. Stokes. *The American Voter*, New York, 1960 [1948, 1952, 1956; SRC].

——*Elections and the Political Order*, New York, 1966 [U.S.; 1948–60 Pres. and mid-term; SRC].

Campbell, Angus and Homer C. Cooper. *Group Differences in Attitudes and Votes*, Ann Arbor, 1956 [U.S.; 1954 mid-term; SRC pre-election].

Campbell, Angus, Gerald Gurin and Warren E. Miller. *The Voter Decides*, Evanston, Ill., 1954 [U.S.; 1952; SRC].

Campbell, Angus and Robert L. Kahn. *The People Elect a President*, Ann Arbor, 1952 [U.S.; 1948; SRC].

Campbell, Angus and Henry Valen. 'Party Identification in Norway and the United States', *Public Opinion Quarterly* (Winter 1961), pp. 505–25.

Carnegie Commission on Educational Television. *Public Television: A Program for Action*, New York, 1967.

Carroll, John B. *Language and Thought*, Englewood Cliffs, N.J., 1964.

Cassinelli, C. W. *The Politics of Freedom: An Analysis of the Modern Democratic State*, Seattle, 1961.

Christie, Richard and Peggy Cook. 'A Guide to Published Literature Relating to the Authoritarian Personality Through 1956', *Journal of Psychology* (April 1958), pp. 171–99.

Christie, Richard and Marie Jahoda (eds.). *Studies in the Scope and Methods of the Authoritarian Personality*, Glencoe, Ill., 1954.

Christophersen, Jens A. *The Meaning of 'Democracy' as Used in European Ideologies from the French to the Russian Revolution*, Oslo, 1966.

Bibliography

Churchman, C. West. *Prediction and Optimal Decision: Philosophical Issues of a Science of Values*, Englewood Cliffs, N.J., 1961.

Cole, G. D. H. *The Future of Local Government*, London, 1921.

——*Guild Socialism Re-stated*, London, 1920.

——*Social Theory*, London, 1930 [1920].

Cole, G. D. H. and Margaret Cole. *A Guide to Modern Politics*, New York, 1934.

Cole, G. D. H. and Raymond Postgate. *The Common People 1746–1946*, London, 1949 [1938].

Coleman, James S. *Community Conflict*, Glencoe, Ill., 1957.

——'Community Disorganization', in Robert Merton and Robert Nisbet (eds.), *Contemporary Social Problems*, New York, 1961, pp. 553–604.

——'Equality of Educational Opportunity: Reply to Bowles and Levin', *Journal of Human Resources* (Spring 1968), pp. 237–46.

Coleman, James S. *et al. Equality of Educational Opportunity*, U.S. Department of Health, Education and Welfare, 1966 [U.S. public schools; 1965; Educational Testing Service survey].

Collingwood, R. G. *An Essay on Metaphysics*, Oxford, 1948 [1940].

——*The Idea of History*, Oxford, 1946.

Committee on Political Parties of the American Political Science Association. *Toward a More Responsible Two-Party System*, New York, 1950.

Converse, Philip E. 'Information Flow and the Stability of Partisan Attitudes', *Public Opinion Quarterly* (Winter 1962), 578–99 [U.S.; 1960; SRC].

——'The Nature of Belief Systems in Mass Publics', in David E. Apter (ed.), *Ideology and Discontent*, New York, 1964, pp. 206–61 [U.S.; 1956, 1960; SRC].

——'Politicization of the Electorate in France and the United States', *Public Opinion Quarterly* (Spring 1962), pp. 1–23.

——'Religion and Politics: The 1960 Election', in Angus Campbell *et al., Elections and the Political Order*, New York, 1966, pp. 96–124 [U.S.; 1956, 1958, 1960; SRC].

——Review of *The Responsible Electorate*, by V. O. Key, Jr., *Political Science Quarterly* (Dec. 1966), pp. 628–33.

Converse, Philip E., Aage R. Clausen and Warren E. Miller. 'Electoral Myth and Reality: The 1964 Election', *American Political Science Review* (June 1965), pp. 321–36 [U.S.; 1964; SRC].

Cooley, Charles H. *Sociological Theory and Social Research*, New York, 1930.

Coons, John E. (ed.). *Freedom and Responsibility in Broadcasting*, Evanston, Ill., 1961.

Cork, Jim. 'John Dewey and Karl Marx', in Sidney Hook (ed.), *John Dewey: Philosopher of Science and Freedom*, New York, 1950, pp. 331–50.

Cox, Robert W. *et al.* 'Workers' Partcipation in Management; Status of a Research Project', *International Institute for Labour Studies Bulletin* (Feb. 1967), pp. 64–125.

Crick, Bernard. *The American Science of Politics*, London, 1959.

Croly, Herbert. *Progressive Democracy*, New York, 1941.

——*The Promise of American Life*, Cambridge, Mass., 1965 [1909].

Cummings, Milton C., Jr. *Congressmen and the Electorate: Elections for the U.S. House and the President, 1920–1964*, New York, 1966 [agg.].

Dahl, Robert A. 'The Behavioral Approach in Political Science: Epitaph for a Monument to a Successful Protest', *American Political Science Review* (Dec. 1961), pp. 763–72.

——'The City in the Future of Democracy', *American Political Science Review* (Dec. 1967), pp. 958–70.

——'Equality and Power in American Society', in William V. D'Antonio and Howard J. Ehrlich, *Power and Democracy in America*, Notre Dame, 1961, pp. 73–89.

——'The Evaluation of Political Systems', in I. Pool (ed.), *Contemporary Political Science*, New York, 1967. pp. 166–81.

——'Further Reflections on "The Elitist Theory of Democracy"', *American Political Science Review* (June 1966), pp. 296–305.

——*Pluralist Democracy in the United States: Conflict and Consent*, Chicago, 1967.

——*A Preface to Democratic Theory*, Chicago, 1963 [1956].

——*Who Governs? Democracy and Power in an American City*, New Haven, 1961 [New Haven leaders, sub-leaders and voters; 1957–8, 1959; 3 Yale sample surveys].

Dahl, Robert A. and Edward R. Tufte. *Size and Democracy*, Stanford, forthcoming.

Dahrendorf, Ralf. *Class and Class Conflict in Industrial Society*, Stanford, 1959.

Daniel, W. W. *Racial Discrimination in England*, Harmondsworth, Middlesex, 1968. [Colored and white immigrants; whites in position to discriminate in six regions; 1966–7; Political and Economic Planning Survey and Report].

Daudt, Harry. *Floating Voters and the Floating Vote: A Critical Analysis of American and English Election Studies*, Leiden, Netherlands, 1961.

Davidson, Donald. 'Actions, Reasons and Causes', *Journal of Philosophy* (7 Nov. 1963), pp. 685–700.

Davidson, W. Phillips. 'On the Effects of Communication', *Public Opinion Quarterly* (Fall 1959), pp. 343–60.

Davis, Lane. 'The Cost of Realism: Contemporary Restatements of Democracy', *Western Political Quarterly* (March 1964), pp. 37–46.

Deakin, Nicholas (ed.). *Colour and the British Electorate: 1964, Six Case Studies*, London, 1965.

Deane, Herbert A. *The Political Ideas of Harold J. Laski*, New York, 1955.

Dewey, John. 'Creative Democracy—The Task Before Us', in Sidney Ratner (ed.), *The Philosopher of the Common Man*. New York, 1940, pp. 220–8.

——*Democracy and Education*, New York, 1961 [1916].

——*The Ethics of Democracy*, Ann Arbor, 1888.

——*Experience and Education*, New York, 1938.

——*Freedom and Culture*, New York, 1939.

——*How We Think*, New York, 1933.

——*Human Nature and Conduct*, New York, 1922.

——*I Believe*, Clifton Fadiman (ed.), New York, 1939.

——*Individualism Old and New*, New York, 1962 [1929].

——*Liberalism and Social Action*, New York, 1935.

——*The Living Thoughts of Thomas Jefferson*, New York, 1940.

——'Practical Democracy', *The New Republic* (2 Dec. 1925), pp. 52–4.

——*Problems of Men*, New York, 1946.

——*The Public and Its Problems*, Denver, 1927.

——'Public Opinion', *The New Republic* (3 May 1922), pp. 286–8.

——*The Quest for Certainty*, New York, 1960 [1929].

——*Reconstruction in Philosophy*, Boston, 1957 [1920].

——*Logic : The Theory of Inquiry*, New York, 1938.

Dewey, John and James H. Tufts. *Ethics*, New York, 1932 [1908].

Diesing, Paul. *Reason in Society*, Urbana, Ill., 1962.

Dilthey, Wilhelm. *Pattern and Meaning in History*: *Thoughts on History and Society*, H. P. Rickman (ed.), New York, 1962.

Downs, Anthony. *An Economic Theory of Democracy*, New York, 1957.

Dray, William. 'The Historical Explanation of Actions Reconsidered', in Sidney Hook (ed.), *Philosophy and History*, New York, 1963, pp. 105–35.

——*Laws and Explanation in History*, Oxford, 1957.

——*Philosophy of History*, Englewood Cliffs, N.J., 1964.

Drucker, Peter F. *The New Society : The Anatomy of the Industrial Order*, New York, 1949.

Duncan, Graeme, and Steven Lukes. 'The New Democracy', *Political Studies* (June 1963), pp. 156–77.

Duncan, Otis Dudley. 'A Socioeconomic Index for All Occupations', in Albert J. Reiss, Jr., *Occupations and Social Status*, New York, 1961, pp. 109–38.

Durant, Henry. 'Voting Behavior in Britain, 1945–1964', in Richard Rose (ed.), *Studies in British Politics*, New York, 1966, pp. 122–8 [Gallup].

Easton, David. 'The Current Meaning of "Behavioralism" in Political Science', in James C. Charlesworth (ed.), *The Limits of Behavioralism in Political Science*, American Academy of Political and Social Science, Oct. 1962, pp. 1–25.

——*The Political System: An Inquiry Into the State of Political Science*, New York, 1953.

Eckstein, Harry. *Authority Relations and Governmental Performance: A Theoretical Framework*, Princeton, 1968, mimeo.

——*Pressure Group Politics: The Case of the British Medical Association*, Stanford, 1960.

——*A Theory of Stable Democracy*, Princeton, 1961.

Edel, Abraham. *Method in Ethical Theory*, London, 1963.

Edelman, Murray. *The Symbolic Uses of Politics*, Urbana, Ill., 1964.

Edwards, Paul. *The Logic of Moral Discourse*, Glencoe, Ill., 1955.

Eldersveld, Samuel J. 'American Interest Groups: A Survey of Research and Some Implications for Theory and Method', in Henry W. Ehrmann (ed.), *Interest Groups on Four Continents*, Pittsburgh, 1958, pp. 173–96.

——'Experimental Techniques and Voting Behavior', *American Political Science Review* (March 1956), pp. 154–65 [Ann Arbor; 1954 city election; student-organized and conducted interviews].

——'The Independent Vote: Measurement, Characteristics, and Implications for Party Strategy', *American Political Science Review* (Sept. 1952), pp. 732–53 [U.S., Mich., Washtenaw Co.; 1948, 1949, 1950; SRC, post-election, agg., survey].

——*Political Parties: A Behavioral Analysis*, Chicago, 1964 [Leaders, precinct leaders and cross-section in Wayne Co., Mich.: 1956 Pres.; post-election interviews except precinct which were pre-election].

Eldersveld, Samuel J. and Richard W. Dodge. 'Personal Contact or Mail Propaganda? An Experiment in Voting Turnout and Attitude Change', in Daniel Katz *et al.* (eds.), *Public Opinion and Propaganda*, New York, 1954, pp. 532–42 [Ann Arbor, Mich.; 1953 City Charter election; survey of two experimental samples and control sample].

Ellsworth, John W. 'Rationality and Campaigning: A Content Analysis of the 1960 Presidential Campaign Debates', *Western Political Quarterly* (Dec. 1965), pp. 794–802.

Erbe, William. 'Social Involvement and Political Activity: A Replication and Elaboration', *American Sociological Review* (April 1964), pp. 198–215 [Three small Iowa towns; survey].

Erskine, Hazel Gaudet. 'The Polls: The Informed Public', *Public Opinion Quarterly* (Winter 1962), pp. 668–77 [U.S.; 1947–62; AIPO, NORC, Roper].

Eulau, Heinz (ed.), *Behavioralism in Political Science*, New York, 1969.

——*Class and Party in the Eisenhower Years: Class Roles and Perspectives in the 1952 and 1956 Elections*, New York, 1962 [U.S.; SRC].

Farrar, Donald E. and Robert R. Glauber. 'Multicollinearity in Regression Analysis: The Problem Revisited', *Review of Economics and Statistics* (Feb. 1967), pp. 92–107.

Feigl, Herbert. 'Validation and Vindication: An Analysis of the Nature and the Limits of Ethical Arguments', in W. Sellars and J. Hospers, *Readings in Ethical Theory*, New York, 1952, pp. 667–80.

Fein, Rashi, 'An Economic and Social Profile of the Negro American', *Daedalus, The Negro American* (Fall 1965), pp. 815–45 [Mainly govt. census].

Fesler, James W. 'Approaches to the Understanding of Decentralization', *Journal of Politics* (August 1965), pp. 536–66.

Fishman, Jacob R. and Frederic Solomon. 'Youth and Social Action: An Introduction', *Journal of Social Issues* (Oct. 1964), pp. 1–27.

Flathman, Richard E. *The Public Interest: An Essay Concerning the Normative Discourse of Politics*, New York, 1966.

Fletcher, Peter. 'The Results Analyzed', in L. J. Sharpe (ed.), *Voting in Cities: The 1964 Borough Elections*, London, 1967, pp. 290–321.

Floud, Jean, A. H. Halsey and F. M. Martin (eds.), *Social Class and Educational Opportunity*, London, 1956 [Southwest section of Hertfordshire and Middlesbrough, Yorkshire; 1952–3; survey].

Foot, Philippa (ed.). *Theories of Ethics*, Oxford, 1967.

Forbes, Hugh D. and Edward R. Tufte. 'A Note of Caution in Causal Modelling', *American Political Science Review* (Dec. 1968), pp. 1258–64.

Foskett, John M. 'Social Structure and Social Participation', *American Sociological Review* (Aug. 1955), pp. 431–38 [Two small Oregon towns; survey].

Fourest, Michel. *Les Théories du Professeur Harold J. Laski: Le declin de l'état moniste et l'avènement de l'état pluraliste*, Paris, 1943.

Frankena, William K. 'Some Aspects of Language', and " 'Cognitive" and "Noncognitive" ', in Paul Henle (ed.), *Language, Thought and Culture*, Ann Arbor, 1958, pp. 121–72.

Friedmann, Georges. *The Anatomy of Work: Labor, Leisure and the Implications of Automation*, trans. Wyatt Rawson, London, 1962.

Friedrich, Carl J. *Constitutional Government and Democracy*, Boston, 1950 [1937].

——*Demokratie als Herrschafts- und Lebensform*, Heidelberg, 1959.

——*Man and His Government*, New York, 1963.

——*The New Image of the Common Man*, Boston, 1950 [1942].

——*The Philosophy of Law in Historical Perspective*, Chicago, 1963 [1958].

——(ed.) *The Public Interest, Nomos V*, New York, 1962.

——(ed.) *Rational Decision, Nomos VII*, New York, 1964.

——*Transcendent Justice: The Religious Dimension of Constitutionalism*, Durham, N.C., 1964.

Froman, Lewis A., Jr. 'A Realistic Approach to Campaign Strategies and Tactics', in M. Kent Jennings and L. Harmon Zeigler (eds.), *The Electoral Process*, Englewood Cliffs, N.J., 1966, pp. 1–20.

Bibliography

Gallie, W. B. 'The Idea of Practice', *Proceedings of the Aristotelian Society* (1967–8), pp. 63–86.

Germino, Dante. *Beyond Ideology: The Revival of Political Theory*, New York, 1967.

Gibson, Quentin. *The Logic of Social Enquiry*, London, 1960.

Glantz, Oscar. 'Unitary Political Behavior and Differential Political Motivation', *Western Political Quarterly* (Dec. 1957), pp. 833–46 [Philadelphia, 1952–7; survey, disproportionately stratified sample].

Glaser, William A. 'Television and Voting Turnout', *Public Opinion Quarterly* (Spring 1965), pp. 71–86 [U.S.; 1956, 1960; SRC, AIPO].

Glazer, Nathan, and Daniel Patrick Moynihan. *Beyond the Melting Pot*, Cambridge, Mass., 1963.

Goldberg, Arthur S. 'Discerning a Causal Pattern Among Data on Voting Behavior', *American Political Science Review* (Dec. 1966), pp. 913–22.

——'Social Determinism and Rationality as Bases of Party Identification', *American Political Science Review* (March 1969), pp. 5–25.

Gosnell, Harold F. *Democracy—The Threshold of Freedom*, New York, 1948.

Grazia, Alfred de. 'The Limits of External Leadership over a Minority Electorate', *Public Opinion Quarterly* (Spring 1956), pp. 113–28 [Large U.S. city; 1955 mayoralty; private poll org.].

——*Public and Republic*, New York, 1951.

——*The Western Public, 1952 and Beyond*, Stanford, 1954 [11 Western states; Pres.; SRC].

Greenstein, Fred I. 'Personality and Political Socialization: The Theories of Authoritarian and Democratic Character', *The Annals of the American Academy of Political and Social Science* (Sept. 1965), pp. 81–95.

Greenstein, Fred I. and Raymond E. Wolfinger. 'The Suburbs and Shifting Party Loyalties', *Public Opinion Quarterly* (Winter 1958–9), pp. 473–82 [U.S.; 1952; SRC].

Hallowell, John H. *The Moral Foundation of Democracy*, Chicago, 1954.

Hampshire, Stuart. *Thought and Action*, London, 1960.

Hanson, Norwood Russell. *Patterns of Discovery: An Inquiry into the Conceptual Foundations of Science*, Cambridge, England, 1965 [1958].

Hare, R. M. *Freedom and Reason*, Oxford, 1963.

——*The Language of Morals*, Oxford, 1952.

Harris, Louis. *Is There a Republican Majority?*, New York, 1954 [U.S.; 1952; seven surveys by Roper organization].

Hart, H. L. A. 'Legal and Moral Obligation', in Abraham I. Melden (ed.), *Essays in Moral Philosophy*, Seattle, 1958, pp. 82–107.

Hastings, Philip K. 'The Voter and the Non-Voter', *American Journal of Sociology* (Nov. 1956), pp. 302–7 [Pittsfield, Mass.; mainly 1954; pre- and post-election survey].

243

Hempel, Carl G. *Aspects of Scientific Explanation*, New York, 1965.
——'The Function of General Laws in History', *Journal of Philosophy* (15 Jan. 1942), pp. 35–48.
Hennessy, Bernard. 'Politicals and Apoliticals: Some Measurements of Personality Traits', *Midwest Journal of Political Science* (Nov. 1959), pp. 336–55 [138 Tucson, Ariz. adults; questionnaire and open-ended interviews].
Herring, E. Pendleton. *The Politics of Democracy*, New York, 1940.
Hobhouse, Leonard T. *Democracy and Reaction*, New York, 1905.
——*The Elements of Social Justice*, London, 1922.
——*Liberalism*, New York, 1964 [1911].
——*The Metaphysical Theory of the State: A Criticism*, London, 1918.
——*Morals in Evolution: A Study in Comparative Ethics*, London, 1929 [1906].
——'The Philosophy of Development', in *Sociology and Philosophy: A Centenary Collection of Essays and Articles*, Cambridge, Mass., 1966, pp. 295–331 [1924].
——*The Rational Good: A Study in the Logic of Practice*, London, 1947 [1921].
——*Social Development: Its Nature and Conditions*, New York, 1924.
——*Social Evolution and Political Theory*, New York, 1928 [1911].
Hoggart, Richard. *The Uses of Literacy*, Harmondsworth, 1958.
Holsti, Ole R. 'Content Analysis', in Gardner Lindzey and Elliot Aronson (eds.), *The Handbook of Social Psychology*, 2nd edition, Reading, Mass., 1968, vol. II, pp. 596–692.
Hook, Sidney. *John Dewey: An Intellectual Portrait*, New York, 1939.
——'The Philosophical Presuppositions of Democracy', *Ethics* (April 1942), pp. 275–96.
——*Reason, Social Myths and Democracy*, New York, 1966 [1940].
Hovland, Carl I., 'Reconciling Conflicting Results Derived from Experimental and Survey Studies of Attitude Change', *American Psychologist* (Jan. 1959), pp. 8–17.
Hovland, Carl I., Irving L. Janis and Harold H. Kelley. *Communication and Persuasion*, New Haven, 1953 [lab.].
Hovland, Carl I. and Walter Weiss. 'The Influence of Source Credibility and Communication Effectiveness', *Public Opinion Quarterly* (Winter 1951–2), pp. 635–50 [lab.].
Hudson, Jay William. *Why Democracy: A Study in the Philosophy of the State*, New York, 1936.
Hume, David. *A Treatise of Human Nature*, L. A. Selby–Bigge (ed.), Oxford, 1960 [1888].
Hyman, Herbert H. *Political Socialization: A Study in the Psychology of Political Behavior*, Glencoe, Ill., 1959.

Bibliography

——'Reference Groups', in David L. Sills (ed.), *International Encyclopedia of the Social Sciences*, New York, 1968, pp. 353–61.

Hyman, Herbert H. and Paul B. Sheatsley. 'Attitudes Toward Desegregation', *Scientific American* (July 1964), pp. 16–23 [U.S.; 1963; NORC].

——'The Political Appeal of President Eisenhower', *Public Opinion Quarterly* (Winter 1953–4), pp. 443–60 [U.S.; also N.Y., Ill., Calif.; 1947–8; NORC].

——'Some Reasons Why Information Campaigns Fail', *Public Opinion Quarterly* (Fall 1947), pp. 412–23 [U.S.; 1947; NORC].

Hyman, Sidney. 'What Trendex for Lincoln?' *New York Times Magazine* (17 Jan. 1960), pp. 26 ff.

Janowitz, Morris and Dwaine Marvick' *Competitive Pressure and Democratic Consent*, Chicago, 1964 [1956] [U.S.; 1952; SRC].

Janowitz, Morris and David R. Segal. 'Social Cleavage and Party Affiliation: Germany, Great Britain and the United States', *American Journal of Sociology* (May 1967), pp. 601–18 [U.K., 1964; four pre-election surveys; U.S., 1961–4, NORC].

Jones, W. H. Morris. 'In Defence of Political Apathy', *Political Studies* (Feb. 1954), pp. 25–37.

Jouvenal, Bertrand de. 'Political Science and Prevision', *American Political Science Review* (March 1965), pp. 29–38.

Kalleberg, Arthur L. 'Concept Formation in Normative and Empirical Studies: Toward Reconciliation in Political Theory', *American Political Science Review* (March 1969), pp. 26–39.

Kant, Immanuel. *Critique of Pure Reason*, Norman Kemp Smith (trans. and ed.), London, 1952.

Kariel, Henry S. *The Decline of American Pluralism*, Stanford, 1961.

——*The Promise of Politics*, Englewood Cliffs, N.J., 1966.

Katz, Elihu. 'The Two-Step Flow of Communication: An Up-to-Date Report on an Hypothesis', *Public Opinion Quarterly* (Spring 1957), pp. 61–78.

Katz, Elihu and Jacob J. Feldman. 'The Debates in Light of Research: A Survey of Surveys', in Sidney Kraus (ed.), *The Great Debates*. Bloomington, Ind., 1962), pp. 173–223.

Katz, Elihu and Paul F. Lazarsfeld. *Personal Influence: The Part Played by People in the Flow of Mass Communications*, Glencoe, Ill., 1955 [Decatur, Ill.: two waves of panel interviews and follow-up interview of influentials; includes survey of other relevant literature].

Katz, Joseph. 'The Student Activists: Rights, Needs and the Powers of Undergraduates', report prepared for the U.S. Office of Education, Stanford, 1967.

Keech, William R. *The Impact of Negro Voting: The Role of the Vote in the Quest for Equality*, Chicago, 1968 [Durham, N.C.; Tuskegee, Ala.].

Kelley, Harold H. 'Salience of Membership and Resistance to Change of Group-Anchored Attitudes', *Human Relations* (Aug. 1955), pp. 275–89 [lab.].

Kelley, Harold H. and John W. Thibaut. 'Group Problem Solving', in Gardiner Lindzey and Elliott Aronson (eds.), *The Handbook of Social Psychology*, 2nd edition, Reading, Mass., 1969, vol. IV, pp. 1–101.

Kelley, Stanley, Jr., 'Campaign Debates: Some Facts and Issues', *Public Opinion Quarterly* (Fall 1962), pp. 351–66.

——*Political Campaigning; Problems in Creating an Informed Electorate*, Washington, 1960.

Kelley, Stanley, Jr., Richard E. Ayres and William G. Bowen. 'Registration and Voting: Putting First Things First', *American Political Science Review* (June 1967), pp. 359–77 [104 U.S. cities over 100,000 population; 1960; agg.].

Kelman, Herbert C. and Carl I. Hovland. 'Reinstatement of the Communicator in Delayed Measurement of Opinion Change', *Journal of Abnormal and Social Psychology* (July 1953), pp. 327–35 [lab.].

Kelsall, R. K. *Report on an Inquiry into Applications for Admission to Universities*, London, 1957.

Kelsen, Hans. 'Absolutism and Relativism in Philosophy and Politics', *American Political Science Review* (Oct. 1948), pp. 906–14.

——'Foundations of Democracy', *Ethics* (Oct. 1955), pt. II, pp. 1–101.

——*General Theory of Law and State*, Cambridge, Mass., 1945.

——*Vom Wesen und Wert der Demokratie*, Tübingen, 1929.

Kendall, Willmoore and George W. Carey. 'The "Intensity" Problem and Democratic Theory', *American Political Science Review* (March 1968), pp. 5–24.

Key, V. O., Jr. *Politics, Parties and Pressure Groups*, 3rd edition, New York, 1958; 5th edition, New York, 1964 [1942].

——*Public Opinion and American Democracy*, New York, 1961.

——'Public Opinion and the Decay of Democracy', *Virginia Quarterly Review* (Autumn 1961), pp. 481–94.

——*The Responsible Electorate: Rationality in Presidential Voting, 1936–1960*, Cambridge, Mass., 1966 [U.S.; AIPO].

——'Secular Realignment and the Party System', *Journal of Politics* (May 1959), pp. 198–210.

——*Southern Politics in State and Nation*, New York, 1949.

——'A Theory of Critical Elections', *Journal of Politics* (Feb. 1955), pp. 3–18.

Key, V. O., Jr. and Frank Munger. 'Social Determinism and Electoral Decision: The Case of Indiana', in Eugene Burdick and Arthur J. Brodbeck (eds.), *American Voting Behavior*, Glencoe, Ill., 1959, pp. 281–99 [Indiana counties; 1868, 1900, 1920–52; Pres.; agg.].

Kitt, Alice S. and David B. Gleicher. 'Determinants of Voting Behavior', *Public Opinion Quarterly* (Fall 1950), pp. 393–412 [Elmira, N.Y.; 1948 Pres.; panel].

Klapper, Joseph T. *The Effects of Mass Communication*, Glencoe, Ill., 1960.

Knight, Rose. 'Changes in the Occupational Structure of the Working Population', *Journal of the Royal Statistical Society*, pt. III (1967), pp. 408–22 [U.K.; 1951, 1961; census].

Knupfer, Genevieve. 'Portrait of the Underdog', *Public Opinion Quarterly* (Spring 1947), pp. 103–14.

Konvitz, Milton R. 'Dewey's Revision of Jefferson', in Sidney Hook (ed.), *John Dewey: Philosopher of Science and Freedom*, New York, 1950, pp. 164–76.

Kornhauser, Arthur. *Mental Health of the Industrial Worker: A Detroit Study*, New York, 1965 [407 workers in 13 auto plants; 1953–4; open-end interviews].

——'Toward an Assessment of the Mental Health of Factory Workers: A Detroit Study', *Human Organization* (Spring 1962), pp. 43–6 [13 auto mfg. plants in Detroit; survey].

Kornhauser, Arthur, Harold L. Sheppard and Albert J. Mayer. *When Labor Votes: A Study of Auto Workers*, New York, 1956 [Detroit auto workers; 1952 Pres.; pre- and post-election surveys].

Kornhauser, William. *The Politics of Mass Society*, Glencoe, Ill., 1959.

Koyré, Alexandre. *Newtonian Studies*, Cambridge, Mass., 1965.

Kuhn, Thomas S. *The Structure of Scientific Revolutions*, Chicago, 1964 [1962].

Kuznets, Simon. 'Income Distribution and Changes in Consumption', in Hoke S. Simpson (ed.), *The Changing American Population*, New York, 1962, pp. 21–58.

Lane, Robert E. *Political Ideology: Why the American Common Man Believes What He Does*, New York, 1962 [15 Eastern urban working-class men randomly selected in one housing unit; in-depth open-ended interviews].

——*Political Life: Why and How People Get Involved in Politics*, New York, 1965 [1959].

——'Political Personality and Electoral Choice', *American Political Science Review* (March 1955), pp. 173–90 [U.S.; 1952; SRC post-election].

Lane, Robert E. and David O. Sears. *Public Opinion*, Englewood Cliffs, N.J., 1964.

Lang, Kurt and Gladys Engel Lang. 'The Inferential Structure of Political Communications: A Study in Unwitting Bias', *Public Opinion Quarterly* (Summer 1955), pp. 168–83 [monitors' reports of 1952 televised party conventions].

——'The Mass Media and Voting', in Eugene Burdick and Arthur J. Brodbeck (eds.), *American Voting Behavior*, Glencoe, Ill., 1959, pp. 217–35.

——'Ordeal by Debate: Viewer Reaction', *Public Opinion Quarterly* (Summer 1961), pp. 277–88 [95 New York City TV viewers; 1960; three waves of non-random interviews (24 self-interviews)].

——*Politics and Television*, Chicago, 1968.

——'The Television Personality in Politics: Some Considerations', *Public Opinion Quarterly* (Spring 1956), pp. 103–12 [85 viewers of nominating conventions south-side of Chicago; 1952; intensive interviews].

——'The Unique Perspective of Television and Its Effect: A Pilot Study', *American Sociological Review* (Feb. 1953), pp. 3–12 [31 participant-observers; MacArthur Day, Chicago, 1951; reports and TV content analysis].

Langer, Susanne. *Philosophy in a New Key*, New York, 1942.

Laski, Harold J. *The American Democracy*, New York, 1948.

——*The American Presidency*, London, 1940.

——*Authority in the Modern State*, New Haven, 1919.

——*Communism*, New York, 1927.

——*The Dangers of Obedience and Other Essays*, New York, 1930.

——*The Decline of Liberalism*, Oxford, 1940.

——'Democracy', *Encyclopedia of Social Sciences*, New York, 1930, pp. 76–85.

——*Democracy in Crisis*, Chapel Hill, N.C., 1933.

——*Democracy at the Crossroads*, London, 1937.

——*Faith, Reason, and Civilization*, New York, 1944.

——*The Foundations of Sovereignty and Other Essays*, New Haven, 1921.

——*A Grammar of Politics*, New Haven, 1930 [1925].

——*Holmes–Laski Letters: The Correspondence of Mr Justice Holmes and Harold J. Laski 1916–1935*, Mark De Wolfe Howe (ed.), Cambridge, Mass., 1953.

——*Introduction to Contemporary Politics*, Seattle, Wash., 1939.

——*Liberty in the Modern State*, London, 1948 [1930].

——*The Limitations of the Expert*, Fabian Tract 235, London, 1931.

——*Parliamentary Government in England*, New York, 1938.

——*Politics*, Philadelphia, 1931.

——'The Present Position of Representative Democracy', *American Political Science Review* (August 1932), pp. 629–41.

——*The Prospects of Democratic Government*, Williamsburg, Va., 1939.

——*Reflections on the Constitution*, Manchester, England, 1951.

——*The Rights of Man*, London, 1940.

——*The State in Theory and Practice*, New York, 1935.

——*The Strategy of Freedom*, New York, 1941.

——*Studies in the Problem of Sovereignty*, New Haven, 1917.

Lasswell, Harold D. 'Introduction', in Sidney Kraus (ed.), *The Great Debates*, Bloomington, Ind., 1962, pp. 19–24.

——*The Political Writings of Harold D. Lasswell*, Glencoe, Ill., 1951.

Lave, James H. 'The Changing Character of the Negro Protest', *The Annals of the American Academy of Political and Social Science* (Jan. 1965), pp. 119–26.

Lazarsfeld, Paul F., Bernard Berelson and Hazel Gaudet. *The People's Choice*, New York, 1948 [1944] [Erie Co., Ohio; 1940 Pres.; six waves, panel surveys].

Levin, Murray B. *The Alienated Voter: Politics in Boston*, New York, 1960 [1959 mayoralty election; post-election survey].

Levy, H. P. *The Press Council: History, Procedure and Cases*, New York, 1967.

Leys, Wayne A. R., and Charner Marquis Perry. *Philsophy and the Public Interest*, Chicago, 1959.

Licklider, J. C. R. 'Televistas: Looking Ahead Through Side Windows', in the Carnegie Commission on Educational Television, *Public Television: A Program for Action*, New York, 1967, pp. 201–25.

Likert, Rensis. *New Patterns of Management*, New York, 1961 [SRC, Research Center for Group Dynamics].

Lindsay, A. D. *The Churches and Democracy*, London, 1934.

——*The Essentials of Democracy*, London, 1951 [1929].

——*The Good and the Clever*, Cambridge, England, 1945.

——*I Believe in Democracy*, London 1940 [BBC broadcasts, 20 May–24 June 1940].

——*Kant*, London, 1934.

——*The Modern Democratic State*, New York, 1962 [1943].

——*The Two Moralities*, London, 1940.

Lippmann, Walter. *The Essential Lippmann: A Political Philosophy for Liberal Democracy*, Clinton Rossiter and James Lare (eds.), New York, 1965 [1963].

——*An Inquiry into the Principles of the Good Society*, Boston, 1938.

——*The Phantom Public*, New York, 1930 [1925].

——*A Preface to Morals*, New York, 1929.

——*Public Opinion*, New York, 1965 [1922].

——*The Public Philosophy*, New York, 1955.

Lipset, Seymour Martin. *The First New Nation: The United States in Historical and Comparative Perspective*, New York, 1963.

——*Political Man: The Social Bases of Politics*, New York, 1960.

——'Student Opposition in the United States', *Government and Opposition* (April 1966), pp. 351–74.

Lipset, Seymour Martin and Reinhard Bendix, *Social Mobility in Industrial Society*, Berkeley, 1959.

Bibliography

Lipsitz, Lewis. 'Work Life and Political Attitudes: A Study of Manual Workers', *American Political Science Review* (Dec. 1964), pp. 951–62. [41 semi-skilled workers in assembly plant, Linden, N.J.; open-ended interviews in homes].

Lipson, Leslie. *The Democratic Civilization*, New York, 1964.

Litt, Edgar. 'Political Cynicism and Political Futility', *Journal of Politics* (May 1963), pp. 312–23 [middle-class Boston ward, matched sample in Brookline, Mass., two Oregon towns (20,000, 50,000); survey].

Logique et Analyse (Dec. 1963).

Lowell, A. Lawrence. *Public Opinion and Popular Government*, New York, 1913.

Lubell, Samuel. 'Personalities v. Issues', in Sidney Kraus (ed.), *The Great Debates*, Bloomington, Ind., 1962, pp. 151–62.

Luce, R. Duncan, and Howard Raiffa. *Games and Decisions*, New York, 1957.

Lundberg, Ferdinand. *The Treason of the People*, New York, 1954.

Lydall, Harold and John B. Lansing. 'A Comparison of the Distribution of Personal Income and Wealth in the United States and Great Britain', *American Economic Review* (March 1959), pp. 43–67 [Oxford Institute of Statistics; SRC].

Maccoby, Eleanor E., Richard E. Matthews and Anton S. Morton. 'Youth and Political Change', *Public Opinion Quarterly* (Spring 1954), pp. 23–39 [21–24 year-olds, Cambridge, Mass., 1952; post-election non-represent. survey].

MacIntyre, Alasdair. 'The Antecedents of Action', in Bernard Williams and Alan Montefiore (eds.), *British Analytical Philosophy*, London, 1966, pp. 205–25.

——'The Idea of a Social Science', *Proceedings of the Aristotelian Society*, supplementary vol. XLI (1967), pp. 95–114.

MacIver, Robert M. *Community: A Sociological Study*, London, 1924 [1917].

——*Leviathan and the People*, University, Louisiana, 1939.

——*The Modern State*, London, 1964 [1926].

——*The More Perfect Union*, New York, 1948.

——*The Ramparts We Guard*, New York, 1950.

——*Social Causation*, New York, 1964 [1942].

——*Society*, New York, 1931.

——*The Web of Government*, New York, 1947.

Marquis, D. G., Harold Guetzkow and R. W. Heyns. 'A Social-Psychological Study of the Decision-Making Conference', in Harold Guetzkow (ed.), *Groups, Leadership and Men*, Pittsburgh, 1951, pp. 55–67.

Martin, Christopher. *The Bored Electors*, London, 1961.

Marx, Gary T. *Protest and Prejudice: A Study of Belief in the Black Community*, New York, 1967 [U.S.; 1964; NORC].

Matthews, Donald R. and James W. Prothro. *Negroes and the New Southern Politics*, New York, 1966 [cross-sections of Negroes and whites in 11 Southern states; March–June 1961; survey. Also SRC data (1964), sample of Negro college students, and 4 Southern counties].

McCallum, R. B. and A. Readman. *The British General Election of 1945*, London, 1947 [agg.].

McClosky, Herbert. 'Consensus and Ideology in American Politics', *American Political Science Review* (June 1964), pp. 361–82 [U.S., national, and delegates and alternates to 1956 Democratic, Republican conventions; 1957–8; AIPO].

——'Conservatism and Personality', *American Political Science Review* (March 1958), pp. 27–45 [Minn., Minneapolis-St Paul; surveys].

McClosky, Herbert, Paul J. Hoffman and Rosemary O'Hara. 'Issue Conflict and Consensus Among Party Leaders and Followers', *American Political Science Review* (June 1960), pp. 406–27 [U.S. national and delegates, alternates, to party conventions; 1957–8; AIPO].

McConnell, Grant. *Private Power and American Democracy*, New York, 1966.

McGuire, William J. 'The Nature of Attitudes and Attitude Change', in Gardner Lindzey and Elliot Aronson (eds.), *Handbook of Social Psychology*, 2nd edition, Reading, Mass., 1969, vol. III, pp. 236–314.

McKenzie, Robert and Allan Silver. *Angels in Marble : Working Class Conservatives in Urban England*, Chicago, 1968 [manual workers who had voted in previous election for Consv. or Lab., in six urban constituencies; surveys in 1958; two open-ended re-interviews of small sub-groups; also general electorate in 36 marginal constituencies, survey 1963. All during non-campaign periods].

——*British Political Parties: The Distribution of Power Within the Conservative and Labour Parties*, London, 1964 [1955].

McKeon, Richard (ed.), *Democracy in a World of Tensions : A Symposium Prepared by UNESCO*, Chicago, 1951.

McPhee, William N. and Jack Ferguson. 'Political Immunization', in William N. McPhee and William A. Glaser (eds.), *Public Opinion and Congressional Elections*, New York, 1962, pp. 155–79 [Colo., Wash., parts of Minn., Iowa; 1950 mid-term; pre- and post-election panel survey].

Melden, A. I. *Free Action*, London, 1961.

Merriam, Charles E. *Civic Education in the United States*, Part VI: *Report of the Commission on the Social Studies, American Historical Association*, New York, 1934.

——'The Education of Charles E. Merriam', in L. White (ed.), *The Future of Government in the United States*, Chicago, 1942, pp. 1–24.

——*Four American Party Leaders*, New York, 1926.

——*The Making of Citizens*, Chicago, 1931.

Bibliography

——*New Aspects of Politics*, Chicago, 1925.

——*The New Democracy and the New Despotism*, New York, 1939.

——*On the Agenda of Democracy*, Cambridge, Mass., 1941.

——*Political Power*, New York, 1964 [1934].

——*Prologue to Politics*, Chicago, 1939.

——*Public and Private Government*, New Haven, 1944.

——*Systematic Politics*, Chicago, 1945.

——*What is Democracy?* Chicago, 1941.

Merriam, Charles E. and Harold F. Gosnell. *Non-Voting: Causes and Methods of Control*, Chicago, 1924.

Merton, Robert K. *Social Theory and Social Structure*, New York, 1968.

Merton, Robert K., Marjorie Fiske and Alberta Curtis. *Mass Persuasion: The Social Psychology of a War Bond Drive*, New York, 1946 [Listeners to radio marathon program and cross-section of New York City; Sept., 1943; detailed interviews with 100 listeners and poll of cross-section].

Meyer, Alan S. 'The Independent Voter', in William N. McPhee and William A. Glaser, *Public Opinion and Congressional Elections*, New York, 1962, pp. 65–77 [U.S.; 1936–58; Roper tabulations of AIPO data].

Milbrath, Lester W. *Political Participation*, Chicago, 1965.

——'Political Participation in the States', in Herbert Jacob and Kenneth Vines (eds.), *Comparative State Politics*, Boston, 1965, pp. 25–60 [agg.].

Mill, James. *An Essay on Government*, in Edwin Burtt (ed.), *The English Philosophers from Bacon to Mill*, New York, 1939, pp. 857–89.

Miller, George A. and David McNeill. 'Psycholinguistics', in Gardner Lindzey and Elliot Aronson (eds.), *Handbook of Social Psychology*, 2nd edition, Reading, Mass., 1969, vol. III, pp. 666–794.

Miller, J. D. B. *The Nature of Politics*, London, 1962.

Miller, Warren E. 'Majority Rule and the Representative System of Government', in E. Allardt and Y. Littunen (eds.), *Cleavages, Ideologies, and Party Systems* (Helsinki, Proceedings of the Westermarck Society, 1964), pp. 343–76.

——'One-Party Politics and the Voter', *American Political Science Review* (Sept. 1956), pp. 707–25 [72 non-Southern counties; 1952; SRC and agg.].

Milne, R. S. 'Second Thoughts on "Straight Fight" ', in Eugene Burdick and Arthur J. Brodbeck (eds.), *American Voting Behavior*, Glencoe, Ill., 1959, pp. 209–16.

Milne, R. S. and H. C. Mackenzie. *Marginal Seat, 1955: A Study of Voting Behavior in the Constituency of Bristol North East at the General Election of 1955*, London, 1958 [pre- and post-election panel; third interview with opinion leaders].

252

Bibliography

——Straight Fight: A Study of Voting Behavior in the Constituency of Bristol North East at the General Election, *1951*, London, 1954 [pre- and post-elected panel surveys].

Montefiore, Alan. 'Fact, Value and Ideology', in Bernard Williams and Alan Montefiore (eds.), *British Analytical Philosophy*, London, 1966, pp. 179–203.

Moore, Barrington, Jr. *Social Origins of Dictatorship and Democracy*, Boston, 1966.

Moore, G. E. *Principia Ethica*, Cambridge, England, 1959 [1903].

Morgan, James N., Martin H. David, Wilbur J. Cohen and Harvey E. Brazer. *Income and Welfare in the United States*, New York, 1962.

Mortimore, G. W. 'An Ideal of Equality', *Mind* (April 1968), pp. 222–42.

Mosca, Gaetano. *Elementi di scienza politica*, 3rd edition, Laterza, 1939.

Myrdal, Gunnar. *Value in Social Theory: A Selection of Essays on Methodology by Gunnar Myrdal*, Paul Streeten (ed.), London, 1958.

Naess, Arne *et al. Democracy, Ideology, and Objectivity*. Oslo, Norway, 1956.

Nagel, Ernest. *The Structure of Science*, New York, 1961.

Nathanson, Jerome. *John Dewey: The Reconstruction of the Democratic Life*, New York, 1951.

Nicholas, H. G. *The British General Election of 1950*, London, 1951 [agg.].

Nixon, Raymond B. and Jean Ward. 'Trends in Newspaper Ownership and Inter-Media Competition', *Journalism Quarterly* (Winter 1961), pp. 3–14.

Nordlinger, Eric A. *The Working-Class Tories: Authority, Deference and Stable Democracy*, Berkeley, 1967 [U.K. urban, manual males who voted for Labour or Conservative in last General Election and intend to vote for same party; 1963; NOP; re-interview, 1964, and second re-interview (open-ended) of smaller sub-group].

Nowell-Smith, Patrick. *Ethics*, Oxford, 1954.

Olson, Mancur, Jr. *The Logic of Collective Action: Public Goods and the Theory of Groups*, Cambridge, Mass., 1965.

Orbell, John M. 'Protest Participation Among Southern Negro College Students', *American Political Science Review* (June 1967), pp. 446–56 [Matthews and Prothro data, 1964].

Orum, Anthony M. 'A Reappraisal of the Social and Political Participation of Negroes', *American Journal of Sociology* (July 1966), pp. 32–46 [black Detroit, white Chicago; 1963–6; NORC; also U.S.; 1955; NORC].

Orwell, George. *The Road to Wigan Pier*, New York, 1958 [1937].

Parsons, Talcott. ' "Voting" and the Equilibrium of the American Party System', in Eugene Burdick and Arthur J. Brodbeck (eds.), *American Voting Behavior*, Glencoe, Ill., 1957, pp. 80–120.

Passmore, John. 'Review Article: Laws and Explanation in History', *Australian Journal of Politics and History* (Nov. 1958), pp. 269–75.

253

Peabody, Dean. 'Authoritarianism Scales and Response Bias', *Psychological Bulletin* (Jan. 1966), pp. 11–23.

Pennock, J. Roland. *Liberal Democracy: Its Merits and Prospects*, New York, 1950.

Pennock, J. Roland and John W. Chapman (eds.), *Equality*, Nomos IX, New York, 1967.

Perelman, Chaim, and L. Olbrechts-Tyteca. *Traité de l'argumentation: la nouvelle rhetorique*, Brussels, 1959.

Perry, Orval, L. 'The Logic of Moral Valuation', *Mind* (Jan. 1957), pp. 42–62.

Pettigrew, Thomas F. *A Profile of the Negro American*, Princeton, 1964.

Pitkin, Hanna. *The Concept of Representation*, Berkeley, and Los Angeles, 1967.

Plamenatz, John. 'Electoral Studies and Democratic Theory, 1: A British View', *Political Studies* (Feb. 1958), pp. 1–9.

——'Interests', *Political Studies* (Feb. 1954), pp. 1–8.

——'The Uses of Political Theory', *Political Studies* (Feb. 1960), pp. 37–47.

Polsby, Nelson. *Community Power and Political Theory*, New Haven, 1963 [see Dahl, *Who Governs?*].

Pool, Ithiel de Sola. 'TV: A New Dimension in Politics'', in Eugene Burdick and Arthur J. Brodbeck (eds.), *American Voting Behavior* Glencoe, Ill., 1959, pp. 236–61 [Calif. college students; 1952 campaign; non-random].

Popper, Karl. 'What Can Logic Do For Philsophy?' *Proceedings of the Aristotelian Society*, supplementary vol. XXII (1948).

Presthus, Robert. *Men at the Top: A Study in Community Power*, New York, 1964 [cross-section and leaders in two small N.Y. towns; 1961; interviews; includes survey of other community studies].

Prothro, James W. and Charles M. Grigg. 'Fundamental Principles of Democracy: Bases of Agreement and Disagreement', *Journal of Politics* (May 1960), pp. 276–94 [registered voters in Ann Arbor and Tallahasseee; survey].

Putnam, Robert D. 'Political Attitudes and the Local Community', *American Political Science Review* (Sept. 1966), pp. 640–54 [non-Southern U.S. counties; 1952; SRC].

Rainwater, Lee and William L. Yancey (eds.), *The Moynihan Report and the Politics of Controversy*, Cambridge, 1967 [includes full text of D. P. Moynihan's *The Negro Family: The Case for National Action*, U.S. Dept. of Labor, 1965].

Randall, John Herman, Jr. 'The Religion of Shared Experience', in Sidney Ratner (ed.), *The Philosopher of the Common Man*, New York, 1940, pp. 106–45.

Ranney, Austin and Willmoore Kendall. *Democracy and the American Party System*, New York, 1956.

Bibliography

Ratner, Sidney (ed.). *The Philosopher of the Common Man: Essays in Honor of John Dewey to Celebrate his Eightieth Birthday*, New York, 1940.

Rawls, John. 'Outline of a Decision Procedure for Ethics', *Philosophical Review* (April 1951), pp. 177–97.

Rees, J. C. 'The Limitations of Political Theory', *Political Studies* (Oct. 1954), pp. 242–57.

Rees, W. J. 'The Public Interest', *Proceedings of the Aristotelian Society*, supplementary vol. XXXVIII (1964), pp. 19–38.

Report of the Committee on Broadcasting, 1960, H.M.S.O., Cmnd. 1753, London, 1962.

Report of the Royal Commission on the Press, 1961–2, H.M.S.O., Cmnd. 1811, London, 1962.

Riesman, David. *The Lonely Crowd*, New Haven, 1950.

Riker, William H. 'Voting and the Summation of Preferences: An Interpretive Bibliographic Review of Selected Developments During the Last Decade', *American Political Science Review* (Dec. 1961), pp. 900–11.

Riker, William H. and Peter C. Ordeshook, 'A Theory of the Calculus of Voting', *American Political Science Review* (March 1968), pp. 25–42.

Robinson, James A. and William H. Standing. 'Some Correlates of Voter Participation: The Case of Indiana', *The Journal of Politics* (Feb. 1960), pp. 96–111 [Ind. counties; 1934–44, 1946–54 (prosecuting attorneys); agg.].

Roelofs, H. Mark. *The Tension of Citizenship: Private Man and Public Duty*, New York, 1957.

Roper, Elmo, and associates. *The Public's View of Television and Other Media, 1959–1964*, New York, 1965 [U.S.; Roper surveys].

Rose, Richard. *Influencing Voters: A Study of Campaign Rationality*, New York, 1967.

Rose, Richard and Harve Mossawir. 'Voting and Elections: A Functional Analysis', *Political Studies* (June 1967), pp. 173–201 [U.K., Stockport North; 1964; survey].

Rosenberg, Morris. 'Some Determinants of Political Apathy', *Public Opinion Quarterly* (Winter 1954–5), pp. 349–66 [Ithaca, N.Y.; 70 non-random, unstructured interviews].

Ross, Alf. *On Law and Justice*, Berkeley, Calif., 1959.

——*Why Democracy?* Cambridge, Mass., 1952.

Rousseas, Stephen W. and James Farganis. 'American Politics and the End of Ideology', *British Journal of Sociology* (Dec. 1963), pp. 347–62.

Rudolph, Lloyd and Susanne H. Rudolph. 'Opinion Surveys in India', *Public Opinion Quarterly* (Fall 1958), pp. 235–44.

Runciman, W. G. *Relative Deprivation and Social Justice: A Study of Attitudes to Social Inequality in Twentieth-Century England*, London, 1966 [U.K.; 1962; survey].

Bibliography

——*Social Science and Political Theory*, Cambridge, England, 1963.

Russett, Bruce M., Hayward R. Alker, Karl W. Deutsch and Harold D. Lasswell. *World Handbook of Economic and Social Indicators*, New Haven, 1964.

Ryle, Gilbert. *The Concept of Mind*, London, 1949.

Sabine, George H. 'The Two Democratic Traditions', *Philosophical Review* (Oct. 1952), pp. 451–74.

Sapir, Edward. 'Language', *Encyclopedia of the Social Sciences*, New York, 1933, pp. 155–69.

Sartori, Giovanni. *Democratic Theory*, New York, 1965 [1962].

Sayre, Wallace S. and Herbert Kaufman. *Governing New York City*, New York, 1960.

Schaar, John H. and Sheldon S. Wolin. 'Review Essay: *Essays on the Scientific Study of Politics:* A Critique', *American Political Science Review* (March 1963), pp. 125–50.

Schattschneider, E. E. *Party Government*, New York, 1942.

Schmandt, Henry J., Paul G. Steinbicker and George D. Hendel. *Metropolitan Reform in St Louis*, New York, 1961.

Schramm, Wilbur. *Responsibility in Mass Communication*, New York, 1957.

Schramm, Wilbur and Richard F. Carter. 'Effectiveness of a Political Telethon', *Public Opinion Quarterly* (Spring 1959), pp. 121–7 [Los Angeles; 1958; telephone interviews].

Schramm, Wilbur and David M. White. 'Age, Education and Economic Status as Factors in Newspaper Reading: Conclusions', in Wilbur Schramm (ed.), *The Process and Effects of Mass Communications*, Urbana, Ill., 1954, pp. 71–3 [Ill. city of 100,000; 1949; survey].

Schubert, Glendon. *The Public Interest: A Critique of the Theory of a Political Concept*. Glencoe, Ill., 1961.

Schumpeter, Joseph A. *Capitalism, Socialism, and Democracy*, London, 1954 [1943].

Searles, Ruth and J. Allen Williams, Jr. 'Negro College Students' Participation in Sit-Ins', *Social Forces* (March 1963), pp. 215–20 [827 students at 3 N.C. colleges; questionnaire; May, 1960].

Sears, David O. and Jonathan L. Freedman. 'Selective Exposure to Information: A Critical Review', *Public Opinion Quarterly* (Summer 1967), pp. 194–213.

Sharp, Harry. 'Migration and Voting Behavior in a Metropolitan Community', *Public Opinion Quarterly* (Summer 1955), pp. 206–9 [Detroit area; 1952, 1954; SRC].

Sharpe, L. J. *A Metropolis Votes: The London County Council Election of 1961*, London, 1962 [Clapham division; post-election survey; also London agg.].

Sheatsley, Paul B. 'White Attitudes Toward the Negro', *Daedalus, The Negro American*—2 (Winter 1966)[U.S.; 1942, 1956, 1963, 1965; NORC].

Siegel, Alberta E. and Sidney Siegel. 'Reference Groups, Membership Groups and Attitude Change', *Journal of Abnormal and Social Psychology* (Nov. 1957), pp. 360–4.

Siepmann, Charles A. 'Were They "Great"?' in Sidney Kraus (ed.), *The Great Debates*, Bloomington, Ind., 1962, pp. 132–41.

Simon, Yves. *Community of the Free*, New York, 1947.

——*A General Theory of Authority*, Notre Dame, 1962.

——*Nature and Functions of Authority*, Milwaukee, 1940.

——*Philosophy of Democratic Government*, Chicago, 1951.

——*The Traditions of Natural Law*, New York, 1965.

Sindler, Allan P. 'Protest Against the Political Status of the Negro', *Annals of the American Academy of Political and Social Science* (Jan. 1965), pp. 48–54.

Skolnick, Jerome H. *The Politics of Protest*, New York, 1969 [report to the National Commission on Causes and Prevention of Violence].

Smith, Thomas Vernor. *The American Philosophy of Equality*, Chicago, 1927.

——*Beyond Conscience*, New York, 1934.

——*The Democratic Tradition in America*, New York, 1941.

——*The Democratic Way of Life*, Chicago, 1939 [1926].

——*Discipline for Democracy*, Chapel Hill, N.C., 1942.

——*The Ethics of Compromise*, Boston, 1956.

——*The Legislative Way of Life in America*, Chicago, 1940.

——*The Philosophic Way of Life in America*, 1943 [1929].

——*The Promise of American Politics*, Chicago, 1936.

Solomon, Frederic and Jacob R. Fishman. 'Youth and Peace: A Psychosocial Study of Student Peace Demonstrators in Washington, D.C. [Feb. 1962]', *Journal of Social Issues* (Oct. 1964), pp. 54–73 [sample of 247 of registered demonstrators; on-the-spot questionnaires and interviews; follow-up questionnaire 18 months later].

Sorauf, Frank J. 'The Public Interest Reconsidered', *Journal of Politics* (Nov. 1957), pp. 616–39.

Spitz, David. *Democracy and the Challenge of Power*, New York, 1958.

Stokes, Donald E. 'Popular Evaluations of Government: An Empirical Assessment', in Harlan Cleveland and Harold Lasswell (eds.), *Ethics and Bigness*, New York, 1962, pp. 61–72 [U.S.; 1958; SRC].

——'Some Dynamic Elements of Contests for the Presidency', *American Political Science Review* (March 1966), pp. 19–28 [U.S.; 1952, 1956, 1960, 1964; SRC].

Storing, Herbert J. (ed.) *Essays on the Scientific Study of Politics*, New York, 1962.

Stouffer, Samuel A. *Communism, Conformity and Civil Liberties*, New York, 1966 [1955] [U.S. and sample of community leaders; May–July 1954; NORC, AIPO].

Bibliography

Strauss, Leo. 'An Epilogue', in Herbert J. Storing (ed.), *Essays on the Scientific Study of Politics*, New York, 1962, pp. 307–27.
——*Natural Right and History*, Chicago, 1953.
Sturmthal, Adolf. *Workers' Councils: A Study of Workplace Organization on Both Sides of the Iron Curtain*, Cambridge, Mass., 1964.
Suchy, John T. 'How Does Commercial Television Affect British Viewing?' *Journalism Quarterly* (Winter 1958), pp. 65–71.
Surface, Samuel J. and Melvin Seeman. 'Some Correlates of Civil Rights Activism', *Social Forces* (Dec. 1967), pp. 197–207 [208 Los Angeles extension college students and 142 civil service personnel; questionnaire].
Survey Research Center. *Who Votes and For Whom*, University of Michigan, 1965, mimeo [U.S.; 1948, 1952, 1956, 1960, 1964; SRC].
Swabey, Marie Collins. *Theory of the Democratic State*, Cambridge, Mass., 1937.
Tawney, R. H. *Equality*, London, 1931.
Taylor, Charles. 'Neutrality in Political Science', in P. Laslett and W. Runciman (eds.), *Philosophy, Politics and Society*, 3rd series, Oxford, 1967, pp. 25–57.
Taylor, Paul W. *Normative Discourse*, Englewood Cliffs, N.J., 1961.
Thompson, Dennis F. 'Electoral Behavior and Democratic Theory', paper delivered at the 1966 Annual Meeting of the American Political Science Association (copyright 1966, APSA).
——'Rational Propaganda', in John D. Montgomery and Arthur Smithies (eds.), *Public Policy*, Cambridge, Mass., 1966.
Thorson, Thomas L. *The Logic of Democracy*, New York, 1962.
Tingsten, Herbert. *Political Behavior: Studies in Election Statistics*, Totowa, N.J., 1963 [1937].
——*The Problem of Democracy*, Totowa, N.J., 1965.
Toulmin, Stephen. *An Examination of the Place of Reason in Ethics*, Cambridge, England, 1953.
Trenaman, Joseph, and Denis McQuail. *Television and the Political Image: A Study of the Impact of Television on the 1959 General Election*, London, 1961 [West Leeds and Pudsey; pre- and post-election survey].
Truman, David B. *The Governmental Process*, New York, 1951.
Tufte, Edward R. *The Civil Rights Movement and Its Opposition*, unpublished doctoral dissertation, Yale, 1968 [107 civil rights leaders and activists and 54 office holders in opposition groups in San Francisco; interviews; summer 1964].
Turner, Ralph H. 'Modes of Social Ascent Through Education: Sponsored and Contest Mobility', in A. H. Halsey *et al.* (eds.), *Education, Economy and Society*, New York, 1961, pp. 121–39.
U.K. Central Statistical Office. *Annual Abstract of Statistics, 1967*, London, H.M.S.O., 1967.

258

U.S. Bureau of the Census. *Statistical Abstract of the United States, 1968*, Washington, 1968.

U.S. Commission on Civil Rights. *1961 Report*, vol. I, 'Voting', Washington, D.C., 1961.

U.S. Congress, Communications Subcommittee of the Senate Committee on Interstate and Foreign Commerce. *Freedom of Communications*, 87th Cong., 1st and 2nd Sess., 1961–2.

——*Review of Section 314*, 87th Cong., 1st Sess., 1961.

U.S. Congress, Senate Special Committee to Investigate Political Activities, Lobbying and Campaign Contributions. *Campaign Contributions, Political Activities and Lobbying*, 85th Cong., 2nd Sess.

Verba, Sidney. 'Organizational Membership and Democratic Consensus', *Journal of Politics* (August 1965), pp. 467–97 [Almond and Verba data].

——*Small Groups and Political Behavior: A Study of Leadership*, Princeton, 1961.

Voegelin, Eric. *The New Science of Politics*, Chicago, 1952.

Walker, Jack L. 'A Critique of the Elitist Theory of Democracy', *American Political Science Review* (June 1966), pp. 285–95.

——'A Reply to "Further Reflections on 'The Elitist Theory of Democracy' " ', *American Political Science Review* (June 1966), pp. 391–92.

——*Sit-ins in Atlanta*, New York, 1964.

Wallace, David. *First Tuesday: A Study of Rationality in Voting*, Garden City, 1964 [Westport, Conn.; 1960; mail panel survey].

Wallas, Graham. *The Art of Thought*, London, 1926.

——*The Great Society*, New York, 1923 [1914].

——*Human Nature in Politics*, Lincoln, Neb., 1962 [1908].

——*Our Social Heritage*, New Haven, 1921.

——*Social Judgement*, New York, 1935.

Walton, John. 'Substance and Artifact: The Current Status of Research on Community Power Structure', *American Journal of Sociology* (Jan. 1966), pp. 430–8.

Weber, Max. 'The Meaning of "Ethical Neutrality" in Sociology and Economics', in *The Methodology of the Social Sciences*, E. Shils and H. Finch (trans. and eds.), Glencoe, Ill., 1949 [originally in *Logos* 1917].

——' "Objectivity" ' in Social Science and Social Policy', in *The Methodology of the Social Sciences*, E. Shils and H. Finch (trans. and eds.), Glencoe, Ill., 1949 [originally in *Archiv für Sozialwissenschaft und Sozial-politik*, vol. XIX (1904)].

——*Wirtschaft und Gesellschaft*, Tübingen, 1925.

Weiss, Walter. 'Effects of the Mass Media of Communication', in Gardner Lindzey and Elliot Aronson (eds.), *The Handbook of Social Psychology*, 2nd edition, Reading Mass., 1969, vol. V.

Weyl, Walter E. *The New Democracy*, New York, 1918.

Bibliography

White, Theodore H. *The Making of the President 1960*, New York, 1961.

Whorf, Benjamin Lee. *Language, Thought, and Reality*, John B. Carroll (ed.), Cambridge, Mass., 1956.

Wiebe, G. D. 'Merchandising Commodities and Citizenship on Television', *Public Opinion Quarterly* (Winter 1951–2), pp. 679–91.

Williams, Bernard, 'The Idea of Equality', in Peter Laslett and W. G. Runciman (eds.), *Philosophy, Politics and Society*, 2nd series, Oxford, 1962, pp. 110–31.

Williams, Francis. *Dangerous Estate: The Anatomy of Newspapers*, London, 1957.

Williams, Raymond. *The Existing Alternatives in Communications*, Fabian Tract 337, London, 1962.

——*The Long Revolution*, London, 1961.

Wilson, James Q. *The Amateur Democrat: Club Politics in Three Cities*, Chicago, 1962.

——'The Negro in Politics', *Daedalus: The Negro American* (Fall 1965), pp. 949–73.

Wilson, James Q. and Edward Banfield. 'Public-Regardingness as a Value Premise in Voting Behavior', *American Political Science Review* (Dec. 1964), pp. 876–87 [Cleveland area, Chicago area, Detroit, St Louis, Kansas City, Miami, Los Angeles; selected elections, 1956–63; agg.].

Wilson, John. *Equality*, New York, 1966.

Winch, Peter. *The Idea of a Social Science and Its Relation to Philosophy*, London, 1963 [1958].

Wittgenstein, Ludwig. *Philosophical Investigations*, G. E. M. Anscombe (trans.), New York, 1953.

Wolfinger, Raymond E. 'The Influence of Precinct Work on Voting Behavior', *Public Opinion Quarterly* (Fall 1963), pp. 387–98 [see Dahl, *Who Governs?*].

——'Some Consequences of Ethnic Politics', in M. Kent Jennings and L. Harmon Zeigler (eds.), *The Electoral Process*, Englewood Cliffs, N.J., 1966, pp. 42–54 [New Haven study: see Dahl, *Who Governs?*],

Wollheim, Richard. 'Democracy', *Journal of the History of Ideas* (April 1958), pp. 225–42.

——*Socialism and Culture*, Fabian tract 331, London, 1961.

Woodward, Julian L., and Elmo Roper. 'Political Activity of American Citizens', *American Political Science Review* (Dec. 1950), pp. 872–85 [U.S.; Roper].

Wright, Charles R. and Herbert H. Hyman. 'Voluntary Association Memberships of American Adults: Evidence From National Sample Surveys', *American Sociological Review* (June 1958), pp. 284–94 [U.S., Denver, New York City, Findley, Ohio; selected periods 1949–55; NORC and others].

Bibliography

Young, Michael. *The Rise of the Meritocracy*, New York, 1959.

Yü, Frederick T. C. *Mass Persuasion in Communist China*, New York, 1964.

Zweig, Ferdynand. *The Worker in an Affluent Society: Family Life and Industry*, New York, 1961 [four U.K. mfg. firms; 1958-9; 672 open-ended interviews].

ABBREVIATIONS

agg.   aggregate election and other statistics

AIPO   American Institute of Public Opinion (Gallup) survey

BIPO   British Institute of Public Opinion (Gallup) survey

lab.   study conducted in a laboratory or under other artificial conditions (as in a classroom)

NOP   National Opinion Poll (U.K.)

NORC   National Opinion Research Center (University of Chicago) survey

Pres.   Presidential election

SRC   Survey Research Center (University of Michigan) pre- and post-election panel survey (unless otherwise specified)

U.S.   national sample of U.S. electorate

U.K.   national sample of U.K. electorate

Index

Index